SCHRIFTENREIHE
MEDIENFORSCHUNG

BAND 83

Mark D. Cole | Christina Etteldorf | Carsten Ullrich

UPDATING THE RULES FOR ONLINE CONTENT DISSEMINATION

Legislative Options of the European Union
and the Digital Services Act Proposal

LANDESANSTALT FÜR MEDIEN NRW
Der Meinungsfreiheit verpflichtet.

Landesanstalt für Medien NRW
Sabrina Nennstiel (Leiterin Kommunikation)
Dr. Meike Isenberg (Leiterin Forschung)
Zollhof 2, 40221 Düsseldorf

www.medienanstalt-nrw.de

The Deutsche Nationalbibliothek lists this publication in the
Deutsche Nationalbibliografie; detailed bibliographic data
are available on the Internet at http://dnb.d-nb.de

ISBN   978-3-8487-8184-3 (Print)
          978-3-7489-2593-4 (ePDF)

British Library Cataloguing-in-Publication Data
A catalogue record for this book is available from the British Library.

ISBN   978-3-8487-8184-3 (Print)
          978-3-7489-2593-4 (ePDF)

Library of Congress Cataloging-in-Publication Data
Cole, Mark / Etteldorf, Christina / Ullrich, Carsten
Updating the Rules for Online Content Dissemination
Legislative Options of the European Union and the Digital Services Act Proposal
Mark D. Cole / Christina Etteldorf / Carsten Ullrich
241 pp.
Includes bibliographic references.

ISBN   978-3-8487-8184-3 (Print)
          978-3-7489-2593-4 (ePDF)

Onlineversion
Nomos eLibrary

Volumes 1–48 published by VS-Verlag,
volumes 49–80 published by VISTAS Verlag.

Published by Nomos Verlagsgesellschaft, Baden-Baden, Germany 2021.
Printed and bound in Germany.

Vorwort

The European Union is based on common values with peace and freedom at the heart. In the reverse, safeguarding this freedom requires rules based on these values. The enforcement of the standards of a free media order in Europe is up to us as independent regulators.

In its study "Cross-Border Dissemination of Online Content" conducted on behalf of the State Media Authority NRW last year (Schriftenreihe Medienforschung der Landesanstalt für Medien NRW, Band 81), the Institute of European Media Law (EMR) explored the legal framework and possible future regulation of the media environment in the EU. It mainly identified areas that need an update to be able to face modern developments in the media sector as well as media regulation.

Today, one year later, the European Commission published a concrete proposal for a possible future regulation of the digital world. The proposed Digital Services Act marks a first European attempt to overhaul the current legal framework. As such, it bears the potential to reduce uncertainty and to make cross-border enforcement more effective. But has the European Commission achieved this? What are the positive aspects, what are the weak points of the proposed regulation?

This study is based on its predecessor and analyses whether the European Commission's proposal improves the identified shortcomings of the existing legal framework. From a media law perspective, the study assesses in particular if the heart of the media market – the Country of Origin principle – is sufficiently safeguarded, if liability and responsibilities of the service providers have been improved and if the envisaged supervisory structure makes cross-border law enforcement more effective.

Down the road, the motto remains the same: Inactivity is not an option.

I want to thank Prof. Dr. Mark D. Cole and his team for their excellent work and wish you, dear readers, an inspiring lecture.

Dr. Tobias Schmid
Director of the State Media Authority of North Rhine-Westphalia

Overview

Table of Contents

Abbreviations

ADR	alternative dispute resolution
AfP	Zeitschrift für Medien- und Kommunikationsrecht
AG	Advocate General
Art.	Article
AVMS	audiovisual media service(s)
AVMSD	Audiovisual Media Services Directive
BEREC	Body of European Regulators for Electronic Communication
B2B	business-to-business
B2C	business-to-consumer
cf.	confer/conferatur (Latin) / compare
CFR	Charter of Fundamental Rights of the EU
CJEU	Court of Justice of the European Union
CLR	California Law Review
CMA	Competition and Markets Authority
COM	Communication
COO	country of origin
CPC	Consumer Protection Cooperation
CYELP	Croatian Yearbook of European Law and Policy
C-	Case-
DMA	Digital Markets Act
DNS	Domain Name System
DSA	Digital Services Act
DSC(s)	Digital Services Coordinator(s)
DSGVO	Datenschutz-Grundverordnung
DSMD	Digital Single Market Directive
EBDS	European Board of Digital Services
EC	European Commission
ECD	e-Commerce Directive
ECN	European Competition Network
ECHR	European Convention on Human Rights
ECtHR	European Court of Human Rights
ed(s).	editor(s)
EDPB	European Data Protection Board

e.g.	exempli gratia (Latin) /for example, for instance
EJLT	European Journal of Law and Technology
EMR	Institute of European Media Law
EP	European Parliament
EPRS	European Parliamentary Research Service
ERGA	European Regulators Group for Audiovisual Media Services
et al.	et alia (Latin) / and others
et seq.	et sequens/sequentes (Latin) / and the following
EU	European Union
EuR	Europarecht (Zeitschrift)
Europol	European Union Agency of Law Enforcement Cooperation
EUV	Vertrag über die Europäische Union
EuZW	Europäische Zeitschrift für Wirtschaftsrecht
GDPR	General Data Protection Regulation
GmbH	Gesellschaft mit beschränkter Haftung
HBI	Hans Bredow Institut
HLEG	High Level Expert Group
IAP	Internet Access Provider
i.e.	that is
IJLIT	International Journal of Law and Information Technology
IMCO	Committee on the Internal Market and Consumer Protection
IMI	Internal Market Information System
INHOPE	International Association of Internet Hotlines
IPR	Internet Policy Review
ISS	Information Society Services
ISSP	Information Society Services Provider
IT	Information Technology
JIL	Journal of Internet Law
JIPITEC	Journal of Intellectual Property, Information Technology and Electronic Commerce Law
KYC	know your customer
lit.	litera (Latin) / letter
MJ	Maastricht Journal of European and Comparative Law
NetzDG	Netzwerkdurchsetzungsgesetz
no.	number
NRA(s)	National Regulatory Authority(ies)
NTD	notice and take down
OCSSP(s)	online content-sharing service provider(s)

OECD	Organisation for Economic Co-operation and Development
OJ/OJEU	Official Journal of the European Union
OJ C	Official Journal – Information and Notices
OJ L	Official Journal – Legislation
p.	page(s)
para.	paragraph
P2B	platform-to-business
REC	Recommendation
SME	small and medium-sized enterprises
SPoC	Single Point of Contact
S.R.L.	Société à Responsabilité Limitée / limited liability company
supra	ut supra / as above
subpara.	subparagraph
SWD	staff and joint staff working documents
TEC	Treaty establishing the European Community
TERREG	Regulation on preventing the dissemination of terrorist content online
TEU	Treaty on European Union
TFEU	Treaty on the Functioning of the European Union
TRIS	Technical Regulation Information System
TV	television
UCPD	Unfair Commercial Practices Directive
UFITA	Archiv für Medienrecht und Medienwissenschaft
URL	Uniform Resource Locator
US	United States
v.	versus
VLOP(s)	very large online platform(s)
VoD	Video on Demand
Vol.	Volume
VSP(s)	video-sharing platform(s)
WTO	Wold Trade Organization
WP	Working Paper

Executive Summary – English

Background of the Study

1. We are living in an age of digitalisation, in which, thanks to the Internet, it is possible to find all forms and types of content, access it, share it with others and disseminate it further. National borders do not matter and, due to the advancing technological developments, language barriers are also disappearing more and more. The digital content market is therefore global, open to development and constantly changing and growing. This not only opens up economic opportunities for companies that can interact with this market, but also offers society a mass of benefits, for example in terms of freedom of information, intercultural exchange or a variety of choices for the consumption of (media) content notwithstanding risks and challenges that come with this globalised exchange. Intermediaries and other platforms that enable or provide access to content, collect and categorise content, provide forums for exchange and content creation by users, are regularly the gatekeepers to these benefits.

2. The regulation of this multi-sided market of dissemination of online content is as diverse as the actors and types of content – whether video, audio, image-based or text-based – involved. Although with respect to Member States competency with regard to media pluralism and the democratic and cultural functions of media actors there is no fully harmonised media regulation at EU level, there are a number of acts which directly or indirectly address or at least have impact on the media and beyond it the creation of content, its distribution and presentation as well as its consumption. Fundamental rights guarantees of freedom and plurality of opinions and the media, internal market freedoms of unhindered cross-border dissemination and a foundation of EU common values that is also relevant for content dissemination result in a complex network of secondary legislation pursuing different objectives and protection goals.

3. The creation of this secondary legal framework partly dates back more than 30 years and thus lies in a time when it was hardly imaginable that digitalisation and its effects would be so profound for media and content dissemination and the way recipients use such content. This is why EU secondary law has been repeatedly reformed over the years. These

reforms, most recently through the Audiovisual Media Services Directive (AVMSD) and the Directive on Copyright and Related Rights in the Digital Single Market (DSMD), were important steps to make the EU "fit for the digital age". The political guidelines of the new Commission President Ursula von der Leyen and the announced work programme of the European Commission are also based on this approach. A large part of the envisaged initiatives at EU level refer to the new role of platforms in the digital environment – including in the context of the online dissemination of content. This addresses above all the provisions of the E-Commerce Directive (ECD), which, as a cross-sectoral piece of legislation, has formed the cornerstone of the internal market for information society services (ISS) for almost 20 years. In December 2020, the Commission published its Proposal of a Digital Services Act Package in order to address the problems arising from the application of a regulatory framework created in a completely different Internet environment. It consisted of two draft Proposals for Regulations, a Digital Services Act (DSA) and a Digital Markets Act (DMA).

4. The application and enforcement of the current legal framework has been confronted with numerous problems, not last due to the above mentioned changes. These include amongst others the following issues, which were extensively analysed in a predecessor study entitled "Cross-Border Dissemination of Online Content – Current and Possible Future Regulation of the Online Environment with a Focus on the EU E-Commerce Directive": The rise of Web 2.0 interactivity led to most intermediaries moving away from being simple "passive hosts" (as is the basic idea and concept of the ECD) to now being interactive content management platforms where the exploitation of user data and network effects are at the centre of the business model. This questions the rather simplistic categorisation of today's platforms as "hosting providers" and blurs the limits of the conditions for claiming liability privileges linked to factors such as "neutrality" and "actual knowledge" of illegal content, despite the fact that the Court of Justice of the European Union (CJEU) has contributed decisively in its case law to clarifying the interpretation of some of these notions responding to referrals by Member States courts which they needed in their interpretation of national transposition acts of the ECD.

5. Furthermore, many users are no longer only passive recipients of content only but rather content creators who promote their views or themselves with the most diverse offers on different platforms in text, image, video or audio. The downside of the opportunities offered by the Inter-

net, technology and digitalisation have also become apparent in the meantime: phenomena such as easy access to illegal or copyright infringing content, content inciting to hatred and terrorist propaganda, but also disinformation, are only examples for a problematic aspect of the possibility for users to create and disseminate widely content via intermediaries whereby the latter can regularly invoke the liability privileges of the ECD when it comes to responsibility for illegal or harmful content. This complex situation, with horizontal liability privileges on the part of gatekeepers on the one hand and growing threats caused by regularly anonymous users on the other, has led to difficulties in regulatory practice and made effective law enforcement more difficult, particularly in the fight against illegal online content disseminated across borders.

6. These developments, in the form of a growing (close to editorial) influence of platforms on content and its exposure to users as well as increasing threats to (fundamental rights of) EU citizens and the values of the EU, have already been taken up and addressed in other secondary legislation and via several instruments of self- and co-regulation, e.g. via rules for video sharing platforms, online intermediation services or online content-sharing services as specific sub-categories of ISS. However, as some of these rules are explicitly based on or refer to the ECD's liability framework and/or are not covered by the ECD's sectoral exceptions, it is becoming increasingly difficult to ensure coherence between these rules and to provide effective enforcement of sectoral provisions. Concerning the cross-border dimension it has to be considered additionally that differing legislative or administrative approaches by the Member States, some of which have recently adopted sectoral rules for certain types of online platforms in exercising their reserved legislative competencies, constitute a certain fragmentation of the regulatory framework.

7. The resulting problems are particularly evident when it comes to cross-border enforcement, which is the norm for online distribution of illegal content due to the cross-border nature of the Internet and also the significant market power of (mainly non-European-) ISS. The ECD, which is based on the country of origin principle (COO) and thus determines both the unhindered provision of ISS under the law of the country of origin and the competence of the regulatory bodies of that Member State, does not contain any specific provisions on the establishment and powers of supervisory bodies, nor mechanisms for coherence and cooperation between sectoral regulatory bodies. The provi-

sions contained on Member States' powers to derogate from the country of origin principle, supervisory cooperation and cross-border information exchange follow a minimum harmonisation approach and have not had a very effective impact in practice with the increasing growth of the market and related tasks.

Aim of the Study

8. Against this background, the present study briefly recalls the applicable regulatory framework of the European Union and Member States for the cross-border dissemination of online content including the interplay between EU legislative acts and Member States law and the implementation of it. It gives an overview of regulatory options on EU level in general terms that are available in the process of adapting this framework. After that five core issues for reform are identified as concerns the specific area of media and (more general:) content dissemination without going discussing other elements such as e.g. new instruments in competition law concerning online platforms. For each of the five issues the study presents different possible solutions and gives an overview of discussed options. It proposes for the question of the future shape of the clarification of the country of origin principle and its exceptions, the scope of application of the framework for ISS, the liability privilege regime, obligations and duties for service providers including the respect for user rights, and finally of specific issues on the institutional set-up for monitoring of compliance and enforcement a concrete way forward.

9. In light of this focus, the study analyses first different legislative options for reforming the framework applicable to online content dissemination in the EU. Based on an outline of the necessity of reforming the current framework and a general overview of the Commission Proposals for a DSA and DMA, the study concentrates on the six most relevant issues in need of reform. In doing so, for each of these issues the status quo and reasons for an update are presented, the relevant parts of the actual Proposal for the DSA are explained and analysed before a detailed assessment of the proposed rules follows including an evaluation of whether further changes or alternative approaches to the options proposed in the DSA should be achieved.

Current Regulatory Framework of the European Union and Members
States

10. Considering the legal framework for the cross-border dissemination of
online content, basis and framework for any solution are fundamental
rights as laid down in the Charter of Fundamental Rights of the EU
(CFR), the European Convention on Human Rights of the Council of
Europe and the provisions of national constitutional law. These rights
feature prominently human dignity, which, according to the CFR, is
"inviolable", i.e. needs to be considered as an overarching goal to be
protected. They include also the protection of minors on their own behalf. On the other hand, freedom of expression (of service users that
create content as well as recipients of this content) and rights of the
service providers that might be confronted with increased legal obligations are to be respected. In the context of safeguarding fundamental
rights, the Member States' competences in the field of media regulation and ensuring diversity must be preserved, particularly where
platforms are concerned which present themselves as media-relevant
gatekeepers.

11. Fundamental freedoms are the core of the single market and, in particular for the functioning of the digital single market in the EU. The
fundamental freedoms include the right to establish oneself in a Member State under the jurisdiction of that state, and to provide goods and
services within the internal market without being subject to stricter restrictions by the receiving Member State as well as relying on the free
movement of capital. In the context of cross-border dissemination of
online content, this does not only concern media companies that can
invoke these freedoms, but also ISS. Derogations from the fundamental freedoms, whether at national or EU level, must be justified in particular by an objective of general interest and be proportionate. This
also applies to varying inclusions in the legislative framework of the
COO, which, although not an overriding requirement of the fundamental freedoms, is an expression of the idea of ensuring a free and
fair internal market enshrined therein.

12. The values on which the EU is founded, which are laid down in the
Treaties and are not merely theoretical in the light of the procedural
mechanisms envisaged, give direction to regulation. In the context of
the threats, but also of the benefits of access to information and communication opportunities in the online sector, human dignity, democracy, the rule of law and protection against discrimination are key factors. Not only as benchmarks for a minimum level of regulation, but

also as common denominators for the EU and all Member States in light of exercising their competencies.

13. At the secondary law level, the AVMSD in particular is an essential part of the relevant legal framework for the dissemination of online content, despite the approach of minimum harmonization pursued therein. This is especially noteworthy with the adoption of rules for video sharing platforms adopted with the revision in 2018, which make these types of platform providers more accountable because they are seen as part of the audiovisual media environment and must therefore be subject to at least similar rules to other media services in order to protect recipients. The transposition of the rules, which in some cases offer far-reaching discretion to Member States encouraging self- and co-regulation mechanisms, is currently taking place at Member State level.

14. However, it is not only the media-specific secondary legislation that is relevant for the online content dissemination, but also other sectoral provisions that, for example, primarily pursue economic or consumer protection policy objectives. The DSMD defines a new category of "online content-sharing service provider" introducing a completely new set of obligations for these; the Platform-to-Business Regulation creates certain information and transparency obligations for online intermediation services and search engines relevant for the visibility of content and products. Existing rules, such as the General Data Protection Regulation (GDPR) with its strictly harmonizing approach establishing the marketplace principle, are just as relevant for the online or platform sector as much as are those currently under discussion, for example the Proposal for a Regulation on tackling terrorist content online. In addition, there are instruments that deliberately leave room for manoeuvre and the possibility of exceptions for the pursuit of media and cultural policy objectives at the national level, which enable supplementary rules concerning content dissemination. This is supplemented by a series of measures encouraging self-regulation at the level of EU coordination and support measures, for example in the area of hate speech and disinformation. Overlaps with the horizontal rules of the ECD are unavoidable. These secondary legal bases must not only be brought into line with any new or to be reformed legal bases, but also shows that there are and must be special rules for certain providers of ISS that address specific objectives and particularities.

Regulatory Options on EU level

15. On this basis of competencies, fundamental rights and values the EU has a wide range of regulatory options using mainly the achievement of a functioning (digital) single market as legal basis. When considering these options there is a need to reconcile this objective, which is fundamentally driven by economic considerations and policy, but has considerable impact on other sectors which are already regulated at the Member State and EU level, with exactly those rules which can also pursue other objectives. However, there is a large variety of players in the online platform sector that offer different services to different recipients using different content, technologies and user interfaces, but still have in common (to varying degrees) that they "only" offer access to certain content or services. Therefore, there is a continued need for horizontally applicable rules which allow for sector-specific approaches to be upheld. The sector-specific perspective – be it consumer protection, media, cultural, telecommunications, competition, criminal, copyright or data protection law, to name relevant examples – through which the regulation of ISS must also be viewed despite their common features as "intermediation services", makes full harmonisation within a single set of rules impossible. For this reason, the horizontal approach that is to be retained in principle calls for a detailed examination of existing legislative approaches and the establishment of sectoral exceptions and room for manoeuvre for the Member States exercising their competencies regarding for example cultural policy or safeguarding pluralism while taking into account impact on the freedom of expression.

16. On the one hand, this requires that the general rules e.g. on duties and obligations of service providers are content-neutral and open enough for the dynamic and continuously changing nature of the online environment which requires a flexible way of responding to new challenges. This could entail laying down fundamental principles and rules in the horizontally applicable act while leaving room for specific additions or supplementary action in the future but also by ensuring an openness for the actual application of the existing rules originating from other legislative acts. The granting of powers to competent and professional authorities to formulate or draw up concretising guidelines is a means that has already been tried and tested in many sectoral legislative acts at EU and Member State level and which enables these to agree on common standards and enforcement procedures.

17. On the other hand, this means that not only the existing rules in the ECD need to be revised or replaced, but a new assessment must also be made as to which sectoral rules should continue to take precedence over the general rules of the ECD and where there must be (additional) sectoral exceptions in the light of competence limitations of the EU. This concretely means that measures taken at (EU or) national level in order to promote cultural and linguistic diversity and to ensure pluralism must still be excluded from a harmonisation approach. This calls for a general clarification of the relationship between existing rules on EU and Member State level, in particular the continued priority of sectoral regulations such as the AVMSD or the DSMD even if these also refer to instruments or rules that will be placed in the horizontal act, too.

18. Regarding the question of the appropriate legal instrument, there are several possible options for binding and non-binding legislative acts. It should be borne in mind that, although previous measures in the area of self-regulation have proven to be beneficial for the development of best practices and the establishment of cooperation and dialogue, shortcomings concerning effective enforcement, not last due to a lack of access to more reliable data needed to assess compliance, have become evident. Co-regulation mechanisms should therefore be a minimum option to be considered but they, too, need to take these shortcomings into account by involving appropriate supervisory mechanisms and provide for sufficiently concrete obligations. A new regulatory framework should be laid down in a Directive to the extent that it would otherwise limit Member State discretion in implementation in a field – media regulation – that is closely connected to their reserved competence. It would be difficult to argue the need for a Regulation as overarching instrument especially considering its quality as horizontal approach, which must take into account a number of sectoral exceptions and Member State competence which is why full harmonization cannot take place anyway. Possibly, different instruments depending on the main legal basis for the provisions will have to be envisaged. If a Regulation is chosen as overall instrument, irrespective of its more limited flexibility with regard to downstream sectoral legislation, it would have to be designed with sufficient opening clauses or connectors to Member State laws.

Clarification of the Country of Origin Principle as Basis and its Exceptions

19. The COO is not only the basis of the ECD, but also of other legal acts regulating services with typically (also) cross-border nature, such as the AVMSD. It is a consequence of establishing an internal market based on the use of the fundamental freedoms. The application of the principle creates legal certainty for providers, as they basically only have to deal with the legal systems of a single Member State and only have to deal with that State or its competent regulatory bodies in procedural terms, even if they provide their services in other Member States, too. This is particularly essential in the online sector, since the services offered are regularly cross-border in nature without the provider necessarily having to actively orientate the service to a specific Member State market. This applies first and foremost to media content. The COO is therefore particularly important not only for large and internationally oriented ISS, but also for SMEs and start-ups, which regularly would have more difficulties to obtain detailed information about the legal requirements in all Member States, let alone to comply with them.

20. For this reason, the fundamental validity of the COO should remain untouched. However, the possibility for Member States of resorting – in urgent cases directly – to measures against (domestic) technical "carriers", in particular Internet Access Providers (IAPs), instead of (foreign) content providers or host providers in case of responding to illegal content without this constituting a breach of the COO per se, needs to be explicitly stated in order to avoid unclarity and resulting hesitation on the part of regulatory authorities to act in this way in high-risk cases. Identified problems, especially in connection with the cross-border dissemination of online content and associated enforcement difficulties, should be clearer addressed by defining derogation cases as well as the possibility to rely on the market location principle for content originating or disseminated by non-domestic providers in certain clearly defined cases. Such a newly found procedural set-up could serve as blueprint for possible future clarifications of COO/market destination distinction also for other parts of the legal framework concerning content, in particular the AVMSD.

21. The Member States' power to derogate from the COO for certain service providers on the grounds that public interests are endangered must be maintained, but the procedure should be clarified and streamlined so it can lead to a binding result within a reasonable and that means short period of time. In particular, it should be assessed whether the general interest objectives contained so far are sufficient

to take account of existing problems. This is especially relevant with respect to the definition of incitement to hatred, which has also been expanded under the AVMSD. Subject clarification should also be foreseen as regards a broad understanding of the protection of minors, which goes beyond protecting against illegal content. The scope of that protection continues to result from Member State law. Furthermore, the possibility of expanding the scope to include threats to democratic elections (e.g. in light of disinformation campaigns) and public safety, explicitly with reference to terrorist propaganda, should be taken into consideration to react current and increasingly relevant threats. The streamlining of the envisaged procedure of participation of the Member State of establishment and the Commission should include the establishment of concrete information and reaction obligations of the participating Member States and tight deadlines to do so. The establishment of a dispute settlement procedure in cases of conflict with the participation of a body composed e. g. of representatives of the regulatory authorities appears useful. This could be based on cooperation of competent bodies (see below) and include fast track and joint discussion/decision-making procedures in order to be both efficient but as mindful as possible for the COO.

22. The same applies to the power of deviation in emergency cases with correspondingly much tighter obligations. In cases of emergency derogation, there should be a tiered system of options, in particular according to the level of risk of the content or infringement, which also takes into account the responsiveness level of enforcement in the competent Member State. Given the fact that, with regard to non-EU providers, it would be possible - with due respect to limits under public international law – to act in accordance with the market location principle under Member State law anyway, since there is no harmonized EU legislation governing the validity of the COO for such providers, the enforcement of law and fight against illegal content within the EU must not be subject to excessive hurdles when it comes to high-risk content such as content that violates human dignity or terrorist propaganda irrespective of where it originates. Details of this should be developed especially within the cooperation of competent bodies.

Defining the Scope of Application of the Framework

23. The need for an update of the definitions concerning the scope of application of the relevant framework for information society services has become evident over the years. Whilst the very general informa-

tion society services definition dating back to 1998 allowed and allows an inclusion of all different types of actors in the online environment, it is not sufficient when it comes to applying specific rules for different actors. For that reason, already the ECD introduced specific categories of providers which under certain circumstances profit from liability exemptions. While the more technical transmission-oriented categories (mere conduit, caching) were hardly problematic in their application, the actually relevant category is that of hosting service provider. The latter has created problems not only its interpretation (namely concerning neutrality/passiveness and actual knowledge criteria as well as the possible reach of preventive injunctions against these), which were not completely resolved by case law of the CJEU, but also through a differing approach on Member State level. In addition to the changed nature of what may have in the past been a more identifiable category of host providers both in terms of business model but also technical capacity, recent years have shown that – in these cases outside of the content dissemination context – even the ISS definition as such may be difficult in its application when distinguishing from more specific definitions (e.g. transportation service) concerning new types of intermediaries or platforms.

24. As a minimum reaction to this, existing definitions regarding the scope of a new or amended act concerning online content dissemination need to be substantially reworked and integrate the elements of interpretation guidance already offered by the CJEU. Preferably, at least the definition of hosting provider is replaced by a broader definition which does not rely any longer on the distinction of active/passive nature of the service provider as this is no longer decisive nor a clear indicator. Beyond having (in continuation of the ISS definition) a very general and broad definition addressing all types of online services providers or more specifically all types of platforms and intermediaries which should be open enough to encompass future new types of services, there should be room for more specific categories of providers so more specific rules can be attached to these. These could be either provided by sector-specific rules which continue to exist besides the horizontally applicable legislative act – examples for which would be the specific type of platform addressed by the AVMSD (VSPs) or the DSMD – or within the horizontal act itself. Taking into consideration the role that platforms play as intermediating instances between content producer and content user/consumer, there has to be at least a specific category of "content platforms/intermediaries" which can be dis-

tinguished from other types of platforms that also act as intermediaries between two parties and also have organisational influence on the interaction but do not concern content. This does not mean that comparable rules cannot be applied to these different types of providers, but it safeguards that the significance in the context of content dissemination can be adequately addressed.

25. Specific online content dissemination platform definitions exist already, such as in the AVMSD and the DSMD, but in creating an additional content intermediary definition, any type of platform contributing to the exchange of content in the public sphere – irrespective of whether it relates to audiovisual content or any other type of content and whether it fulfils the detailed requirements laid down in existing definitions – could be addressed and included in the regulatory framework. The broader definition should limit the criteria to a few, namely addressing information society service providers that offer the storage of or access to content (created/uploaded/shared) by recipients of the service with the aim of making it available to other recipients of the service and clarifying that (for this activity) the content producer is not under the authority or control of the provider (in which case the provider anyway falls in other categories). Only when it comes to applicability of specific rules should a further differentiation be made which reflects the degree of organisational involvement (actual and potential) as the differentiating standard. This would still allow for a distinction by editorial influence (= e.g. AVMS categories in the AVMSD), curatorial influence (organisation, presentation etc. of the content, = AVMSD-VSP- or DSMD-type, but also as in the Proposal TERREG) and merely technical transmission which is in principle reduced to direct communication forms or technical facilitation (e.g. Internet access providers).

26. In addition, to (a) newly formulated category/ies, the different impact of providers can also be reflected. This would allow for certain exemptions in the substantive rules concerning certain types of providers that otherwise would fulfil the criteria (e.g. non-profit types of services) or for considering economic disparities between major players and smaller market participants. However, these should not be entirely excluded from the category. Instead, while the core elements of the rules such as treatment of illegal content should fully apply to all providers within the scope, such providers could only be confronted with a subset of rules in the implementation. Further, it should be considered how regulatory transparency can be increased by providing – either based

on an own categorization in a registration process reviewed by a supervisory authority or established by the latter – lists of content intermediaries falling under the definition and, where applicable, jurisdiction of a specific Member State. A periodic evaluation of the definition – which would be more difficult if it is exclusively integrated in a Directive or even Regulation – or, preferably, the empowerment of competent bodies to give application guidance of the definition by listing criteria (also of new types of services) that can be regarded as fulfilling an element of the definition.

Reforming the Liability Privilege Regime

27. The starting point concerning the disputed liability privilege regime in the ECD is the following: without having harmonised EU rules on liability under certain conditions providers including host providers were shielded against application of liability rules on Member State level. While the original introduction of this regime was meant to safeguard innovation and offer legal certainty for „new" service providers when developing especially services allowing content exchange, the situation has changed entirely: the unclear reach of the liability exemption has partly led to a limited contribution by providers in taking a more active role in preventing dissemination of illegal or harmful content and partly made enforcement against such content especially by competent bodies difficult. This lack of enforcement online has not only led to a significantly different approach towards ensuring content standards in more traditional forms of content dissemination and via intermediaries. Fundamental values of the EU including an efficient protection of fundamental rights necessitate, however, a comparable approach concerning (from user perspective) comparable types of content dissemination. Therefore, the question of upholding or amending the liability privilege regime has to be looked at through an entirely different lens than when it was introduced.

28. Without having to question the liability privilege per se, it needs to be shaped in a way that it does not hinder or limit efficient enforcement of rules e.g. concerning illegal types of content. Although it is already possible to be introduced under the current ECD, a clarification in that sense should be undertaken that the question of liability privilege is a separate matter from imposing certain obligations on intermediaries that go beyond the reactive measures needed to be able to benefit from the liability privilege. The latter currently is based on providers' expeditious reaction by removing or disabling access to illegal content

when gaining actual knowledge. The criteria such as "knowledge" could be defined more clearly and ideally accompanied by the obligation of introducing specific procedures leading to this knowledge. In addition, the limited set of reactive measures should be elaborated including possible measures in reaction to illegal content that go beyond a simple removal. As mentioned, already the current ECD and the interpretation by the CJEU allow Member States to request measures that reflect due care of the providers without these conflicting with the prohibition to introduce general monitoring obligations. This prohibition should be upheld in as far as it constitutes an element in protecting the widest possible use of freedom of expression by recipients of the service, but should be clarified as not hindering proactive duties of content intermediaries depending on certain conditions as set out below.

29. The combination of liability privilege with separate obligations and duties of providers would better reflect the crucial position of content intermediaries in facilitating the use of fundamental rights but also suppressing illegal use. It would further allow a dependence on compliance with the obligations and duties in order to be able to continuously profit from the liability exemption as well as foreseeing sanctioning instruments in case of non-compliance. To recall in this context: the liability exemption for content dissemination is dependent on the relevant content not being own content of the intermediary in which case normal liability would apply. In that context the circumstances should be defined under which intermediaries become liable for illegal user content if they do not disclose the identity of that user to supervising bodies in order for them to be able to take action against the user. In order to avoid further unclarity about when "curation" (i.e. organisational involvement of the intermediary in the content dissemination) comes close to "editorial control" (which would establish liability directly), adding the layer of responsibility (= obligations and duties) at least clarifies that irrespective of the liability exemption these types of providers have compliance obligations. Underlining in a reformed framework that such responsibility can include not only the way "illegal" but also harmful content as defined by the laws of the Member States is treated, would contribute to a better balancing of the diverging interests at stake. Finally, in the context of liability exemption it should be noted that although technical services, such as IAPs are not the primary addressee for enforcement measures against illegal content dissemination, they too can be target of actions taken by com-

petent bodies with which they have to comply irrespective of their liability exemption.

Introducing Obligations and Duties for Service Providers

30. As mentioned above, obligations and duties can be introduced for service providers in a more spelled out way than just referring to the possibility of foreseeing duty of care standards as is currently the case. These responsibility-oriented instruments do not concern the question of liability (or its exemption) in individual cases of violation of the applicable legal framework, but a separate regime which allows holding the content intermediaries accountable in case of non-compliance with the structural expectations concerning their responsibility. The advantage of introducing responsibility requirements in a harmonising legislative act at EU level is responding to the pan-European (and typically global) activity of most relevant service providers and thereby giving these legal clarity in a comparable way as it was done with the initial ECD and the introduction of (common) liability exemptions. In addition, these would allow for applying joint enforcement standards even if specificities of national law need to be taken into account by competent national bodies. Finally, it would clarify the possibilities of introducing such measures beyond the current step-by-step evaluation of national measures by the jurisprudence of the CJEU.

31. The expectations towards intermediary responses to their responsibility should – respecting a proportionality approach – take into consideration the type and position of the service provider concerned as well as the level of harm and the risk of its occurrence. Concerning the intermediaries, a graduated approach will be applied depending on the impact of the service for the general public, which in turn concerns both the actual service offered as well as the market or opinion power allowing for exempting certain categories of especially small or emerging providers from certain obligations and imposing potentially stricter obligations for platforms with significant intermediary powers. Concerning the level of harm this means that the measures expected should be more strict for high-risk, high-impact and high-probability types of content compared to responses to risks at the lower end of the scale. This approach needs to refer to the types of harms that should be prevented by responsibility measures, without, however, having to define them in detail. For that purpose, existing sector-specific provisions can be referred to or used and it also allows Member States to uphold

their legislative framework defining the categories of illegal or harmful content to which such measures would then correspond.

32. The carving out of responsibility requirements as mentioned in a summarized form below can lean itself on the approach of the revised AVMSD concerning appropriate measures to be taken by VSPs, as it already establishes a detailed responsibility standard which is separate from the other rules of the Directive that concern providers of content with editorial (and therefore increased) responsibility. The AVMSD-approach also refers to the use of codes of conduct in a co-regulatory setting, which allows to include established practices by industry as long as there is an inclusion of some form of robust and independent oversight e.g. through endorsement by competent regulatory bodies.

33. The obligations (so-to-speak the rules within the responsibility framework) and duties (the tasks to be fulfilled) require diligent economic operators to follow the concept of risk management which is based on an initial risk assessment and the responses to identified risks. As is established practice in other areas such as for financial services or for personal data processing the assessment equates to a systematic preparation and preparedness for reacting to risk situations in practice. Risk thereby does not mean individual cases in which a potential violation of content standards occur and necessitate a reaction but include avoidance measures so that risks do not even materialize. Depending on the outcome of the risk assessment the expected risk responses or mitigation strategies can derive from practices and standards that are commonly accepted and laid down by certified standard-setting bodies which regularly will include reference to state of the art technology. A further possibility to enhance legal certainty for content intermediaries as far as their responsibility is concerned, is to list the basic measures in the legislative act but foresee the further concretisation by Guidelines adopted by the Commission or competent national regulatory bodies or other designated institutions.

34. The responsibility framework will include a number of areas for which (certain) intermediaries need to have measures in place complying with accepted standards. These will partly be of a proactive nature, partly reactive and concerning the latter also be a link to the question of liability: measures to be taken as a reaction to a notification about illegal content can expand from merely taking down that content (failure to do so leading to actual liability) to ensuring future non-reappearance of that content ("staying down") as well as following up the action with information to concerned parties as well as to competent

bodies in a reporting mechanism. Therefore, a clear distinction between types of duties is not necessary.

35. Guidance concerning the procedures to be installed and followed for notification of illegal content is a minimum request for the future act, especially if the liability privilege remains unchanged and is therefore dependent on the adequate response to such notifications. These procedural elements should include the way reporting is possible and facilitated, the conditions for response measures and redress possibilities, whereas especially the technologies to be used need not be specified in the law itself. The same applies for other types of technical measures that might be within the measures expected from intermediaries, such as e.g. age verification systems or content flagging systems.

36. Another main area for which more detailed requirements are needed in the legislation concerns transparency. This entails transparency towards users and affected recipients of the service in case of content blocking or removal, through informing about the use of algorithmic instruments and their main functionalities, it also includes transparency towards competent bodies charged with supervision of the service both as a general reporting obligation as well as responding to individual requests. Concerning content moderation policies, transparency is not sufficient nor the above-mentioned reaction in case of notification. In light of the role of content intermediaries these have to be able to demonstrate that they are using policies that do not limit freedom of expression beyond the combatting of illegal and harmful content and how they adhere to the idea of a rule of law-approach in case of disputes about decisions made by guaranteeing different levels of challenging these in an easily accessible manner.

37. This basic set of requirements which has been exemplified above is complemented by relying on accepted standards in the way the requirements are to be reached. This combination of laying down the responsibility approach in the law but relying strongly on such standards allows on the one hand for a flexible and continuous evolution of these standards as well as a close involvement of the industry in identifying possible standards. The system then allows – beyond the question of liability in specific cases – to hold content intermediaries accountable and imposing potentially also a sanctioning regime which does not respond to individual cases of illegal content dissemination but the lack of readiness by disregarding the expected standards. In that way, burden of proof lies with the providers and encourages compliant behaviour. As a result, the limiting of dissemination of illegal or

harmful content online seems more promising than by only relying on individual cases brought forward by private parties or public authorities.

Institutional Setup for Monitoring of Compliance and Enforcement

38. Creating rules necessitates ensuring their enforcement in case they are not complied with. Besides enforcement by private parties, designated bodies – typically public authorities – are in charge of monitoring compliance of supervised persons or entities and reacting in case of violations. The rules not only have to allow for an efficient enforcement by taking into account procedures and an institutional set-up, but there also has to be an adequate implementation of this set-up by the competent entity. This holds especially true if the subject matter of regulation requires specific types of enforcement bodies, as is the case for oversight of media and other types of content communication for which freedom of expression prohibits direct state influence in the monitoring. Although the creation of rules on an EU level may seem to call for bodies enforcing these rules on EU level, the application of rules deriving from EU law in most cases is still dependent on and assigned to authorities of the Member States. Even though the existing and future rules on ISS concern activities that typically have a cross-border dimension and will often concern providers active in all or the majority of EU Member States, the enforcement should continue to rely on the Member State level. This concerns at least the category of providers relevant for this study, the content intermediaries. For those there is a comparability to media-type regulatory conditions that allocate the competence with Member States not last because of national, regional or local specificities which – at least for media regulation including the extended scope of the AVMSD – should be able to be included in enforcement approaches. Irrespective of this competency assignment cooperation structures are possible.

39. The COO is reason for both giving the supervisory power to Member States' (country of origin's) bodies while calling for the improvement of cooperation between these competent bodies on a pan-European level in order to ensure the effective enforcement across borders within the single market. Firstly, however, the rules have to frame the supervisory structure either by defining it on EU level or by requesting Member States to do so along a certain amount of given criteria in their national law. The COO clearly not only attaches jurisdiction to the establishment of providers but also the obligation of the Member

States with jurisdiction to use their supervisory powers. Efficient oversight of content-related activity therefore necessitates not only independence from influence by public or private parties, the adequate equipment by assigning relevant competence and providing sufficient means and ensuring relevant expertise, as well as the authorization to contribute to a transnational cooperation. For this purpose and because of the comparability of the monitoring task relating to content intermediaries a reliance on regulatory bodies charged with this type of supervision since a long time seems an obvious solution. But even if such expanded coverage of content-related supervision is not assigned to national regulatory authorities equivalent to the ones under the AVMSD, that Directive can serve as blueprint for the criteria to establish adequate bodies. Where supervision of content intermediaries necessitates new powers, such as e.g. in order to measure compliance with responsibility requirements or, to name a concrete example, transparency obligations, these have to be expressly assigned, such as in the example information rights vis-a-vis providers or the possibility for auditing. These new powers can extend to sanctioning possibilities for non-compliance with the responsibility requirement which is to be seen separate from the question of potential liability in specific cases of content dissemination.

40. Concerning the cooperation on EU level different degrees can be conceived: national competent bodies could come together for a loose exchange of viewpoints and comparable non-binding activity; they could be part of a specifically created body in which they contribute to formalized cooperation which includes joint decision-making in some cases by majority opinion; finally, they could be part of a cooperation system with a separate body created on EU level. The lowest form of engagement is inappropriate, as it does not ensure any form of joint agreements on directions of regulatory action. The example of the European Regulators Group for Audiovisual Media Services (ERGA) clearly shows how changing the format from a more loosely structured group (then based on a Commission Decision) to a formally established body with assigned tasks in the revised AVMSD allowed it to elevate the exchange of best practices and development of common guidelines by its Members. For both above mentioned degrees of more intensive cooperation there are a number of examples in more recent legislative acts of the EU. Namely the European Data Protection Board (EDPB) brings together the national supervisory authorities which in a formalized consistency procedure can issue joint opinions on proce-

dures of individual authorities and in the event of disputes even make binding majority decisions concerning cross-border cases. It can be regarded as the main source of inspiration when considering the further enhancement of cooperation – laid down in law – of competent bodies charged with media and content communication oversight. Especially concerning possible specific EU rules for systemic platforms (which can include content intermediaries) an even more enhanced form of cooperation in supervision that includes the creation of an additional body can be envisaged. It could lean on the creation of the Single Supervisory Mechanism for banking supervision, which foresees direct authority only for significant banks, however taking into consideration the very specific nature of that system and the pre-existence of a relevant body with the European Central Bank.

41. The actual form of cooperation will depend on the agreed substantive rules and its structure can use existing models which are adapted to the specifics of the market for online content dissemination and which is put in context with other forms and institutions charged with oversight of other types of platforms covered by the new rules. This can include regulatory structures for consumer protection, competition law or newly created dedicated bodies concerning the platform sector. Defining the cooperation and the powers assigned to the cooperation structure, which could include establishing e.g. sanctioning powers, in detail is easier possible in form of a Regulation, which potentially would have to be created separate to the substantive ruleset (as was the case for the Body of European Regulators for Electronic Communications (BEREC)). However, the example of ERGA shows that it is also possible within a Directive containing provisions that need transposition by Member States. In whatever form it is laid down, the cooperation tasks should extend at least to concretising the application of the rules where assigned to do so, agreeing on common enforcement standards, giving opinions on cases of cross-border content dissemination in case of dispute about the treatment in the country of origin, ensuring efficient information provision between each other in concrete cases and participating in fast-track-procedures for urgent cases which justify a market destination oriented exception to the COO. Beyond the cooperation between national competent bodies, cooperation (on national but also on EU level) includes working together with supervised entities especially in co-regulatory approaches, but with other supervisory bodies e.g. in data protection or competition law, too.

Evaluation of the approaches chosen in the DSA Proposal

42. The European Commission's two Proposals for a DSA and a DMA constitute, as announced, the suggested new horizontal approach to the regulation of intermediary service providers of which online platforms are a specific category. Content intermediaries are not treated as a separate category differently compared to other types of providers, but there are certain rules which are of more relevant in the context of such intermediaries, namely the ones about online platforms. The DMA Proposal takes a general approach to responding to a market situation in which few gatekeepers provide essential services ("core platform services") for connecting business and users. For such gatekeeper platforms an ex ante regulatory approach is chosen that resembles a competition law approach. It is relevant also for content dissemination as some of the key channels for online dissemination are via platforms that will fulfil the criteria to be designated as gatekeepers. The main instrument in the context of this study is the DSA Proposal which introduces a set of due diligence obligations applicable to all intermediary service providers, some additional for hosting services, some more detailed for online platforms and finally specific obligations to manage systemic risks for very large online platforms (VLOPs); integrates the liability privilege regime of the ECD with some clarifications and additional liability conditions regarding authority orders, while leaving the above due diligence obligations untouched by the question of liability; and suggests a new structure for the supervision and enforcement of the rules.

43. Both legislative acts are proposed as Regulations, although the scope of the DSA and the principle of subsidiarity speak in favour of an approach that leaves Member States more room for manoeuvre and thereby opting for a Directive. Both Proposals use Art. 114 TFEU, the internal market harmonisation clause, as legal basis. This approach regulating economic aspects may not conflict with the Member States retained competence for rules concerning media and content. The cross-border nature of online dissemination alone does not justify the choice of a Regulation, which is why a solution needs to be found that respects the allocation of competences, but even more important the continued relevance of sectoral EU legislation. Concerning the latter, it is to be welcomed that a lex specialis rule is aimed for concerning the AVMSD, DSMD and other relevant acts, but a further clarification is needed in order to avoid uncertainty as to the national transposition measures for those Directives status in comparison to the DSA.

Finally, the continuation of the ECD besides the new DSA (and only a transferal of the liability privilege rules) should be reconsidered.

44. The DSA Proposal moves towards a market location principle which on the one hand clearly extends the scope of the rules to all providers offering services to EU citizens, thereby making it applicable to EU domestic and foreign ISS. On the other hand, it opens up more possibilities for action initiated by regulatory authorities that do not regularly have jurisdiction as they are not from the establishment State. The proposed rules consider the genuine link requirement under public international law to justify the application of rules to foreign providers, with detailed criteria to identify a substantial connection of the provider to the market of a given Member State. There is an obligation for such providers to designate a legal representative in one of the EU Member States which shall also facilitate supervisory actions against the providers in question.

45. The DSA Proposal creates several categories of intermediary service providers in order to differentiate the newly foreseen rules in their application to the categories according to their relevance. However, the basic distinction of intermediary service providers as it is contained in the ECD in order to define the application of liability privileges, is upheld. By moving it into a Regulation there is potential for overcoming existing differing national transpositions or interpretations of the provider categories, but due to a lack of further precision of mere conduits, caching and hosting services, it is not unlikely that uncertainty remains. In addition, no further differentiation was made even though the relevant Recital aims at clarifying that new types of services that have emerged can potentially fall under the existing definitions. It is, however, an important step that online platforms are identified as a separate, more specific category of hosting services, to which specific obligations can be attached. The reluctance of clarifying further the relevance of "neutrality" of platforms and continuing to rely on the distinction of active and passive hosts will likely lead to further interpretation difficulties in the future and should therefore be revisited in the legislative procedure. The Proposal considers size of platforms as a relevant criterion for either limiting or expanding obligations, while it needs to be discussed further which of those should be applicable to all providers.

46. The virtually unchanged liability exemptions in the DSA Proposal have only been narrowed down to the extent that there is a clear obligation to react to authority orders concerning illegal content or re-

questing information on users. Separating the question of liability (exemption) from the need to comply with additional (newly introduced) due diligence obligations has advantages, but the interconnection of those two chapters of the Proposal need to be further discussed, especially concerning the question when under national law failure to comply with obligations can justify assuming liability of the provider. The Proposal achieves a clarification of criteria for actual knowledge and introduces harmonised notice and action procedures. The accompanying Recitals to the upheld "no general monitoring" rule will likely not be sufficient to end uncertainty of what type of specific measures aimed at keeping content down or proactively identify specific, new illegal acts, are allowed without being in conflict with that rule. The newly inserted provisions in the chapter on liability show the need to enable courts and authorities to be able to order timely and consistent reactions of providers especially in urgent cases. In that context, the final version of the future framework should address clearly that Member States approaches to treating harmful content (or other sectoral approaches in EU legislation) are possible even when the DSA Proposal itself does not deal with the matter itself.

47. The comprehensive list of due diligence obligations introduced in the DSA Proposal is to be welcomed. Although it is not entirely clear that all of these would need to be addressed in an EU Regulation, especially when they touch media-oriented content regulation which is Member State competence, the graduated, cumulative allocation of obligations is a necessary step to include intermediaries in the enforcement. For some of the proactive obligations in the context of risk management an inclusion of other providers than the VLOPs should be considered. The notice and action mechanisms suggested follow previous Recommendations of the Commission and especially the reporting obligations will help to have a clearer picture about provider behaviour. Mandating the introduction of complaint handling systems and out-of-court dispute settlements improve the user position. However, there is no consistent reliance on industry standards but rather on codes of conduct, for which it needs to be critically questioned whether they are adequate and effective for this area. The enhanced procedural framework for trusted flaggers is an additional improvement compared to the status quo, while the limitation of Know-Your-Customer obligations to online marketplaces should be reconsidered in favour of a more general expectation concerning knowledge about and verification of users by the platforms.

48. The DSA Proposal offers a new supervisory framework enabling cooperation in cross-border cases including a sanctioning regime. There could, however, be a stronger reliance on administrative structures of the Member States instead of a concentration of certain powers in the Commission, which – other than for the DMA approach that resembles the situation in competition law – is not an evident need for the scope of the DSA. This also applies to the set-up of the newly proposed joint body of the national regulatory bodies on EU level, which allows for institutionalized cooperation forms, but to a rather limited extent without decision-making powers. The "accountability" of the national regulatory authorities towards those of other Member States is an important step towards efficient enforcement in cross-border cases, especially as there is a procedural consequence if there are differing opinions. However, no consistency procedure similar as for the area of data protection cooperation between national supervisory authorities is foreseen so far. Existing cooperation structures which reflect specific requirements in sectoral approaches such as the AVMSD need to be more clearly safeguarded against an overlap by the DSA-structures. Requiring Member States to focus their oversight structures on one Digital Services Coordinator may not be an adequate solution for federal states or states without a convergent regulatory authority. In the further legislative procedure a careful assessment should be made of the procedural steps for any type of violation of the substantive provisions of the proposed Regulation in order to see whether the changes would facilitate or complicate the procedures in cross-border cases.

Conclusions

49. Based on these findings, some main conclusions about a future framework for online platforms on EU level can be drawn. The suggestions presented in this study concern specifically content intermediaries. Because of the relevance of such platforms for the dissemination and availability of media and communication content more generally, it is justified to pay specific attention to these in reforming the horizontally applicable framework for intermediaries. Such a framework promises a unified and overarching approach but can also be problematic in addressing specificities of certain categories of platforms or services. Therefore, the basic rules can and should apply to any type of intermediary, but the requirements for rules that impact media and communication content are different to that of a marketplace where goods and services are traded. For such content intermediaries, not only the

Member States' retained power to regulate in this field needs to be considered, but also the existing framework for supervision and enforcement of rules concerning content dissemination. This is especially important in view of the goal that for content the same rules should apply (and be enforced) online as offline. A further clarification of how the new general rules relate to existing or future rules specifically enacted for regulating content dissemination should be achieved.

50. The study proposes solutions based on the approach that regulating content intermediaries results from and respects the fundamental rights basis and the core European values and is not only motivated by ensuring a single market with expansive use of the fundamental freedoms with only very limited restrictions. Therefore, additional burdens for intermediaries are reflective of their position, in many cases amounting to dominant market power, but certainly having a crucial function between content creation and consumption by users. These rules are not meant to hamper the ability of platforms to act as economic operators in the single market, but integrate them in a more clearly defined manner in the safeguarding of a functioning public communication sphere. Although it would be conceivable to limit a new framework to laying down certain common regulatory goals (such as fairness, transparency and accountability) and enabling supervisory authorities or other bodies charged with the oversight and enforcement of such standards to further detail the requirements, the DSA Proposal goes the way of providing detailed rules and delegating further clarifications to the Commission. It is very important that the shaping of the enforcement or rules concerning content intermediaries is done by competent bodies that fulfil criteria of efficiency and independence from state powers, supervised entities and private parties. Such bodies are the established national regulatory authorities in the field of audiovisual media services which have developed in their joint body on EU level advanced forms of cooperation in cross-border matters. These structures could be used or at least the proposed supervisory framework should take more inspiration from that monitoring and enforcement experience.

51. Without any doubt, the DSA and DMA Proposals are to be welcomed as they promise at the end of the legislative procedure to be the basis for a sustainable regulatory framework for the digital sector and can put the EU in the position of setting standards in a way that was already successfully done in the data protection field. The Proposals are ambitious in the way they are aimed at addressing not only intermedi-

aries overall, but that they identify specific categories of providers that are essential for the connection between businesses and users and are then under special scrutiny as gatekeepers or have to comply with specific additional obligations. Applicability of the proposed Regulations as well as jurisdiction will not be dependent on establishment of the concerned providers in an EU Member State which is another important signal to the market. Assuming that the new ruleset will stand in principle for a long period of time and will shape the digital intermediaries market at least for a decade, the suggested rules should be seen as a good basis but which can be further improved in the legislative procedure in the way described in the study in order to reach a solution that responds in a promising way to the challenges previously identified.

Executive Summary – Deutsch

Hintergrund der Studie

1. Wir leben im Zeitalter der Digitalisierung, in dem es im Internet jederzeit möglich ist, die unterschiedlichsten Arten von Inhalten online zu finden, auf sie zuzugreifen, sie mit anderen zu teilen und weiterzuverbreiten. Ländergrenzen spielen dabei ebenso wenig eine Rolle wie Sprachbarrieren, die durch die fortschreitende technologische Entwicklung zunehmend verschwinden. Der Markt für digitale Inhalte ist daher global, entwicklungsoffen und befindet sich in ständigem Wandel und Wachstum. Das eröffnet nicht nur wirschaftliche Chancen für Unternehmen, die in diesem Markt operieren können, sondern bietet auch der Gesellschaft eine Reihe von Vorteilen, z. B. in Bezug auf die Informationsfreiheit, den interkulturellen Austausch oder breitere Auswahlmöglichkeiten für die Nutzung von (Medien-)Inhalten, ungeachtet der Risiken und Herausforderungen, die dieser globalisierte Austausch mit sich bringt. Intermediäre und andere Plattformen, die den Zugang zu Inhalten eröffnen, diese bereitstellen, sammeln und kategorisieren, die Foren für den Austausch und die Erstellung von Inhalten durch Nutzende bieten, sind daher auch regelmäßig Gatekeeper für die Inanspruchnahme der genannten Vorteile.

2. Die Regulierung dieses mehrseitigen Marktes der Verbreitung und Vermittlung von Online-Inhalten ist so vielfältig wie die beteiligten Akteure und die Arten der Inhalte – ob video-, audio-, bild- oder textbasiert. Obwohl es aufgrund der Zuständigkeitsverteilung zwischen der EU und ihren Mitgliedstaaten vor dem Hintergrund der Sicherung von Medienpluralismus und der Funktionen der Medien im demokratischen und kulturellen Gefüge keine vollständige Harmonisierung der Medienregulierung auf EU-Ebene gibt, bestehen verschiedene Rechtsakte, die sich mittelbar oder unmittelbar auf die Medien selbst, die Erstellung von Inhalten, ihre Verbreitung und Präsentation sowie ihre Nutzung beziehen oder zumindest auswirken. Grundrechtliche Garantien der Meinungsfreiheit sowie der Medienfreiheit und -pluralität, grundfreiheitliche Garantien einer grundsätzlich ungehinderten grenzüberschreitenden Verbreitung von Waren und Dienstleistungen (auch „Inhalten") sowie ein Fundament gemeinsamer Werte der EU, das auch für die Vermittlung von Inhalten relevant ist, münden in ein komple-

xes Netz von Sekundärrechtsakten, die unterschiedliche Ziele und Schutzrichtungen verfolgen.

3. Die Schaffung dieses sekundärrechtlichen Rahmens reicht zum Teil mehr als 30 Jahre zurück und damit in eine Zeit, in der die Digitalisierung und die mit ihr einhergehenden tiefgreifenden Auswirkungen auf die Verbreitung von Medien, die Vermittlung von Inhalten sowie die Art und Weise ihres Gebrauchs durch die Nutzer kaum vorstellbar waren. Daher wurde das EU-Sekundärrecht immer wieder angepasst. Diese Reformen, wie etwa jüngst durch die Richtlinie über audiovisuelle Mediendienste (AVMD-Richtlinie) und die Richtlinie über das Urheberrecht und verwandte Schutzrechte im digitalen Binnenmarkt (DSM-Richtlinie), waren wichtige Schritte, um die EU „fit für das digitale Zeitalter" zu machen. Dies ist zugleich das zentrale Motiv für die politischen Leitlinien der neuen Kommissionspräsidentin Ursula von der Leyen und das angekündigte Arbeitsprogramm der Europäischen Kommission für 2020. Ein großer Teil der geplanten Initiativen auf EU-Ebene bezieht sich dabei auf die neue Rolle von Plattformen im digitalen Umfeld – auch im Zusammenhang mit der Online-Verbreitung von Inhalten. Hierbei geht vor allem um die Bestimmungen der E-Commerce-Richtlinie (ECRL), die als sektorübergreifender Sekundärrechtsakt seit fast 20 Jahren den Grundpfeiler des (digitalen) Binnenmarkts für die Dienste der Informationsgesellschaft bildet. Im Dezember 2020 hat die Europäische Kommission ihre Vorschläge für ein Paket mit neuen Vorschriften für digitale Dienste („Digital Services Act Package") veröffentlicht, die auf diejenigen Probleme reagieren sollen, die sich aus der Anwendung eines Rechtsrahmens ergeben, der noch aus einer völlig anderen Internetumgebung stammt. Das Paket beinhaltet zwei Legislativvorschläge für Verordnungen: ein Gesetz über digitale Dienste (Digital Services Act, DSA) und ein Gesetz über digitale Märkte (Digital Markets Act, DMA).

4. Anwendung und Durchsetzung des geltenden Rechtsrahmens haben sich als problematisch herausgestellt, nicht zuletzt aufgrund der bereits angeführten Veränderungen der Umgebungsbedingungen. Dazu gehören unter anderem die folgenden Aspekte, die in einer Vorgängerstudie mit dem Titel „Cross-Border Dissemination of Online Content – Current and Possible Future Regulation of the Online Environment with a Focus on the EU E-Commerce Directive" ausführlich 4 analysiert wurden: Die Zunahme der Web-2.0-Interaktivität hat dazu geführt, dass die meisten Intermediäre sich von lediglich „passiven Vermittlern" (wie es der ECRL als Grundidee und Konzept zugrunde liegt) zu interaktiven

Content-Management-Plattformen entwickelt haben, deren Geschäftsmodelle regelmäßig auf der Verwertung von Nutzerdaten und der Ausnutzung von Netzwerkeffekten basieren. Dies stellt die eher vereinfachende Kategorisierung der heutigen Plattformen als „Hosting-Provider" in Frage und lässt eine klare Einordnung der Kriterien wie „Neutralität" und „tatsächliche Kenntnis" von illegalen Inhalten, die Elemente sind für die Entscheidung über Haftungsprivilegien, nicht mehr zu – obwohl der Gerichtshof der Europäischen Union (EuGH) in seiner Rechtsprechung entscheidend dazu beigetragen hat, die Auslegung einiger dieser Begriffe als Reaktion auf Vorlagen von mitgliedstaatlichen Gerichten, die diese für ihre Auslegung der nationalen Umsetzungsakte der ECRL benötigten, zu klären.

5. Darüber hinaus sind auch viele Nutzer nicht mehr lediglich passive Rezipienten von Inhalten, sondern erstellen vielmehr aktiv Inhalte, die ihre Ansichten oder ihre Eigendarstellung als Person in unterschiedlichen Angeboten auf den verschiedensten Plattformen in Text, Bild, Video oder Audio enthalten. Auch dadurch ist mittlerweile die Kehrseite der Vorteile, die das Internet, der technologische Fortschritt und die Digitalisierung insgesamt gebracht haben, deutlich geworden: Phänomene wie der leichte Zugang zu illegalen oder urheberrechtsverletzenden Inhalten, zu Hass und terroristischer Propaganda aufstachelnde Inhalte, aber auch Desinformation sind nur Beispiele für die problematischen Aspekte der Möglichkeiten für Nutzer, Inhalte zu erstellen und über Intermediäre weiter zu verbreiten, wobei die vermittelnden Plattformen sich regelmäßig auf die Haftungsprivilegien der ECRL berufen können, wenn es um die Verantwortung für illegale oder schädliche Inhalte geht. Diese komplexe Situation mit horizontalen Haftungsprivilegien der Gatekeeper auf der einen Seite und wachsenden Bedrohungen durch (regelmäßig anonyme) Nutzer auf der anderen Seite hat zu Schwierigkeiten in der regulatorischen Praxis geführt und eine wirksame Strafverfolgung erschwert, insbesondere im Kampf gegen grenzüberschreitend verbreitete illegale Online-Inhalte.

6. Diese Entwicklungen in Richtung eines steigenden (annähernd redaktionellen) Einflusses von Plattformen auf Inhalte und deren Darstellung gegenüber Nutzern sowie einer zunehmenden Bedrohung der (Grundrechte der) EU-Bürger und der Werte der EU wurden bereits in anderen sekundärrechtlichen Bestimmungen und durch verschiedene Instrumente der Selbst- und Koregulierung aufgegriffen und adressiert, z. B. durch spezielle Regeln für Video-Sharing-Plattformen, Online-Vermittlungsdienste oder Diensteanbietende für das Teilen von On-

line-Inhalten als spezifische Unterkategorien des Oberbegriffs „Dienste der Informationsgesellschaft". Da sich jedoch einige dieser Regeln ausdrücklich auf den Haftungsrahmen der ECRL beziehen und/oder nicht unter die sektoralen Ausnahmen der ECRL fallen, wird es schwieriger, die Kohärenz zwischen diesen Regeln und damit auch eine wirksame Durchsetzung der betreffenden sektoralen Bestimmungen zu gewährleisten. In Bezug auf die grenzüberschreitende Dimension muss zusätzlich berücksichtigt werden, dass verschiedene legislative oder administrative Ansätze der Mitgliedstaaten, von denen einige vor kurzem sektorale Regeln für bestimmte Arten von Online-Plattformen in Ausübung ihnen vorbehaltener Kompetenzen verabschiedet haben, eine gewisse Fragmentierung des Rechtsrahmens begründen.

7. Die daraus resultierenden Probleme werden umso deutlicher, wenn es um die grenzüberschreitende Rechtsdurchsetzung geht, die aufgrund des globalen Charakters des Internets und auch der beträchtlichen Marktmacht der (hauptsächlich nicht-EU-ansässigen) Anbieter von Diensten der Informationsgesellschaft den Regelfall im Rahmen des Vorgehens gegen die Verbreitung illegaler Online-Inhalte darstellt. Die ECRL, die auf dem Herkunftslandprinzip basiert und damit sowohl die ungehinderte Bereitstellung von Diensten der Informationsgesellschaft nach dem Recht des Herkunftslandes als auch die Zuständigkeit der Regulierungsstellen dieses Mitgliedstaates bestimmt, enthält weder spezifische Bestimmungen über die Einrichtung und die Befugnisse der Regulierungseinrichtungen noch ausdifferenzierte Kohärenz- und Kooperationsmechanismen für die Zusammenarbeit zwischen den sektoralen Regulierungsstellen. Die Regelungen über die Befugnisse der Mitgliedstaaten, vom Herkunftslandprinzip abzuweichen, zur Zusammenarbeit der Aufsichtsbehörden und zum grenzüberschreitenden Informationsaustausch folgen einem Mindestharmonisierungsansatz und haben sich in der Praxis mit dem zunehmenden Wachstum des Marktes und den damit verbundenen Aufgaben als nicht ausreichend effektiv erwiesen.

Ziel der Studie

8. Vor diesem Hintergrund verweist die vorliegende Studie zunächst kurz auf den anwendbaren Rechtsrahmen für die grenzüberschreitende Verbreitung von Online-Inhalten, einschließlich des Zusammenspiels zwischen EU-Rechtsakten und dem Recht der Mitgliedstaaten und dessen Umsetzung. Sie gibt einen allgemeinen Überblick über die Regulierungsmöglichkeiten, die der EU im Prozess der Anpassung dieses

Rechtsrahmens zur Verfügung stehen. Danach werden fünf Kernfragen einer möglichen Reform identifiziert, die den spezifischen Bereich der Medien und – allgemeiner – der Verbreitung von Inhalten betreffen, ohne auf andere Elemente wie z. B. die Etablierung neuer Instrumente innerhalb des Wettbewerbsrechts bzgl. Online-Plattformen einzugehen. Für jede dieser fünf Kernfragen stellt die Studie verschiedene Lösungsmöglichkeiten vor und gibt einen Überblick über die diskutierten Optionen: Für Fragen zur künftigen Ausgestaltung des Herkunftslandprinzips, des Anwendungsbereichs der Regeln für Dienste der Informationsgesellschaft, des Haftungsregimes, der Pflichten der Anbieter einschließlich der Wahrung von Nutzerrechten und schließlich der Rechtsdurchsetzung und Aufsicht werden konkrete Lösungswege vorgeschlagen.

9. Vor dem Hintergrund des Schwerpunkts dieser Studie werden dabei verschiedene regulatorische Möglichkeiten zur Anpassung des Rechtsrahmens für die Verbreitung von Online-Inhalten in der EU analysiert. Aufbauend auf der bereits festgestellten Notwendigkeit einer Reform des aktuellen Rechtsrahmens und einem allgemeinen Überblick über die Vorschläge der Kommission für einen DSA und einen DMA, konzentriert sich die Studie auf die sechs relevantesten Kernpunkte der Reform. Dabei werden für jeden der sechs Punkte sowohl der gegenwärtige Regulierungsstand als auch die tragenden Gründe für die Notwendigkeit einer Aktualisierung dargestellt sowie anschließend die entsprechenden Ansätze aus dem DSA-Vorschlag im Detail beleuchtet. Darauf aufbauend erfolgt eine Analyse und eine umfassende Bewertung der vorgeschlagenen Regeln, die auch beantwortet, welcher weiterer Anpassungen es im Rahmen des DSA bedarf oder welche alternativen Ansätze verfolgt werden sollten.

Aktueller Rechtsrahmen innerhalb der EU und ihrer Mitgliedstaaten

10. Bei Betrachtung des Rechtsrahmens für die grenzüberschreitende Verbreitung von Online-Inhalten sind Basis und Bezugsrahmen zunächst die Grundrechte, wie sie in der Charta der Grundrechte der EU (GRC), der Europäischen Menschenrechtskonvention des Europarats (EMRK) und den Bestimmungen des nationalen Verfassungsrechts verankert sind. Diese Rechte heben vor allem die Würde des Menschen hervor, die nach der GRC „unantastbar" ist, d. h. als ein übergeordnetes Ziel betrachtet werden muss, das es zu gewährleisten gilt. Sie umfassen auch den Schutz von Minderjährigen als eigene Rechtsposition. Andererseits sind die Freiheit der Meinungsäußerung (sowohl der

Dienste-Nutzer, die Inhalte erstellen, als auch der Empfänger dieser Inhalte) und die Rechte der Dienstleistungsanbieter, die durch die Auferlegung von Regeln mit erhöhten rechtlichen Verpflichtungen konfrontiert werden könnten, zu respektieren. Im Zusammenhang mit der Wahrung der Grundrechte sind dabei auch die Kompetenzen der Mitgliedstaaten im Bereich der Medienregulierung und der Vielfaltssicherung zu wahren, insbesondere wenn es sich bei Regulierungsadressaten um Plattformen handelt, die sich als medienrelevante Gatekeeper darstellen.

11. Die Grundfreiheiten sind das Herzstück des Binnenmarkts und insbesondere relevant für das Funktionieren des digitalen Binnenmarkts in der EU. Zu den Grundfreiheiten gehört das Recht, sich in einem Mitgliedstaat und damit unter dessen Hoheitsgewalt niederzulassen und Waren und Dienstleistungen innerhalb des Binnenmarkts anzubieten, ohne dabei strengeren Bestimmungen durch den Empfangsmitgliedstaat unterworfen zu sein, sowie sich auf den freien Kapitalverkehr zu stützen. Im Zusammenhang mit der grenzüberschreitenden Verbreitung von Online-Inhalten betrifft dies nicht nur Medienunternehmen, die sich auf diese Freiheiten berufen können, sondern auch die Dienste der Informationsgesellschaft. Ausnahmen von den Grundfreiheiten, ob auf nationaler oder EU-Ebene, müssen insbesondere durch ein Ziel von allgemeinem Interesse gerechtfertigt und verhältnismäßig sein. Dies gilt auch für unterschiedliche Ausgestaltungen des Herkunftslandprinzips im Rechtsrahmen, das zwar kein vorrangiges Erfordernis der Grundfreiheiten darstellt, aber Ausdruck des Gedankens der Gewährleistung eines freien und fairen Binnenmarkts ist.

12. Die in den Verträgen niedergelegten Werte, auf denen die EU gründet, sind nicht nur theoretischer Natur, was sich auch in prozeduralen Vorkehrungen zu ihrem Schutz niederschlägt. Sie sind auch Orientierungspunkte für die Regulierung von Plattformen. Vor dem Hintergrund der beschriebenen Gefährdungen, aber auch der Vorteile für den Informationszugang und die Kommunikationsmöglichkeiten im Online-Sektor, kommt dabei insbesondere den Werten Menschenwürde, Rechtsstaatlichkeit und Schutz vor Diskriminierung eine Schlüsselrolle zu. Nicht nur als Gradmesser für ein Mindestmaß an notwendiger Regulierung, sondern auch als gemeinsamer Nenner, dem die EU und ihre Mitgliedstaaten im Lichte der ihnen zugewiesenen Kompetenzen unterworfen sind.

13. Auf der Ebene des Sekundärrechts ist insbesondere die AVMD-Richtlinie – trotz des darin verfolgten Ansatzes lediglich einer Mindesthar-

monisierung – ein wesentlicher Bestandteil des einschlägigen Rechtsrahmens, auch für die Verbreitung von Online-Inhalten. Bemerkenswert sind insbesondere die mit der letzten Anpassung 2018 einbezogenen Regeln für Video-Sharing-Plattformen (VSPs), die diese Art von Plattformanbieter stärker in die Verantwortung nehmen, weil sie als Teil des audiovisuellen Mediensektors gesehen werden und daher zum Schutz der Empfänger mindestens ähnlichen Regeln wie andere Mediendienste in diesem Sektor unterliegen müssen. Die Umsetzung der Vorschriften, die den Mitgliedstaaten in einigen Aspekten einen weitreichenden Ermessensspielraum belassen und zur Einbeziehung von Selbst- und Koregulierungsmechanismen auffordern, erfolgt aktuell durch die Mitgliedstaaten.

14. Für die Verbreitung von Online-Inhalten ist jedoch nicht nur das medienspezifische Sekundärrecht relevant, sondern auch andere sektorale Bestimmungen, die z.B. primär wirtschafts- oder verbraucherschutzpolitische Ziele verfolgen. So definiert die DSM-Richtlinie etwa eine neue Kategorie von „Diensteanbietern für das Teilen von Online-Inhalten" und führt für diese einen neuen Pflichtenkatalog ein; die Verordnung zur Förderung von Fairness und Transparenz für gewerbliche Nutzer von Online-Vermittlungsdiensten (Platform-to-Business (P2B)-Verordnung) schafft Informations- und Transparenzverpflichtungen für Online-Vermittlungsdienste und Suchmaschinen, die für die Sichtbarkeit von Inhalten und Produkten relevant sind. Bestehende Regelungen wie die Datenschutz-Grundverordnung (DS-GVO), die mit ihrem harmonisierenden Ansatz das Marktortprinzip festlegt, sind für den Online- bzw. Plattformbereich ebenso relevant wie einige der derzeit diskutierten Initiativen, z. B. der Vorschlag für eine Verordnung zur Bekämpfung terroristischer Online-Inhalte (TERREG). Hinzu kommen Instrumente, die bewusst Spielräume und Ausnahmemöglichkeiten für die Verfolgung medien- und kulturpolitischer Ziele auf nationaler Ebene belassen, die wiederum ergänzende Regelungen in Bezug auf die Verbreitung von Inhalten ermöglichen. Ergänzt wird dies durch eine Reihe von Maßnahmen zur Förderung der Selbstregulierung auf der Ebene von EU-Koordinierungs- und Unterstützungsmaßnahmen, beispielsweise im Bereich von Hassrede und Desinformation. Überschneidungen mit den horizontalen Regeln der ECRL sind dabei unvermeidlich. Diese sekundärrechtlichen Grundlagen müssen nicht nur mit etwaigen neuen oder zu ändernden Elementen des Rechtsrahmens in Einklang gebracht werden, sondern zeigen auch, dass es für bestimmte Anbieter von Diensten der Informationsgesell-

schaft spezielle Regeln gibt und geben muss, die spezifische Ziele und Besonderheiten adressieren.

Regelungsoptionen auf EU-Ebene

15. Auf Basis der genannten Zuständigkeiten, der Grundrechte und Werte verfügt die EU über ein breites Spektrum an Regulierungsmöglichkeiten, wobei als rechtliche Handlungsgrundlage vor allem das Ziel der Verwirklichung eines funktionierenden (digitalen) Binnenmarkts dient. Bei der Prüfung der verschiedenen Optionen ist es notwendig, dieses Ziel, das grundsätzlich von wirtschaftlichen Erwägungen und Politikansätzen bestimmt wird, aber erhebliche Auswirkungen auf andere Sektoren hat, die bereits auf der Ebene der Mitgliedstaaten und der EU reguliert sind und dabei auch andere Ziele verfolgen können, mit eben diesen sektoralen Vorschriften in Einklang zu bringen. Es existiert zwar eine Vielzahl von Akteuren im Online-Plattformbereich, die unterschiedliche Dienste für verschiedene Empfänger mit heterogenen Inhalten, Technologien und Benutzeroberflächen anbieten, die aber dennoch (in unterschiedlichem Maße) gemeinsam haben, dass sie „lediglich" den Zugang zu bestimmten Inhalten oder Diensten anbieten. Aus diesem Grund besteht auch weiterhin Bedarf an horizontal anwendbaren Regeln, die es ermöglichen, sektorspezifische Ansätze beizubehalten. Die sektorspezifische Perspektive – sei es Verbraucherschutz-, Medien-, Kultur-, Telekommunikations-, Wettbewerbs-, Straf-, Urheber- oder Datenschutzrecht, um einschlägige Beispiele zu nennen –, die für Dienste der Informationsgesellschaft trotz der Gemeinsamkeit als „vermittelnde Dienste" im Rahmen der Regulierung berücksichtigt werden muss, macht eine vollständige Harmonisierung innerhalb eines einzigen Regelungswerks unmöglich. Der grundsätzlich beizubehaltende horizontale Ansatz erfordert daher eine eingehende Prüfung der bestehenden Gesetzgebung und die Festlegung von sektoralen Ausnahmen und Gestaltungsspielräumen für die Mitgliedstaaten bei der Ausübung ihrer Kompetenzen, z. B. im Rahmen der Kulturpolitik oder bei der Sicherung des Pluralismus unter Berücksichtigung der Auswirkungen auf die Meinungsfreiheit.

16. Auf der einen Seite bedarf es hierzu allgemeiner Regeln, beispielsweise im Hinblick auf Verpflichtungen und Obliegenheiten von Diensteanbietern, die inhaltsneutral und offen genug sind, um der dynamischen und sich stets im Wandel befindlichen Natur der Online-Umgebung gerecht zu werden, was in Bezug auf Veränderungen flexible Reaktionsmöglichkeiten erfordert. Das könnte mit der Festlegung von

50

grundlegenden Prinzipien und Regeln in dem horizontal anwendbaren Rechtsakt verbunden sein, die Raum für spezifische Ergänzungen oder Maßnahmen in der Zukunft lassen, dabei aber auch eine Offenheit für die tatsächliche Anwendung der bestehenden Regeln, die aus anderen Rechtsakten stammen, sicherstellen. Die Übertragung von Befugnissen an zuständige und entsprechend eingerichtete Behörden zur Formulierung oder Konkretisierung von Leitlinien ist dabei ein Mittel, das sich bereits in vielen sektoralen Rechtsakten auf EU- und mitgliedstaatlicher Ebene bewährt hat und es diesen ermöglicht, sich auf gemeinsame Standards und Durchsetzungsverfahren zu einigen.

17. Auf der anderen Seite bedeutet dies, dass nicht nur die bestehenden Bestimmungen der ECRL überarbeitet oder ersetzt werden müssen, sondern dass auch neu beurteilt werden muss, welche sektoralen Regelungen weiterhin Vorrang vor den allgemeinen Regelungen der ECRL haben sollen und in welchen Bereichen es angesichts der kompetenzrechtlichen Grenzen für die EU (zusätzliche) sektorale Ausnahmen geben muss. Konkret dürfen Maßnahmen, die auf (EU- oder) nationaler Ebene ergriffen werden, um die kulturelle und sprachliche Vielfalt zu fördern und den Pluralismus zu gewährleisten, nicht von einem Harmonisierungsansatz erfasst werden. Dies erfordert eine generelle Klärung des Verhältnisses zwischen bestehenden Regelungen auf Ebene der EU und ihrer Mitgliedstaaten, insbesondere die weiterhin bestehende Vorrangigkeit von sektoralen Regelungen wie der AVMD- oder der DSM-Richtlinie, auch wenn diese an Instrumente oder Regeln anknüpfen, die auch in den horizontalen Rechtsakt aufgenommen werden.

18. Hinsichtlich der Frage nach dem geeigneten Rechtsinstrument gibt es mehrere mögliche Optionen rechtsverbindlicher und nicht rechtsverbindlicher Natur. Es ist zu bedenken, dass frühere Maßnahmen im Bereich der Selbstregulierung sich zwar als vorteilhaft für die Entwicklung von Best Practices und die Einrichtung von Verfahren der Zusammenarbeit und des Dialogs erwiesen haben, dass jedoch Mängel bei der wirksamen Durchsetzung deutlich geworden sind – nicht zuletzt aufgrund des fehlenden Zugangs zu zuverlässigeren Daten, die zur Beurteilung der Einhaltung der Vorschriften benötigt werden. Koregulierungsmechanismen sollten daher als Mindestoption angesehen werden. Aber auch solche müssen den genannten Mängeln durch die Etablierung geeigneter Aufsichtsmechanismen Rechnung tragen und ausreichend konkrete Verpflichtungen vorsehen. Ein neuer Regulierungsrahmen sollte in einer Richtlinie festgelegt werden, da oder so-

weit er ansonsten den Ermessensspielraum der Mitgliedstaaten bei der Umsetzung in einem Bereich (der Medienregulierung) einschränken würde, der in engem Zusammenhang mit der ihnen vorbehaltenen Zuständigkeit steht. Es wäre schwierig, die Notwendigkeit einer Verordnung als übergreifendes Instrument zu begründen, insbesondere bei einem horizontalen Ansatz, der eine Reihe von sektoralen Ausnahmen und die Zuständigkeit der Mitgliedstaaten berücksichtigen muss, weshalb eine vollständige Harmonisierung ohnehin nicht stattfinden kann. Möglicherweise müssen unterschiedliche Rechtsinstrumente vorgesehen werden, je nachdem, auf welche Rechtsgrundlage sie hauptsächlich gestützt werden sollen. Wenn eine Verordnung als übergreifendes Instrument gewählt wird, müsste diese – ungeachtet ihrer begrenzteren Flexibilität in Bezug auf nachgelagerte sektorale Rechtsvorschriften – mit ausreichenden Öffnungsklauseln oder Anknüpfungspunkten an die Rechtsakte der Mitgliedstaaten konzipiert werden.

Klarstellung des Herkunftslandprinzips als Basis und dessen Ausnahmen

19. Das Herkunftslandprinzip ist nicht nur die Grundlage der ECRL, sondern auch anderer Rechtsakte, die Dienstleistungen mit typischerweise (auch) grenzüberschreitendem Charakter regeln, wie der AVMD-Richtlinie. Das Prinzip ist eine Folge der Errichtung eines Binnenmarkts, der die Nutzung der Grundfreiheiten ermöglicht. Seine Anwendung schafft Rechtssicherheit für Anbieter, da sie sich grundsätzlich nur mit der Rechtsordnung eines Mitgliedstaates befassen und sich verfahrenstechnisch nur mit diesem Staat bzw. seinen zuständigen Regulierungsbehörden auseinandersetzen müssen, auch wenn sie ihre Dienstleistungen in anderen Mitgliedstaaten erbringen. Dies ist im Online-Bereich besonders wichtig, da die angebotenen Dienstleistungen regelmäßig von Natur aus grenzüberschreitend sind, ohne dass der Anbieter die Dienstleistung unbedingt aktiv auf einen bestimmten mitgliedstaatlichen Markt ausrichten muss. Dies gilt gerade auch für Medieninhalte. Das Herkunftslandprinzip ist daher nicht nur für große und international ausgerichtete Dienste der Informationsgesellschaft von besonderer Bedeutung, sondern auch für kleine und mittelständische Unternehmen sowie Start-ups, die regelmäßig Schwierigkeiten hätten, sich über die rechtlichen Anforderungen in allen Mitgliedstaaten informiert zu halten, geschweige denn diesen umfänglich zu entsprechen.

20. Aus diesem Grund sollte die grundsätzliche Verankerung des Herkunftslandprinzips unangetastet bleiben. Die Möglichkeit der Mitgliedstaaten, mit Maßnahmen – in dringenden Fällen auch direkt – gegen (inländische) technische „Zugangsvermittler", insbesondere Internet-Access-Provider (IAP), anstelle von (ausländischen) Content-Providern oder Host-Providern vorzugehen, wenn sie auf illegale Inhalte reagieren, ohne dass dies per se einen Verstoß gegen das Herkunftslandprinzip darstellt, sollte ausdrücklich klargestellt werden, um Unklarheiten und eine daraus resultierende Zurückhaltung der Regulierungsstellen in Fällen mit hohem Risikopotenzial zu vermeiden. Identifizierte Probleme, insbesondere im Zusammenhang mit der grenzüberschreitenden Verbreitung von Online-Inhalten und den damit verbundenen Durchsetzungsschwierigkeiten, sollten deutlicher adressiert werden, indem Ausnahmefälle sowie die Möglichkeit festgelegt werden, sich in bestimmten, klar definierten Fällen auf das Marktortprinzip zu berufen in Bezug auf Inhalte, die von nicht-EU-ansässigen Anbietern stammen oder verbreitet werden. Ein solchermaßen neu gefasster Verfahrensaufbau könnte als Vorlage für mögliche künftige Klarstellungen der Unterscheidung zwischen Herkunftslandprinzip und Marktortprinzip dienen, auch für andere Elemente des einschlägigen Rechtsrahmens, insbesondere die AVMD-Richtlinie.

21. Die Befugnis der Mitgliedstaaten, für bestimmte Dienstleistungsanbieter vom Herkunftslandprinzip abzuweichen, wenn die Gefährdung öffentlicher Interessen begründet werden kann, muss beibehalten werden. Jedoch sollte das Verfahren klarer gestaltet und gestrafft werden, sodass es innerhalb einer angemessenen, d. h. kurzen Zeitspanne zu einem verbindlichen Ergebnis geführt werden kann. Insbesondere sollte geprüft werden, ob die bisher innerhalb des Rechtsrahmens aufgeführten Ziele von allgemeinem Interesse ausreichend sind, um den vorgefundenen Problemen Rechnung zu tragen. Dies bezieht sich etwa auf die Formulierung des Tatbestands der Aufstachelung zum Hass, die schon bei der Novelle der AVMD-Richtlinie angepasst wurde. Eine inhaltliche Klärung sollte auch bzgl. eines breiten Verständnisses des Jugendschutzes vorgenommen werden, der weiter reicht als der Schutz vor illegalen Inhalten. Der Umfang des Schutzes ergibt sich dabei nach wie vor aus dem Recht der Mitgliedstaaten. Darüber hinaus sollte die Möglichkeit in Betracht gezogen werden, den Geltungsbereich auf Gefahren für demokratische Wahlen (z. B. im Hinblick auf Desinformationskampagnen) und für die öffentliche Sicherheit auszudehnen, insbesondere ausdrücklich bzgl. terroristischer Propaganda,

um auf aktuelle und zunehmende Bedrohungen zu reagieren. Die Straffung des vorgesehenen Verfahrens der Beteiligung des Niederlassungsmitgliedstaats und der Kommission sollte die Festlegung konkreter Informations- und Reaktionspflichten der beteiligten Mitgliedstaaten und enge Fristen hierfür umfassen. Die Einrichtung eines Streitbeilegungsverfahrens in Konfliktfällen mit der Beteiligung eines Gremiums, das sich z. B. aus Vertretern der Regulierungsbehörden zusammensetzt, wäre nützlich. Dieses könnte auf der Zusammenarbeit der zuständigen Stellen beruhen (siehe unten) und schnelle sowie gemeinsame Diskussions- und Entscheidungsverfahren umfassen, um sowohl effizient als auch für das Herkunftslandprinzip möglichst minimalinvasiv zu sein.

22. Dasselbe gilt für die Abweichungsbefugnis in Eilfällen mit entsprechend strengeren Verpflichtungen. In solchen Fällen sollte es ein abgestuftes System von Reaktionsmöglichkeiten geben, die sich insbesondere nach dem Risikograd des Inhalts oder des Verstoßes richten und den Grad der Rechtsdurchsetzung im zuständigen Mitgliedstaat berücksichtigen. Angesichts der Tatsache, dass im Hinblick auf Anbieter aus Nicht-EU-Staaten – unter Beachtung völkerrechtlicher Grenzen – ohnehin nach dem Marktortprinzip auf Grundlage mitgliedstaatlichen Rechts gehandelt werden könnte, da es keine Harmonisierung durch EU-Rechtsakte gibt, die die Gültigkeit des Herkunftslandprinzips für solche Anbieter regelt, darf die Rechtsdurchsetzung und Bekämpfung illegaler Inhalte innerhalb der EU bei besonders gefährlichen Inhalten wie Verletzungen der Menschenwürde oder terroristischer Propaganda unabhängig von deren Herkunft nicht übermäßig erschwert werden. Einzelheiten hierzu sollten insbesondere im Rahmen der Zusammenarbeit der zuständigen Stellen entwickelt werden.

Die Definition des Anwendungsbereichs des Rechtsrahmens

23. Die Notwendigkeit einer Aktualisierung der Definitionen bzgl. des Geltungsbereichs des Rechtsrahmens für die Dienste der Informationsgesellschaft ist in den vergangenen Jahren deutlich geworden. Während die allgemein gehaltene Definition der Dienste der Informationsgesellschaft aus dem Jahr 1998 eine Einbeziehung aller verschiedenen Arten von Akteuren im Online-Umfeld ermöglichte und weiterhin ermöglicht, reicht sie nicht aus, wenn es darum geht, spezifische Regeln für die verschiedenen Akteure anzuwenden. Aus diesem Grund hat bereits die ECRL spezifische Kategorien von Anbietern definiert, die unter bestimmten Umständen von Haftungsprivilegien profitieren. Wäh-

rend die eher technisch-übertragungsorientierten Kategorien (reine Durchleitung, Caching) in ihrer Anwendung kaum problematisch waren, ist die eigentlich relevante Kategorie die der Hosting-Service-Provider. Zu dieser gab es Auslegungsprobleme (namentlich hinsichtlich Neutralität/Passivität und der Kriterien für „tatsächliche Kenntnis" von Rechtsverletzungen sowie der möglichen Reichweite präventiver Unterlassungsklagen gegen diese), die durch die Rechtsprechung des EuGH nicht vollständig gelöst wurden, sowie Probleme durch unterschiedliche Herangehensweisen der Mitgliedstaaten. Abgesehen von der veränderten Natur einer – möglicherweise in der Vergangenheit sowohl hinsichtlich des Geschäftsmodells als auch der technischen Kapazität stärker identifizierbaren – Kategorie von Host-Providern haben die vergangenen Jahre gezeigt, dass selbst die allgemeine Definition von Diensten der Informationsgesellschaft als solche in ihrer Anwendung schwierig sein kann, wenn sie von spezifischeren Definitionen (z. B. Transportdienst) in Bezug auf neue Arten von Vermittlern oder Plattformen unterschieden wird, auch wenn es in diesen Fällen um Sachverhalte außerhalb des Kontexts der Verbreitung von Inhalten ging.

24. Als Mindestreaktion hierauf müssen die bestehenden Definitionen hinsichtlich des Geltungsbereichs eines neuen oder geänderten Rechtsakts in Bezug auf die Verbreitung von Online-Inhalten grundlegend überarbeitet werden und dabei die bereits vom EuGH als Auslegungshilfe vorgegebenen Elemente integriert werden. Vorzugsweise wird zumindest die Definition des Host-Providers durch eine weiter gefasste Definition ersetzt, die sich nicht mehr auf die Unterscheidung zwischen aktivem/passivem Charakter des Dienstes stützt, da dies nicht mehr entscheidend für die Einordnung und kein klarer Indikator mehr ist. Abgesehen davon, dass es sich (bei Fortführung der Definition der Dienste der Informationsgesellschaft) um eine sehr allgemeine und weit gefasste Definition handelt, die sich auf alle Arten von Online-Diensteanbietern oder, genauer gesagt, auf alle Arten von Plattformen und Vermittlern bezieht und die offen genug sein sollte, um künftige neue Arten von Diensten zu erfassen, sollte es Raum für spezifischere Kategorien von Anbietern geben, damit diese jeweils mit eigenen Regeln adressiert werden können. Letztere könnten entweder durch sektorspezifische Vorschriften etabliert werden, die neben dem horizontal anwendbaren Rechtsakt weiterbestehen – Beispiele hierfür wären die Regeln für spezifische Arten von Plattformen, die von der AVMD-Richtlinie (für VSPs) oder der DSM-Richtlinie erfasst werden

–, oder innerhalb des horizontalen Rechtsaktes selbst. Unter Berücksichtigung der Rolle, die Plattformen als vermittelnde Instanzen zwischen Inhalteerstellern und Rezipienten/ Verbrauchern spielen, muss es zumindest eine spezifische Kategorie von „Inhaltsplattformen/Intermediären" geben, die von anderen Arten von Plattformen unterschieden werden kann, die zwar ebenfalls als Vermittler zwischen zwei Parteien fungieren und auch organisatorischen Einfluss auf die Interaktion haben, aber keine Inhalteverbreitung vornehmen. Dies bedeutet nicht, dass keine vergleichbaren Regeln auf diese verschiedenen Arten von Anbietern angewendet werden können, aber es stellt sicher, dass die Bedeutung von Inhaltsplattformen/Intermediären im Zusammenhang mit der Verbreitung von Inhalten angemessen berücksichtigt werden kann.

25. Spezifische Definitionen für Plattformen zur Verbreitung von Online-Inhalten existieren wie erwähnt bereits, z. B. in der AVMD-Richtlinie und der DSM-Richtlinie. Bei der Schaffung einer weiteren Definition für Inhaltevermittler könnte jede Art von Plattform, die zum Austausch von Inhalten in der öffentlichen Sphäre beiträgt – unabhängig davon, ob sie sich auf audiovisuelle Inhalte oder andere Arten von Inhalten bezieht und ob sie die in den bestehenden Definitionen festgelegten detaillierten Anforderungen erfüllt –, angesprochen und in den Rechtsrahmen aufgenommen werden. Die weiter gefasste Definition sollte sich dabei auf einige wenige Kriterien beschränken, nämlich auf Anbieter von Diensten der Informationsgesellschaft, die die Speicherung von oder den Zugang zu erstellten/hochgeladenen/ geteilten Inhalten durch Nutzer des Dienstes mit dem Ziel anbieten, sie anderen Nutzern zur Verfügung zu stellen, sowie auf die Klarstellung, dass (für diese Tätigkeit) der Inhalteerstellende nicht der Weisung oder Kontrolle des Anbieters unterliegt – in diesem Fall fällt der Anbieter ohnehin unter eine andere Kategorie. Nur wenn es um die Anwendbarkeit spezifischer Regeln geht, sollte eine weitere Differenzierung vorgenommen werden, die den Grad der organisatorischen Beteiligung (tatsächlich und potenziell) als differenzierenden Maßstab widerspiegelt. Damit wäre noch eine Unterscheidung nach redaktioneller Einflussnahme (d.h. z. B. AVMD-Kategorien in der AVMD-Richtlinie), lediglich kuratorischer Einflussnahme (Organisation, Präsentation etc. des Inhalts, d.h. AVMD-, VSP- oder DSM-Kategorien, aber auch wie im TER-REG-Vorschlag vorgesehen) und rein technischer Übertragung möglich, die im Prinzip auf direkte Kommunikationsformen oder die tech-

nische Leistungserbringung (d.h. z. B. Internet-Zugangsprovider) re-
duziert ist.

26. Zusätzlich zu einer oder mehreren neu formulierten Kategorien könnten auch die unterschiedlichen Möglichkeiten der Einflussnahme der
Anbieter berücksichtigt werden. Dies würde gewisse Ausnahmen in
den materiellrechtlichen Vorschriften für bestimmte Arten von Anbietern ermöglichen, die ansonsten die Kriterien erfüllen würden (z. B.
nicht gewinnorientierte Anbieter von Dienstleistungen), oder die Berücksichtigung wirtschaftlicher Ungleichheiten zwischen großen Plattformen und kleineren Marktteilnehmern erlauben. Solche Anbieter
sollten jedoch nicht von vornherein aus der Kategorie ausgeschlossen
werden. Stattdessen sollten zwar die Kernelemente der Regeln wie die
Behandlung illegaler Inhalte in vollem Umfang für alle Anbieter innerhalb des Geltungsbereichs anwendbar sein, jedoch könnten diese
Anbieter bei der Umsetzung nur mit einem Teil der Regeln konfrontiert werden. Ferner sollte in Betracht gezogen werden, wie die regulatorische Transparenz erhöht werden kann, indem – entweder auf der
Grundlage einer eigenen Kategorisierung in einem von einer Auf-
sichtsbehörde überprüften oder von dieser aufgestellten Registrie-
rungsprozess – Listen von Inhaltevermittlern bereitgestellt werden, die
unter die Definition und gegebenenfalls die Rechtsprechung eines bestimmten Mitgliedstaates fallen. Eine periodische Evaluierung der Definition – was schwieriger wäre, wenn sie ausschließlich in eine Richtlinie oder sogar in eine Verordnung aufgenommen würde – oder, vorzugsweise, die Ermächtigung der zuständigen Stellen, durch Auflistung von Kriterien (auch von neuen Arten von Diensten), von denen
angenommen werden kann, dass sie ein Element der Definition erfüllen, Anwendungshinweise für die Definition zu geben, wäre sinnvoll.

Die Reform des Regimes zur Haftungsprivilegierung

27. Der Ausgangspunkt in Bezug auf das umstrittene Regime der Haf-
tungsprivilegierungen innerhalb der ECRL ist folgender: Ohne dass es
harmonisierte Haftungsvorschriften auf EU-Ebene gibt, werden Anbieter (einschließlich HostProvider) vor der Anwendung mitgliedstaatlicher Haftungsvorschriften durch die EU-Haftungsprivilegien ge-
schützt. Während die ursprüngliche Einführung dieses Regimes dazu
gedacht war, Raum für Innovationen zu ermöglichen und „neuen"
Diensteanbietern bei der Entwicklung insbesondere von Diensten, die
den Austausch von Inhalten ermöglichen, Rechtssicherheit zu bieten,
hat sich die Situation mittlerweile vollkommen verändert: Die unklare

Reichweite der Haftungsbefreiung hat teilweise dazu geführt, dass die Anbieter nur einen begrenzten Beitrag dazu leisten, eine aktivere Rolle bei der Verhinderung der Verbreitung illegaler oder schädigender Inhalte zu übernehmen. Dies hat teilweise die Bekämpfung solcher Inhalte auf Ebene der Rechtsdurchsetzung insbesondere durch die zuständigen Stellen erschwert. Der Mangel an effektiver Rechtsdurchsetzung im Online-Bereich hat zu deutlichen Unterschieden bei der Gewährleistung von inhaltlichen Standards zwischen traditionelleren Formen der Vermittlung von Inhalten einerseits und der Vermittlung durch Intermediäre andererseits geführt. Die Grundwerte der EU – einschließlich eines effizienten Schutzes der Grundrechte – erfordern jedoch einen (aus Perspektive der Nutzer) vergleichbaren Ansatz hinsichtlich vergleichbarer Arten der Verbreitung von Inhalten. Die Frage der Aufrechterhaltung oder Änderung des Systems der Haftungsprivilegierung muss daher aus einer völlig anderen Perspektive betrachtet werden als bei seiner Einführung.

28. Ohne das Haftungsprivileg an sich in Frage stellen zu müssen, sollte es so ausgestaltet werden, dass es die effiziente Durchsetzung von Vorschriften, z. B. über illegale Inhalte, nicht behindert oder einschränkt. Obwohl dies bereits innerhalb des gegenwärtigen ECRL-Rahmens möglich ist, sollte eine Klarstellung in dem Sinne vorgenommen werden, dass die Frage des Haftungsprivilegs zu differenzieren ist von der Auferlegung bestimmter Verpflichtungen an Vermittler, die über die reaktiven Maßnahmen hinausgehen, die für die Anwendbarkeit des Haftungsprivilegs erforderlich sind. Letzteres hängt derzeit von der unverzüglichen Reaktion der Anbieter ab, indem sie bei Erlangung tatsächlicher Kenntnis den Zugang zu illegalen Inhalten entfernen oder sperren. Kriterien wie die „Kenntnis" von illegalen Inhalten könnten klarer definiert werden und idealerweise mit der Festlegung von spezifischen Verfahren einhergehen, was zu einer „Kenntnis" in diesem Sinn führt. Darüber hinaus sollte die bislang begrenzte Auswahl reaktiver Maßnahmen weiter ausgebaut werden, einschließlich möglicher Maßnahmen als Reaktion auf illegale Inhalte, die über eine bloße Entfernung dieser Inhalte hinausgehen. Wie bereits erwähnt, erlauben bereits die gegenwärtigen Regeln der ECRL und die Auslegung durch den EuGH den Mitgliedstaaten, Maßnahmen von den Anbietern zu verlangen, die sich an deren Sorgfaltspflicht orientieren, ohne dass diese im Widerspruch zum Verbot der Einführung einer allgemeinen Überwachungspflicht stehen. Dieses Verbot sollte insofern aufrechterhalten werden, als es ein Element des Schutzes der größtmöglichen

Wahrnehmung der Meinungsfreiheit durch die Nutzer des Dienstes darstellt. Es sollte aber klargestellt werden, dass es nicht proaktive Pflichten von Inhaltevermittlern verhindert, die von bestimmten Bedingungen abhängig sind, wie sie unten dargelegt werden.

29. Die Kombination des Haftungsprivilegs mit davon getrennt zu betrachtenden Pflichten und Obliegenheiten (im Sinne von Aufgabenerfüllung) der Anbieter würde die bedeutende Rolle der Inhaltevermittler bei der Wahrnehmung der Grundrechte widerspiegeln, aber gleichzeitig auch deren Rolle bei der Eindämmung der illegalen Nutzung. Damit könnten die Einhaltung der Pflichten und Obliegenheiten als Voraussetzung der dauerhaften Haftungsbefreiung bedingt sowie Sanktionsinstrumente für den Fall der Nichteinhaltung vorgesehen werden. Es ist daran zu erinnern, dass der Haftungsausschluss für die Verbreitung von Inhalten davon abhängt, ob der betreffende Inhalt nicht ein eigener Inhalt des Vermittlers ist, weil dann die normale Haftung greift. In diesem Zusammenhang sollten auch die Umstände definiert werden, unter denen Vermittler für illegale Benutzerinhalte haftbar gemacht werden können, wenn sie die Identität dieses Benutzenden gegenüber Aufsichtsorganen, die gegen den Benutzenden vorgehen wollen, nicht offenlegen. Um weitere Unklarheit darüber zu vermeiden, wann das „Kuratieren" (die organisatorische Einbindung des Vermittlers in die Inhalteverbreitung) nahe an die „redaktionelle Kontrolle" (die die Haftung direkt begründen würde) heranreicht, wird durch die Hinzufügung der Verantwortlichkeitsebene (= Pflichten und Obliegenheiten) zumindest klargestellt, dass diese Art von Anbietern unabhängig von der Haftungsfreistellung Compliance-Pflichten hat. Die Betonung in einem reformierten Rechtsrahmen, dass eine solche Verantwortung nicht nur die Art und Weise umfassen kann, wie „illegale", sondern auch schädigende Inhalte behandelt werden, wie sie in den Rechtsordnungen der Mitgliedstaaten definiert sind, würde zu einem besseren Ausgleich der divergierenden Interessen beitragen. Schließlich ist darauf hinzuweisen, dass technische Dienste wie z. B. Internetzugangsanbieter zwar nicht primärer Adressat von Durchsetzungsmaßnahmen gegen die Verbreitung illegaler Inhalte sind, dass aber auch sie Ziel von Maßnahmen der zuständigen Stellen sein können, denen sie unabhängig von ihrer Haftungsbefreiung nachzukommen haben.

Die Einführung von Pflichten und Obliegenheiten für Diensteanbieter

30. Wie bereits erwähnt, können Pflichten und Obliegenheiten für die Anbieter von Diensten der Informationsgesellschaft in präzisierter Form eingeführt werden, anstatt lediglich die mitgliedstaatliche Befugnis hervorzuheben, Regelungen über Sorgfaltspflichten vorzusehen, wie es derzeit der Fall ist. Bei diesen verantwortlichkeitsorientierten Instrumenten geht es nicht um die Frage der Haftung (bzw. der Freistellung davon) bei Verletzung des geltenden Rechtsrahmens im Einzelfall, sondern um eine gesonderte Regelung, die es erlaubt, Inhaltevermittler bei Nichteinhaltung der strukturellen Erwartungen an ihre Verantwortungsposition zur Rechenschaft zu ziehen. Der Vorteil der Einführung von Verantwortlichkeitsanforderungen in einen harmonisierenden Rechtsakt auf EU-Ebene besteht darin, der gesamteuropäischen (und typischerweise globalen) Tätigkeit der meisten relevanten Diensteanbieter Rechnung zu tragen und damit für diese Rechtsklarheit in vergleichbarer Weise zu schaffen, wie dies bereits mit der ursprünglichen ECRL und der dortigen Einführung von (mitgliedstatenübergreifend anwendbaren) Haftungsausschlüssen geschehen ist. Darüber hinaus würde dies die Anwendung gemeinsamer Durchsetzungsstandards ermöglichen, auch wenn zuständige nationale Stellen Besonderheiten des nationalen Rechts berücksichtigen müssten. Schließlich würde damit die Möglichkeit der Einführung solcher Maßnahmen endgültig geklärt werden und es käme nicht mehr – wie derzeit – auf die schrittweise Bewertung nationaler Maßnahmen durch den EuGH und die damit einhergehende Klärung an.

31. Die Erwartungen an die Intermediäre hinsichtlich der Wahrnehmung ihrer Verantwortung sollten – unter Beachtung des Verhältnismäßigkeitsgrundsatzes – die Art und Position des betreffenden Dienstleisters sowie die Schwere der möglichen Rechtsverletzung und das Risiko ihres Eintretens berücksichtigen. In Bezug auf die Intermediäre wird ein abgestufter Ansatz angewandt, der von den Auswirkungen der jeweiligen Dienstleistung auf die Allgemeinheit abhängt, was sich sowohl auf die angebotene Dienstleistung selbst als auch auf die Markt- oder Meinungsmacht des Anbieters bezieht. Damit würde ermöglicht, bestimmte Kategorien besonders kleiner oder im Entstehen begriffener Anbieter von bestimmten Verpflichtungen zu befreien und Plattformen mit erheblichem Einfluss potenziell strengere Verpflichtungen aufzuerlegen. Hinsichtlich des Gefährdungsgrades bedeutet dies, dass die erwartbaren Maßnahmen für Inhalte mit hohem Risiko, hoher Auswirkung und hoher Wahrscheinlichkeit strenger sein sollten als

Reaktionen auf Risiken am unteren Ende der Skala. Dieser Ansatz muss sich auf die Arten von Schäden beziehen, die durch Verantwortlichkeitsmaßnahmen verhindert werden sollen, ohne diese jedoch im Einzelnen definieren zu müssen. Zu diesem Zweck kann auf bestehende sektorspezifische Bestimmungen verwiesen oder auf sie zurückgegriffen werden, was den Mitgliedstaaten auch ermöglicht, ihren Rechtsrahmen beizubehalten, in welchem die Kategorien illegaler oder schädlicher Inhalte definiert werden, auf die sich solche Maßnahmen dann beziehen würden.

32. Das Herausarbeiten von Verantwortlichkeitsanforderungen, wie sie im Folgenden in zusammengefasster Form erwähnt werden, kann sich auf den Ansatz der revidierten AVMD-Richtlinie bzgl. geeigneter Maßnahmen stützen, die von den VSPs zu ergreifen sind, da dort bereits ein detaillierter Verantwortungsstandard festgelegt wird, der von den anderen auf Anbieter von Inhalten mit redaktioneller (und daher erhöhter) Verantwortung gerichteten Bestimmungen der Richtlinie getrennt ist. Das AVMD-System befürwortet die Anwendung von Verhaltenskodizes in einem koregulierenden Ansatz, mit dem etablierte Praktiken der Industrie einbezogen werden können, solange diese mit einer Form robuster und unabhängiger Aufsicht verbunden werden, etwa indem die Standards z. B. durch die zuständigen Regulierungsstellen gebilligt werden.

33. Die Verpflichtungen (sozusagen die Regeln innerhalb des Verantwortlichkeitsrahmens) und Obliegenheiten (die zu erfüllenden Aufgaben) verlangen von sorgfältig agierenden Wirtschaftsteilnehmern ein Risikomanagement, das auf einer anfänglichen Risikobewertung und der Planung notwendiger Reaktionen auf identifizierte Risiken beruht. Wie in anderen Bereichen, z. B. bei Finanzdienstleistungen oder bei der Verarbeitung personenbezogener Daten, ist diese Form der Risikoeinschätzung gleichbedeutend mit einer systematischen Vorbereitung und einem Bereithalten zur Reaktion auf Risikosituationen in der Praxis. Risiken sind dabei nicht Einzelfälle, in denen eine potenzielle Verletzung inhaltlicher Standards auftritt, die eine Reaktion erforderlich machen, sondern schließen Vermeidungsmaßnahmen ein, damit Risiken gar nicht erst entstehen. Je nach Ergebnis der Risikoabschätzung können sich die zu erwartenden Risikoreaktionen oder Abwehrstrategien aus allgemein akzeptierten Praktiken und Normen ableiten, die etwa von zertifizierten Normungsgremien festgelegt und regelmäßig einen Verweis auf den aktuellen Stand der Technik enthalten werden. Eine weitere Möglichkeit, die Rechtssicherheit für Inhaltevermittler

hinsichtlich ihrer Verantwortung zu erhöhen, besteht darin, die grundlegenden Maßnahmen im Rechtsakt aufzunehmen, aber die weitere Konkretisierung durch Leitlinien vorzusehen, die von der Kommission oder den zuständigen nationalen Regulierungsstellen oder anderen benannten Institutionen verabschiedet werden.

34. Der Verantwortungsrahmen wird so eine Reihe von Bereichen erfassen, für die (bestimmte) Vermittler Maßnahmen vorsehen müssen, die den anerkannten Standards entsprechen. Diese werden teils proaktiver, teils reaktiver Natur sein und bei Letzteren auch eine Verbindung zur Frage der Haftung herstellen: Maßnahmen, die als Reaktion auf eine Meldung über illegale Inhalte zu ergreifen sind, können sich von der bloßen Entfernung dieser Inhalte („take down", wobei das Unterlassen dieser Handlung zu tatsächlicher Haftung führt) bis hin zur Sicherstellung des zukünftigen Nicht(wieder-)auftauchens dieser Inhalte („stay down") sowie zur Weiterverfolgung dieser Maßnahmen mit entsprechenden Informationen an die betroffenen Parteien sowie an die zuständigen Stellen in einem Meldemechanismus erstrecken. Daher ist eine klare Unterscheidung zwischen verschiedenen Arten von Pflichten nicht notwendig.

35. Ein zukünftiger Rechtsakt muss mindestens auch Leitlinien bzgl. der Verfahren vorgeben, die für die Meldung illegaler Inhalte durch die Nutzer an die Anbieter von Letzteren zu installieren und zu befolgen sind, insbesondere wenn das Haftungsprivileg unverändert bestehen bleibt und daher von einer angemessenen Reaktion auf solche Meldungen abhängig ist. Hierzu sollten die Art und Weise, wie Beschwerden ermöglicht und auch erleichtert werden, sowie die Bedingungen für Reaktionsmechanismen und Rechtsbehelfe gehören, wobei insbesondere die zu verwendenden Technologien nicht im Gesetz selbst festgelegt werden müssen. Dasselbe gilt für andere Arten von technischen Maßnahmen, die zu den von Intermediären erwarteten Maßnahmen gehören können, z. B. Altersverifikationssysteme oder Systeme zur Kennzeichnung von Inhalten.

36. Ein weiterer Hauptbereich, für den im Hinblick auf den zukünftigen Rechtsrahmen detailliertere Anforderungen nötig sind, betrifft die Transparenz. Dazu gehört die Transparenz gegenüber Nutzern und betroffenen Empfängern des Dienstes im Falle der Sperrung oder Entfernung von Inhalten durch Information über die Verwendung algorithmischer Instrumente und deren Hauptfunktionalitäten, aber auch die Transparenz gegenüber den zuständigen Stellen, die mit der Überwachung des Dienstes beauftragt sind, sowohl in Form allgemeiner Be-

richtspflichten als auch als Pflicht zur Antwort auf individuelle Anfragen. Soweit es um Richtlinien zur Moderation von Inhalten geht, sind weder Transparenzvorgaben noch die oben erwähnten Reaktionsmaßnahmen im Falle einer Meldung allein ausreichend. Angesichts der Rolle der Intermediäre müssen diese in der Lage sein, nachzuweisen, dass sie Richtlinien anwenden, die die Meinungsfreiheit nicht über die Bekämpfung illegaler und schädlicher Inhalte hinaus einschränken, und wie sie bei Streitigkeiten über getroffene Entscheidungen dem Gedanken eines rechtsstaatlichen Ansatzes folgen, indem sie verschiedene Ebenen der Anfechtung dieser Entscheidungen auf leicht zugängliche Weise garantieren.

37. Dieser grundlegende Anforderungskatalog, der oben beispielhaft dargestellt wurde, wird ergänzt durch den Verweis auf anerkannte Standards hinsichtlich der Art und Weise, wie die Anforderungen erreicht werden sollen. Diese Kombination aus der gesetzlichen Verankerung des Verantwortlichkeitsansatzes und dem intensiven Rückgriff auf solche Standards ermöglicht einerseits eine flexible und kontinuierliche Weiterentwicklung dieser Vorgaben und andererseits eine enge Beteiligung der Industrie an der Festlegung möglicher Standards. Das System erlaubt damit – über die Frage der Haftung in konkreten Fällen hinaus – die Inhaltevermittler zur Rechenschaft zu ziehen und möglicherweise auch ein Sanktionssystem zu etablieren, das nicht auf einzelne Fälle illegaler Inhalteverbreitung, sondern auf die mangelnde Bereitschaft der Anbieter im Allgemeinen durch Missachtung der erwarteten Standards reagiert. Auf diese Weise liegt die Beweislast bei den Anbietern und ermutigt zu rechtskonformem Verhalten. Die Begrenzung der Verbreitung illegaler oder schädlicher Online-Inhalte scheint daher erfolgversprechender zu sein, als sich nur auf Einzelfälle zu verlassen, die von privaten Beschwerdeführenden oder öffentlichen Stellen vorgebracht werden.

Die institutionelle Ausgestaltung der Überwachung und der Rechtsdurchsetzung

38. Die Schaffung solcher Regelungen macht es auch erforderlich, ihre Durchsetzung im Falle der Nichteinhaltung sicherzustellen. Neben der Durchsetzung durch private Beschwerdeführende haben beauftragte Stellen – in der Regel Behörden – die Aufgabe, die Beachtung der Regeln durch die beaufsichtigten Personen oder Einrichtungen zu überwachen und bei Verstößen darauf zu reagieren. Der Regelungsrahmen muss daher nicht nur eine effiziente Durchsetzung durch vor-

zusehende Verfahren und einen geeigneten institutionellen Aufbau ermöglichen, sondern es muss auch eine angemessene Umsetzung dieses
Aufbaus durch die jeweils zuständige Stelle gewährleistet sein. Dies
gilt insbesondere dann, wenn der Gegenstand der Regulierung eine
bestimmte Art von Aufsichtsorgan erfordert, wie dies bei der Aufsicht
über Medien und andere Arten der Inhaltskommunikation der Fall ist,
bei denen wegen der Meinungsfreiheit eine direkte staatliche Einflussnahme auf die Aufsicht verboten ist. Selbst wenn die Schaffung von
materiellen Vorschriften auf EU-Ebene die damit einhergehende Einrichtung von Organen zur Durchsetzung dieser Vorschriften auch auf
EU-Ebene nahezulegen scheint, ist die Anwendung von Vorschriften,
die sich aus dem EU-Recht ableiten, in den meisten Fällen immer
noch von Behörden der Mitgliedstaaten abhängig und diesen zugeord-
net. Auch wenn die bestehenden und künftigen Vorschriften für
Dienste der Informationsgesellschaft Aktivitäten betreffen, die typischerweise eine grenzüberschreitende Dimension haben und oft Anbieter adressieren werden, die in allen oder den meisten EU-Mitgliedstaaten tätig sind, sollte auch für diesen Bereich die Durchsetzung weiterhin auf der Ebene der Mitgliedstaaten erfolgen. Dies betrifft zumindest die für diese Studie relevante Kategorie von Anbietern, den
Inhaltevermittlern. Für diese gibt es eine Vergleichbarkeit mit medien-
typischen Regulierungsbedingungen, die die Zuständigkeit nicht zuletzt aufgrund nationaler, regionaler und lokaler Besonderheiten den
Mitgliedstaaten zuweisen, die – zumindest für die Medienregulierung
einschließlich des erweiterten Anwendungsbereichs der AVMD-Richtlinie – in Ansätzen zur Rechtsdurchsetzung einbezogen werden sollen.
Unabhängig von dieser Kompetenzverteilung sind Kooperationsstrukturen möglich.

39. Das Herkunftslandprinzip ist sowohl der Grund für die Übertragung
der Aufsichtsbefugnisse an die Organe der Mitgliedstaaten (Herkunfts-
staaten) als auch der Grund für die Forderung nach einer Verbesserung der Zusammenarbeit zwischen diesen zuständigen Organen auf
gesamteuropäischer Ebene, um eine effektive grenzüberschreitende
Durchsetzung im Binnenmarkt zu gewährleisten. Zunächst müssen
die Vorschriften jedoch die Aufsichtsstruktur entweder durch eine Definition auf EU-Ebene vorgeben oder durch eine Pflicht für die Mitgliedstaaten nach vorgegebenen Kriterien im nationalen Recht veran-
kern. Das Herkunftslandprinzip legt eindeutig nicht nur die Zuständigkeit für die Niederlassung von Anbietern fest, sondern auch die
Verpflichtung der zuständigen Mitgliedstaaten, von ihren Aufsichtsbe-

fugnissen Gebrauch zu machen. Eine effiziente Aufsicht über inhalts-
bezogene Aktivitäten erfordert daher nicht nur die Unabhängigkeit
von der Einflussnahme öffentlicher oder privater Parteien, sondern
auch die angemessene Ausstattung durch die Zuweisung einschlägiger
Kompetenzen und die Bereitstellung ausreichender Mittel, die Gewährleistung einschlägigen Fachwissens sowie die Ermächtigung, zu
einer transnationalen Zusammenarbeit beizutragen. Zu diesem Zweck
und wegen der Vergleichbarkeit der Überwachungsaufgabe in Bezug
auf die Inhaltevermittler scheint ein Rückgriff auf die seit langem mit
dieser Art der Überwachung beauftragten Aufsichtsbehörden eine na-
heliegende Lösung zu sein. Aber selbst wenn eine solche erweiterte
Abdeckung der inhaltebezogenen Aufsicht nicht den nationalen Regulierungsbehörden zugewiesen wird, die denjenigen nach der AVMD-
Richtlinie entsprechen, kann die AVMD-Richtlinie als Vorlage für die
Kriterien zur Einrichtung geeigneter Stellen dienen. Soweit die Aufsicht über Inhaltevermittler neue Befugnisse erfordert, etwa zur Kontrolle der Einhaltung von Verantwortlichkeitsanforderungen oder, um
ein konkretes Beispiel zu nennen, von Transparenzverpflichtungen,
müssen diese ausdrücklich den Stellen als Kompetenz zugewiesen werden, wie im Beispiel durch Informationsansprüche gegenüber Anbietern oder die Möglichkeit zur Durchführung von Audits. Diese neuen
Befugnisse können sich auf Sanktionsmöglichkeiten bei Nichteinhaltung der Verantwortlichkeitserfordernisse erstrecken, die getrennt von
der Frage nach einer möglichen Haftung in konkreten Fällen der Verbreitung von Inhalten zu sehen ist.

40. Hinsichtlich der Zusammenarbeit auf EU-Ebene sind verschiedene Ab-
    stufungen denkbar: Nationale zuständige Stellen könnten zu einem lo-
    ckeren Meinungsaustausch und vergleichbarer unverbindlicher Tätig-
    keit zusammenkommen; sie könnten Teil eines eigens geschaffenen
    Gremiums sein, in dem sie zu einer formalisierten Zusammenarbeit
    beitragen, die eine gemeinsame Beschlussfassung – in einigen Fällen
    durch Mehrheitsentscheidungen – einschließt; schließlich könnten sie
    Teil eines Kooperationssystems mit einem gesonderten, auf EU-Ebene
    geschaffenen Gremium sein. Die erstgenannte, am wenigsten intensive
    Form der Zusammenarbeit ist allerdings ungeeignet, da sie keine ge-
    meinsamen Vereinbarungen über die Ausrichtung von Regulierungs-
    maßnahmen gewährleistet. Das Beispiel der Gruppe Europäischer Re-
    gulierungsstellen für audiovisuelle Mediendienste (ERGA) zeigt deut-
    lich, wie es die Änderung des Formats von einer eher locker struktu-
    rierten Gruppe (damals auf der Grundlage eines

Kommissionsbeschlusses) zu einem formell eingerichteten Gremium mit ausdrücklich zugewiesenen Aufgaben in der überarbeiteten AVMD-Richtlinie der ERGA ermöglichte, den Austausch bewährter Praktiken und die Entwicklung gemeinsamer Leitlinien durch ihre Mitglieder effektiv zu fördern. Für beide oben genannten Grade einer intensiveren Zusammenarbeit gibt es eine Reihe von Beispielen in neueren Rechtsakten der EU. So sind im Europäischen Datenschutzausschuss (EDSA) die nationalen Aufsichtsbehörden zusammengeschlossen, die in einem formalisierten Kohärenzverfahren gemeinsame Stellungnahmen zu Verfahren einzelner Behörden abgeben und im Streitfall sogar verbindliche Mehrheitsentscheidungen in grenzüberschreitenden Fällen treffen können. Der EDSA kann als wichtigste Inspirationsquelle angesehen werden, wenn es darum geht, die gesetzlich verankerte Zusammenarbeit der mit der Aufsicht über die Medien- und Inhaltekommunikation betrauten Stellen weiter zu verstärken. Insbesondere im Hinblick auf mögliche spezifische EU-Regelungen für systemische Plattformen (zu denen auch Inhaltevermittler zählen können) ist eine noch intensivere Form der Zusammenarbeit bei der Aufsicht denkbar, die die Schaffung eines zusätzlichen Gremiums einschließt. Sie könnte sich auf die Etablierung des einheitlichen Bankenaufsichtsmechanismus stützen, der direkte Überwachungsbefugnisse nur bzgl. systemrelevanter Banken vorsieht, allerdings unter Berücksichtigung der sehr spezifischen Natur dieses Systems und der Tatsache, dass es mit der Europäischen Zentralbank bereits eine entsprechende Institution gab, auf die aufgebaut werden konnte.

41. Die tatsächliche Form der Zusammenarbeit wird von den vereinbarten materiellen Regeln abhängen, und ihre Struktur kann auf bestehende Modelle zurückgreifen, die an die Besonderheiten des Marktes für die Verbreitung von Online-Inhalten angepasst sind und mit anderen Formen und Institutionen in Zusammenhang gebracht werden, die mit der Überwachung anderer Plattformarten betraut sind, die unter die neuen Regeln fallen. Dazu können Regulierungsstrukturen für den Verbraucherschutz, das Wettbewerbsrecht oder neu geschaffene spezielle Gremien für den Plattformsektor gehören. Die detaillierte Definition der Zusammenarbeit und der der Kooperationsstruktur zugewiesenen Befugnisse, die z. B. die Festlegung von Sanktionsmöglichkeiten einschließen kann, ist einfacher in Form einer Verordnung möglich, die gegebenenfalls getrennt vom materiellen Regelwerk geschaffen werden müsste (wie dies beim Gremium der Europäischen Regulierungsbehörden für elektronische Kommunikation (GEREK) der Fall

war). Das Beispiel der ERGA zeigt jedoch, dass eine solche Lösung auch innerhalb einer Richtlinie möglich ist, die daneben Bestimmungen enthält, die von den Mitgliedstaaten umgesetzt werden müssen. In welcher Form auch immer die Festlegung erfolgt, die Kooperationsaufgaben sollten sich zumindest auf die Zuweisung des Rechts zur Konkretisierung der Anwendung der Regeln erstrecken, auf die Vereinbarung gemeinsamer Durchsetzungsstandards, auf die Abgabe von Stellungnahmen zu Fällen grenzüberschreitender Verbreitung von Inhalten bei Streitigkeiten über die Behandlung im Herkunftsstaat, auf die Sicherstellung einer effizienten Informationsbereitstellung untereinander in Einzelfällen und auf die Teilnahme an Eilverfahren für dringende Fälle, die eine marktortbezogene Ausnahme vom Herkunftslandprinzip rechtfertigen. Über die Kooperation zwischen den zuständigen nationalen Stellen hinaus umfasst diese (auf nationaler, aber auch auf EU-Ebene) die Zusammenarbeit mit den beaufsichtigten Unternehmen, insbesondere im Rahmen von Koregulierungsansätzen, aber auch mit anderen Aufsichtsbehörden, z. B. im Datenschutz- oder Wettbewerbsrecht.

Bewertung der im DSA vorgeschlagenen Ansätze

42. Wie bereits im Vorfeld angekündigt, bilden die Entwürfe der Kommission für einen DSA und einen DMA den vorgeschlagenen neuen horizontalen Ansatz für die Regulierung von Vermittlungsdiensten, zu denen auch auch Online-Plattformen als spezielle Unterkategorie gehören. Zwar sind darin Inhaltevermittler nicht als eigenständige Kategorie von Anbietern adressiert, die sich von anderen Arten von Anbietern unterscheidet. Allerdings werden bestimmte Regeln vorgeschlagen, die im Zusammenhang mit solchen Intermediären besondere Relevanz besitzen, und zwar durch die Regeln, die Online-Plattformen adressieren. Der DMA-Vorschlag basiert dabei auf einem generellen Ansatz, der auf Marktsituationen reagiert in denen zentrale Plattformdienste wesentliche Dienste erbringen und durch ihren erheblichen Einfluss auf den Binnenmarkt eine Schlüsselrolle bei der Vermittlung von Geschäftskunden und Verbrauchern/Nutzern einnehmen („Gatekeeper"). Für solche Plattformen wird ein ex ante-Regulierungsrahmen vorgeschlagen, der einem wettbewerbsrechtlichen Ansatz gleicht. Dies ist auch im Bereich der Verbreitung von (medialen) Inhalten relevant, da sich Plattformen, die den Kriterien zur Einordnung als Gatekeeper entsprechen werden, auch Schlüsselkanäle für die Online-Verbreitung sind. Im Kontext dieser Studie ist aber vor al-

lem der DSA-Vorschlag relevant, der eine Reihe von Sorgfaltspflichten („due dilligence"-Pflichten) für alle Vermittlungsdienste, einige weitere für Hosting-Dienste, zusätzliche, noch weiter detaillierte für Online-Plattformen sowie schließlich darüber hinaus spezifische Pflichten zum Management systemischer Risiken für sehr große Online-Plattformen einführt; der das Haftungsprivilegierungssystem der ECRL mit einigen Klarstellungen und zusätzlichen Haftungsbedingungen in Bezug auf behördliche Anordnungen in das vorgeschlagene Regelungskonstrukt überführt, wobei die darüber hinaus auferlegten Sorgfaltspflichten aber unberührt bleiben; und der schließlich eine neue Struktur für die Aufsicht und Rechtsdurchsetzung dieser Regeln vorschlägt.

43. Beide Rechtsakte werden als Verordnungen vorgeschlagen, obwohl sowohl der Anwendungsbereich im Sinne des Regelungsumfangs als auch das Subsidiaritätsprinzip in Bezug auf den DSA mehr für einen Ansatz streiten, der den Mitgliedstaaten größere Gestaltungsspielräume belässt und daher regelmäßig entlang des Rechtscharakters einer Richtlinie umzusetzen wäre. Beide Vorschläge stützen sich als kompetenzrechtliche Grundlage auf die Binnenmarktharmonisierungsklausel des Art. 114 AEUV. Dieser Ansatz, der auf die Regulierung wirtschaftlicher Aspekte gestützt ist, darf aber nicht mit den Mitgliedstaaten verbleibenden Kompetenzen zum Erlass von Regeln im Bereich der Medien- und Inhalteregulierung in Konflikt geraten. Der grenzüberschreitende Charakter der Online-Verbreitung allein rechtfertigt noch nicht die Wahl der Rechtsform einer Verordnung, so dass zum einen eine Lösung gefunden werden muss, die der Kompetenzverteilung zwischen EU und Mitgliedstaaten, und zum anderen, und das ist besonders wichtig, der fortgeführten Bedeutung des EU-Sekundärrechts in diesem Bereich ausreichend Rechnung trägt. In Bezug auf letzteren Aspekt ist es zu begrüßen, dass der DSA-Vorschlag der AVMD-Richtlinie, der DSM-Richtlinie und anderen relevanten Rechtsakten einen lex specialis-Vorrang einräumen will. Allerdings werden hier vor dem Hintergrund des Status der Umsetzung dieser Richtlinien im Vergleich zum DSA weitere Klarstellungen erforderlich sein, um Rechtsunsicherheiten zu vermeiden. Zudem sollte auch die Beibehaltung der ECD neben dem neuen DSA (bei lediglich der Übertragung der dort enthaltenen Regeln zur Haftungsprivilegierung) nochmals überdacht werden.

44. Der DSA-Vorschlag wählt den Ansatz des Marktortprinzips, was einerseits den Anwendungsbereich der Regeln in deutlicher Weise auf alle Anbieter erweitert, die ihre Dienste an EU-Bürgerinnen und -Bürger

anbieten, und damit sowohl EU-inländische als auch Anbieter aus Drittstaaten adressiert. Andererseits eröffnet dies auch größere Initiativmöglichkeiten für Maßnahmen von Regulierungsbehörden, die grundsätzlich keine eigene Zuständigkeit auf Basis des Niederlassungsstaates ableiten könnten. Die vorgeschlagenen Regeln ziehen dabei das Erfordernis einer „wesentlichen Verbindung" zum Markt eines Mitgliedstaates als völkerrechtliches „genuine link"-Kriterium heran, um die Anwendung der Regeln zu rechtfertigen. EU-ausländische Anbieter werden verpflichtet, einen Rechtsvertreter in einem EU-Mitgliedstaat zu benennen, durch den unter anderem Aufsichtsmaßnahmen gegen die in Rede stehenden Anbieter erleichtert werden sollen.

45. Der DSA-Vorschlag schafft verschiedene Kategorien von Anbietern von Vermittlungsdiensten, um die Anwendung der neu vorgeschlagenen Regeln in Bezug auf deren Relevanz für die jeweiligen Anbieter zu unterscheiden. Allerdings wird die grundsätzliche Unterscheidung, wie sie in der ECRL zur Bestimmung der Anwendbarkeit der verschiedenen Haftungsprivilegien enthalten ist, aufrechterhalten. Mit der Überführung der Regeln in den Rechtsrahmen einer Verordnung besteht zwar grundsätzlich die Chance, dass die bisherige unterschiedliche Umsetzung oder Auslegung auf nationaler Ebene überwunden werden kann. Aufgrund der mangelnden Präzisierung der reinen Durchleitung, von Caching- und Hosting-Diensten, ist jedoch eine rechtliche Unsicherheit weiterhin zu erwarten. Darüber hinaus wird keine weitere Differenzierung vorgenommen, obwohl der zugehörige Erwägungsgrund gerade unterstreicht, dass neu entstandene Arten von Diensten potenziell unter die bestehenden Definitionen fallen können. Allerdings ist es ein bedeutender Schritt, dass Online-Plattformen als eine separate, spezifischere Kategorie von Hosting-Diensten identifiziert werden, an die besondere Verpflichtungen geknüpft werden können. Die Zurückhaltung dabei, die Frage der "Neutralität" von Plattformen weiter zu konkretisieren, sowie das Weiterführen der Unterscheidung zwischen aktiven und passiven Hostern, werden voraussichtlich in Zukunft zu weiteren Auslegungsschwierigkeiten führen. Deshalb sollten diese Ansätze im Gesetzgebungsverfahren nochmals überdacht werden. Der Vorschlag berücksichtigt die Größe der Plattformen als relevantes Kriterium, um den Umfang bestimmter Verpflichtungen zu erweitern bzw. zu begrenzen, wobei es noch der weiteren Diskussion darüber bedarf, welche davon für alle Anbieter gelten sollen.

46. Die praktisch unveränderten Haftungsfreistellungen im DSA-Vorschlag wurden nur insoweit begrenzt, als eine klare Verpflichtung eingeführt wurde, auf behördliche Anordnungen zum Vorgehen gegen illegale Inhalte und zu Auskunftsersuchen zu reagieren. Zwar hat die
Trennung der Frage der Haftung(sfreistellung) von der Notwendigkeit
der Einhaltung zusätzlicher (neu eingeführter) Sorgfaltspflichten Vorteile. Die Verbindung dieser beiden Kapitel des Vorschlags bedarf allerdings der weiteren Diskussion, insbesondere hinsichtlich der Frage-
stellung, wann nach nationalem Recht die Nichteinhaltung von
Pflichten eine Haftung des Anbieters rechtfertigen kann. Der Vorschlag führt zu einer weiteren Klarstellung der Kriterien für die An-
nahme der "tatsächlichen Kenntnis" und führt harmonisierte Melde-
und Abhilfeverfahren ein. Allerdings ist nicht zu erwarten, dass die be-
gleitenden Erwägungsgründe zur beibehaltenen Regel, wonach „generelle Überwachungspflichten" unzulässig sind, ausreichen werden, um
die bestehende Unsicherheit darüber zu beenden, welche spezifischen
Maßnahmen zur Verhinderung der Wiedereinstellung rechtswidriger
Inhalte („stay down") oder welche proaktiven Identifizierungspflich-
ten in Bezug auf neue rechtswidrige Inhalte von den Anbietern erwar-
tet werden können, ohne mit dieser Regel in Konflikt zu geraten. Die
neu eingefügten Bestimmungen im Kapitel zur Haftung zeigen die
Notwendigkeit, Gerichte und Behörden in die Lage zu versetzen, insbesondere in dringenden Fällen zeitnahe und konsequente Maßnahmen der Anbieter anordnen zu können. In diesem Zusammenhang
sollte in der finalen Fassung eines zukünftigen Rechtsrahmens klar ge-
regelt werden, dass Ansätze der Mitgliedstaaten zur Behandlung schädigender Inhalte (oder andere diesbezügliche sektorale Ansätze in Le-
gislativakten der EU) auch dann möglich bleiben, auch wenn der
DSA-Vorschlag selbst diese Frage nicht regelt.

47. Die umfassende Liste an Sorgfaltspflichten, die mit dem DSA-Vorschlag eingeführt wird, ist zu begrüßen. Auch wenn nicht auf den ers-
ten Blick nachvollziehbar ist, dass alle diese Pflichten im Rahmen
einer EU-Verordnung zu regeln sind, insbesondere wenn sie die mitgliedstaatliche Kompetenz der medienorientierten Inhalteregulierung
berühren, ist die abgestufte, kumulierte Auflistung solcher Pflichten
ein notwendiger Schritt, um Vermittlungsdiensteanbieter in die
Rechtsdurchsetzung einzubeziehen. Für einige der proaktiven Pflichten im Zusammenhang mit dem Risikomanagement sollte eine Einbeziehung auch anderer Anbieter als derjenigen, die in die Kategorie der
sehr großen Online-Plattformen fallen, erwogen werden. Die vorge-

schlagenen Melde- und Abhilfemechanismen folgen dabei früheren Empfehlungen der Kommission und insbesondere die Berichtspflichten werden dazu beitragen, ein klareres Bild über den Umgang der Anbieter mit eben diesen zu gewinnen. Die Verpflichtung zur Einführung von Beschwerdemanagementsystemen und zur außergerichtlichen Streitbeilegung verbessert die Situation der Nutzer. Allerdings wird hier nicht konsequent auf Industriestandards gesetzt, sondern auf Verhaltenskodizes, bei denen kritisch hinterfragt werden muss, ob sie für diesen Bereich angemessen und effektiv sind. Der erweiterte verfahrensrechtliche Rahmen für vertrauenswürdige Hinweisgeber ist eine weitere Verbesserung gegenüber dem Status quo, während die Beschränkung der Know-Your-Customer-Pflichten auf Online-Marktplätze zugunsten einer allgemeineren Erwartung an die Kenntnis über und Verifizierung der Nutzer durch die Plattformen überdacht werden sollte.

48. Der DSA-Vorschlag führt einen neuen Aufsichtsrahmen ein, der die Zusammenarbeit in grenzüberschreitenden Sachverhalten ermöglicht und ein Sanktionierungsregime vorsieht. Es könnte jedoch ein stärkerer Rückgriff auf die behördlichen Strukturen der Mitgliedstaaten anstelle einer Konzentration bestimmter Befugnisse bei der Kommission erfolgen, was – anders als in Bezug auf die Ansätze im DMA, der an die Gegebenheiten im Wettbewerbsrecht angelehnt ist – im Rahmen des Anwendungsbereichs des DSA nicht offensichtlich nötig ist . Dies gilt auch für die Schaffung des neu vorgeschlagenen gemeinsamen Gremiums der nationalen Regulierungsstellen auf EU-Ebene, das zwar institutionalisierte Kooperationsformen vorsieht, aber dies auch in eher begrenztem Umfang und darüber hinaus ohne konkrete Entscheidungsbefugnisse. Die "Rechenschaftspflicht" der nationalen Regulierungsstellen gegenüber denen anderer Mitgliedstaaten ist ein wichtiger Schritt in Richtung einer effizienten Rechtsdurchsetzung in grenzüberschreitenden Sachverhalten, zumal eine verfahrensrechtliche Konsequenz im Fall von Meinungsverschiedenheiten über die Behandlung eines Sachverhalts vorgesehen ist. Ein ähnliches Kohärenzverfahren wie es beispielsweise für den Bereich der datenschutzrechtlichen Zusammenarbeit zwischen den nationalen Aufsichtsbehörden existiert, ist bisher jedoch nicht vorgesehen. Bestehende Kooperationsstrukturen, die spezifische Anforderungen aus sektoralen Bereichen wie der AVMD-Richtlinie adressieren, müssen durch die DSA-Strukturen deutlicher gegen potentielle Überschneidungen abgesichert werden. Die Verpflichtung der Mitgliedstaaten, ihre Aufsichtsstrukturen auf einen

Koordinator für digitale Dienste zu konzentrieren, ist für Föderalstaaten oder Staaten ohne eine konvergente Regulierungsbehörde möglicherweise keine angemessene Lösung. Im weiteren Gesetzgebungsverfahren sollte eine sorgfältige Bewertung aller Verfahrensschritte für jede Art von Verstoß gegen die materiellen Bestimmungen des DSA-Vorschlags vorgenommen werden, um festzustellen, ob die vorgeschlagenen Änderungen die Verfahren in grenzüberschreitenden Fällen tatsächlich erleichtern oder eher erschweren würden.

Schlussfolgerungen

49. Aus diesen Erkenntnissen lassen sich einige wesentliche Schlussfolgerungen für einen zukünftigen Rechtsrahmens für Online-Plattformen auf EU-Ebene ableiten. Die Vorschläge, die in dieser Studie präsentiert werden, betreffen insbesondere Informationsintermediäre. Aufgrund der Relevanz solcher Plattformen für die Verbreitung und Verfügbarkeit von Medien- und Kommunikationsinhalten im Allgemeinen ist es gerechtfertigt, diesen bei der Reform des horizontal anwendbaren Rahmens für Vermittlungsdienste besondere Aufmerksamkeit zu widmen. Ein solcher Rechtsrahmen verspricht zwar einen einheitlichen und übergreifenden Ansatz, kann aber auch Schwierigkeiten bei der Berücksichtigung der Spezifika bestimmter Kategorien von Plattformen oder Diensten bereiten. Daher können und sollten die Grundregeln zwar für alle Arten von Vermittlern gelten, aber die Anforderungen an Regeln, die sich auf Medien- und Kommunikationsinhalte auswirken, unterscheiden sich von denen für einen Marktplatz, auf dem Waren und Dienstleistungen angeboten werden. Für solche Inhaltevermittler ist nicht nur die den Mitgliedstaaten verbliebene Regelungskompetenz in diesem Bereich zu berücksichtigen, sondern auch der bestehende Rechtsrahmen für die Aufsicht über die Verbreitung von Inhalten und die Durchsetzung dieser Regeln. Dies ist insbesondere im Hinblick auf die Zielvorgabe wichtig, dass für Inhalte online die gleichen Regeln gelten (und durchgesetzt werden) sollen wie offline. Es sollte klarer herausgestellt werden, wie sich die neuen allgemeinen Regeln zu bestehenden oder künftigen Regeln verhalten, die speziell zur Regulierung der Verbreitung von Inhalten erlassen wurden.
50. Die Studie schlägt Lösungen vor, die dem Ansatz folgen, dass die Regulierung von Informationsintermediären auf den Grundrechten und Werten der EU basiert, diese respektiert werden und nicht nur eine Sicherung des Binnenmarkts mit möglichst weitreichender Gewährleistung der Grundfreiheiten – verbunden mit nur sehr begrenzten Ein-

schränkungen dieser Grundfreiheiten – angestrebt wird. Zusätzliche Einschränkungen für diese Diensteanbieter resultieren aus deren Position, die in vielen Fällen einer marktbeherrschenden Stellung gleichkommt, jedenfalls aber einer entscheidenden Rolle zwischen der Schaffung von Inhalten und deren Nutzung durch die Rezipienten entspricht. Diese Regeln sollen die Möglichkeiten von Plattformen, als Wirtschaftsakteure im Binnenmarkt zu agieren, nicht behindern, sondern sie in einer klarer definierten Weise in die Gewährleistung einer funktionierenden öffentlichen Kommunikationssphäre integrieren. Obwohl es denkbar wäre, den neuen Rechtsrahmen auf bestimmte gemeinsame Regulierungsziele (wie Fairness, Transparenz und Verantwortlichkeit) zu beschränken und auf dieser Grundlage die Beteiligung von Aufsichtsbehörden oder anderen mit der Überwachung und Durchsetzung dieser Standards betrauten Stellen bei der weiteren Konkretisierung der Anforderungen zu ermöglichen, geht der DSA-Vorschlag in Richtung der Schaffung von detaillierten Regeln, deren weitere Konkretisierung der Kommission überlassen wird. Es ist von besonderer Bedeutung, dass die Ausformung der Rechtsdurchsetzung bzw. der Regeln für Inhaltevermittler durch kompetente Stellen erfolgt, die Kriterien erfüllen, die deren Effizienz und deren Unabhängigkeit von einer Einflussnahme seitens des Staates, der beaufsichtigten Unternehmen und anderer privater Stellen garantieren. Solche Stellen sind die bereits etablierten nationalen Regulierungsbehörden im Bereich der audiovisuellen Mediendienste, die in ihrem gemeinsamen Gremium auf EU-Ebene fortgeschrittene Formen der Zusammenarbeit in grenzüberschreitenden Angelegenheiten entwickelt haben. Diese Strukturen könnten genutzt werden oder zumindest sollte sich der vorgeschlagene Aufsichtsrahmen stärker an diesen Erfahrungen mit der Überwachung und Durchsetzung orientieren.

51. Zweifellos sind die Vorschläge von DSA und DMA zu begrüßen, da sie am Ende des Legislativverfahrens die Grundlage für einen nachhaltigen Regulierungsrahmen für den digitalen Sektor zu bilden versprechen und die EU in die Lage versetzen können, Standards zu setzen, wie es im Bereich des Datenschutzes bereits erfolgreich geschehen ist. Die Vorschläge sind insofern ambitioniert, als dass sie nicht nur Vermittlungsdienste insgesamt adressieren, sondern bestimmte Kategorien von Anbietern identifizieren, die für die Verknüpfung zwischen Unternehmen und Nutzern essentiell sind und deshalb als Gatekeeper einer besonderen Überwachung bedürfen bzw. spezifische zusätzliche Pflichten zu erfüllen haben. Die Anwendbarkeit der vorgeschlagenen

Verordnungen sowie die Zuständigkeit werden nicht von der Niederlassung der betroffenen Anbieter in einem EU-Mitgliedstaat abhängig gemacht, was ein weiteres wichtiges Signal an den Markt ist. Davon ausgehend, dass das neue Regelwerk grundsätzlich für einen langen Zeitraum Bestand haben und den Markt für digitale Vermittlungsdienste mindestens für ein Jahrzehnt prägen wird, sind die vorgeschlagenen Regeln als gute Grundlage zu sehen, die aber im Legislativverfahren in der in der Studie beschriebenen Weise weiter verbessert werden können, um zu einer Lösung zu gelangen, die auf die zuvor identifizierten Herausforderungen erfolgversprechend reagiert.

A. Background of the Study

We are living in an age of digitalisation, in which, thanks to the Internet, it is possible to find online all forms and types of content, access it, share it with others and disseminate it further. In that respect, borders of states have become superfluous and, due to the advancing technological developments, language barriers are also disappearing more and more. The market for digital content is therefore global, open to development and constantly changing and growing. This not only opens up economic opportunities for companies that can interact with participants on this market, but it also offers society a large amount of benefits, for example in terms of freedom of expression and information, intercultural exchange or the variety of choices for consumption of (media) content. At the same time there are significant risks and challenges that come with this globalised exchange. Intermediaries and other platforms that enable or provide access to content, collect and categorise content and provide forums for exchange and content creation by users are regularly the gatekeepers to these benefits.

This digital environment could not have been imagined 20 years ago, not least because of the state of development of the Internet in those early days of increasing use of the Internet by the general population. In terms of stability (i.e. transmission rates), distribution, price and versatility, access to and use of Internet services were still real hurdles. Search engines were in their infancy; multimedia platforms with personalization possibilities were considered a possibility in the future but did not actually exist yet due to the described limitations.[1] This observation is even more obvious considering social networks or video sharing platforms[2] in their current form and popularity, which were unthinkable under the given circumstances at the turn of the millennium. The big players at that time were access providers and the few electronic commerce platforms that already existed.

---

1 For an insight into the status and environmental conditions at that time see for example *Joint Research Centre*, Multimedia information society.
2 The first video hosting service was founded 1997 with "ShareYourWorld.com", enabling users to upload small videoclips. Cf., e.g., *Haarkötter*, Journalismus.online: Das Handbuch zum Online-Journalismus, p. 288.

However, it was precisely in light of this environment that the E-Commerce Directive (ECD)[3] was established with the aim "of ensuring a high level of Community legal integration in order to establish a real area without internal borders for information society services"[4] (ISS). The liability privileges, information obligations, cooperation mechanisms and other provisions created in that EU legislative act on the basis of the pursuit of this objective still apply today without the ECD having been reformed since then. Instead of reforming the ECD itself, in recent years a threefold strategy had been pursued at EU level to nevertheless adapt the regulatory environment to the more advanced, modern internet age:

- adapting sector-specific legislation that responds to certain problems identified;
- providing (more) guidance on the interpretation of less clear provisions of the ECD, in particular regarding notice-and-takedown measures and the reliance on voluntary preventive actions;
- promoting coordinated EU-wide self- (and partly co-) regulation concerning illegal materials which are particularly harmful.[5]

As a result, the regulation of the multi-sided market of dissemination of online content is as diverse as the actors and types of content – whether video, audio, image-based or text-based – involved. The horizontal regulatory approach of the ECD still contains the relevant provisions for ISS, divided by the categories of access, hosting and caching providers, while other secondary legislation that addresses these providers in addition has been created or developed, thereby acknowledging the significantly changed role of ISS. The rise of Web 2.0 interactivity led to most intermediaries moving away from being simple hosts and becoming interactive content management platforms where the exploitation of user data and network effects are at the centre of the business model. Users are no longer passive recipients of content only but rather content creators that promote themselves with very diverse offers on different platforms in text, image, video or sound. The "dark side" of the great opportunities offered by the Internet, technology and digitalisation has also become very apparent over the

---

3 Directive 2000/31/EC of the European Parliament and of the Council of 8 June 2000 on certain legal aspects of information society services, in particular electronic commerce, in the Internal Market (Directive on electronic commerce), OJ L 178, 17.7.2000, p. 1–16.
4 Cf. Recital 3 ECD.
5 Cf. on this de *Streel/Husovec*, The e-commerce Directive as the cornerstone of the Internal Market, p. 32 et seq.

years. Phenomena such as easy access to (and continued dissemination of) illegal content, content inciting to hatred and terrorist propaganda, but also disinformation, are only examples of the problematic aspect that comes with the possibility for users to create and disseminate content via intermediaries without direct editorial control whereby the intermediaries can regularly invoke the liability privileges of the ECD when it comes to the question of responsibility for illegal or harmful content.

The complex situation, with horizontal liability privileges on the part of intermediaries which can be characterised as gatekeepers on the one side and growing threats caused by regularly anonymous users on the other, has led to difficulties in the regulatory practice. Particularly combatting the cross-border spread of illegal online content in an effective manner has turned out to be very difficult for authorities enforcing the law. Against this background and the – at the time not yet officially announced – plans of the European Commission to review the rules of the ECD and propose an amended regulatory framework in the coming years, the State Media Authority of North Rhine-Westphalia commissioned a study conducted by the Institute of European Media Law (EMR) in 2019. That study on "Cross-border Dissemination of Online Content"[6] examined in detail the applicable legal framework and enforcement issues with regard to the cross-border dissemination of online content, taking into account EU primary law, in particular fundamental rights and freedoms, as well as relevant secondary law.

A special focus was given to the liability privileges of the ECD resulting in the conclusion that the cross-sectoral regulatory approach of the year 2000 no longer takes sufficient account of the structural change of the actors on the Internet: despite the emerging case law of the Court of Justice of the European Union (CJEU) the rapid change of these service providers from formerly neutral information intermediaries to today's active and multilaterally acting as well as content selecting and curating intermediaries and platforms called for a need to update the rules. Those rules do not (any longer) interconnect in harmony with other existing legislative approaches which were, or are being, pursued both concerning content directly or other sectorial approaches that are also content-related. Such rules – as for audiovisual media services, copyright or the fight against online

---

6 *Cole/Etteldorf/Ullrich*, Cross-border Dissemination of Online Content. Open access at https://www.nomos-elibrary.de/10.5771/9783748906438/cross-border-dissemination-of-online-content.

"hate speech", disinformation and terrorist propaganda – are making intermediaries and platform providers more accountable.

In order to avoid further fragmentation of the rules applicable to different types of online service providers and to avoid the need to continuously introduce new categories of service providers depending on the further development of the online sector, the study therefore proposed either to replace at EU level the existing cross-sectoral approach with a new horizontally applicable legal instrument, which takes into account the different roles of different intermediaries and platforms, or to amend the existing rules in order to clarify the conditions under which previous exemptions from liability do not apply and the types of providers to be included in the scope of this instrument. The main challenges identified in this context are both substantive and procedural implications against the background of the country-of-origin (COO) principle as the hitherto fundamental principle in the regulatory treatment of the cross-border dissemination of online content, but there are also questions of a possible institutional structure that would be both sufficient to meet the risks and preserve competence allocation between the EU and Member States.

Based on the findings of that study, its presentation in several stakeholder meetings and conferences and in light of more concrete announcements for legislative plans of the European Commission, the State Media Authority of North Rhine-Westphalia tasked the Institute of European Media Law (EMR) with a follow-up study focussing on the most pressing areas for reform of the regulatory framework for the online sector as far as content dissemination is concerned. That study, which is the basis for this published version, was conducted during summer and autumn 2020, and its conclusions were presented by the scientific lead of the project at the conference "Safeguarding Freedom – Stabilising Democracy" on 27 October 2020.[7] At that time, the European Commission had already announced the

---

7 Cf. Mark D. Cole, Updating the Legal Framework and Enforcement Concerning Cross-Border Dissemination of Online Content (presentation available at https://e mr-sb.de/wp-content/uploads/2021/02/Updating-the-Legal-Framework-and-Enforce ment-Concerning-Cross-Border-Dissemination-of-Online-Content.pdf). The conference was organised by the German Media Authorities in cooperation with the Media Authority of North Rhine-Westphalia, the EMR and the Representation of the State of North Rhine-Westphalia to the European Union; see for more details https://www.medienanstalt-nrw.de/termine/safeguarding-freedom-stabilising-d emocracy.html.

"Digital Services Act" as a legislative measure in its work programme 2020[8] by highlighting that the legislative package would aim to modernise the current regulatory framework for digital services through two main pillars: firstly, to propose clear rules that define the responsibilities of digital services in order to address the risks faced by their users and protect their rights; secondly, to propose competition-based ex-ante rules for large online platforms that can act as "gatekeepers", thereby setting the "rules of the game" for their users and competitors.

After the Commission presented the Digital Services Act package with two draft proposals for a Digital Services Act (DSA Proposal)[9] and a Digital Markets Act (DMA Proposal)[10] to the European Parliament and the Council on 15 December 2020,[11] the study was updated in order to integrate the concrete provisions in the existing analysis and to highlight suggested areas for potential improvement of the proposals in the further legislative procedure.[12] The study continues to focus on those elements that are relevant in the context of media and content dissemination online. From the perspective of the media sector, the proposed reform is an opportunity to take account of existing problems with regard to the legal framework for, and enforcement of, the law in the online environment as far as the cross-border distribution of media content is concerned. In substantive

---

8 Communication from the Commission to the European Parliament, the Council, the European Economic and Social Committee and the Committee of Regions, Adjusted Commission Work Programme 2020, COM(2020) 37 final, https://eur-l ex.europa.eu/resource.html?uri=cellar%3A7ae642ea-4340-11ea-b81b-01aa75ed71a 1.0002.02/DOC_1&format=PDF, p. 4.

9 Proposal for a Regulation of the European Parliament and of the Council on a Single Market For Digital Services (Digital Services Act) and amending Directive 2000/31/EC, COM/2020/825 final, https://eur-lex.europa.eu/legal-content/en/TXT /?uri=COM:2020:825:FIN.

10 Proposal for a Regulation of the European Parliament and of the Council on contestable and fair markets in the digital sector (Digital Markets Act), COM/ 2020/842 final, https://eur-lex.europa.eu/legal-content/en/TXT/?uri=COM%3A202 0%3A842%3AFIN.

11 Cf. in addition the press releases and Q&A overviews, available for the DSA at https://ec.europa.eu/info/strategy/priorities-2019-2024/europe-fit-digital-age/digita l-services-act-ensuring-safe-and-accountable-online-environment_en, and for the DMA at https://ec.europa.eu/info/strategy/priorities-2019-2024/europe-fit-digital-a ge/digital-markets-act-ensuring-fair-and-open-digital-markets_en.

12 For a first overview of both acts *Ukrow*, Die Vorschläge der EU-Kommission für einen Digital Services Act und einen Digital Markets Act; *Woods*, Overview of Digital Services Act; *Woods*, The proposed Digital Markets Act: overview and analysis.

terms, this relates in particular to the review of the existing liability privileges of intermediaries and platform providers, the protection and safety of users on the Internet, especially with regard to disinformation, hate, violence and other illegal or harmful content, and the treatment of the dominant providers as gatekeepers. From a procedural and organisational point of view, it concerns above all the effective monitoring and enforcement of substantive rules, including an organisational structure that is adapted to situations of danger and at the same time takes sufficient account of restrictions of EU competences.[13]

The present study is structured as follows: it briefly recalls the applicable regulatory framework of the European Union and its Member States for the cross-border dissemination of online content, including the interplay between EU legislative acts and Member States' law and the implementation of it. The study then highlights the problems identified in connection with this framework. After that, the Commission Proposals for a DSA and a DMA are presented in a nutshell. The study then gives a general overview of regulatory options at EU level in the process of adapting this framework. Subsequently five core issues for reform are identified that concern the specific area of media and, more general, content dissemination, without discussing in detail the other elements which are also contained in the Commission Proposals. For each of the five issues the study presents different possible solutions and gives an overview of discussed options as well as the provisions proposed by the European Commission and assessment of the way forward: the country-of-origin principle and its exceptions, the scope of application of the framework for ISS, the liability privilege regime, new obligations and duties for service providers, including the respect for user rights, and, finally, specific issues about the institutional set-up for monitoring of compliance and enforcement.

---

13 On the latter aspect a further detailed analysis in light of the forthcoming reform of the platform rules of the EU was made by *Cole/Ukrow/Etteldorf*, On the Allocation of Competences between the European Union and its Member States in the Media Sector.

B. Summarising the Applicable Legal Framework

This chapter gives an overview on the existing framework for the media- and content-related online environment. In doing so, it summarises relevant findings of the preceding study "Cross-border Dissemination of Online Content".[14]

I. On Fundamental Rights, Fundamental Freedoms and EU Values

Considering the legal framework for the cross-border dissemination of online content, the fundamental rights as laid down in the Charter of Fundamental Rights of the EU (CFR)[15], the European Convention on Human Rights of the Council of Europe (ECHR)[16] and the provisions of national constitutional law lay the basis and have to be the foundation for any approach that is chosen.[17] These rights include prominently human dignity, which, according to the CFR, is "inviolable", i.e. needs to be considered as an overarching goal that has to be protected by State efforts. In the area of online content, there are many ways to violate rights of others, including attacking the human dignity of others. This can be true in particular for audiovisual content containing certain forms of pornography or depictions of violence. Concerning non-fictional depictions, this can be assumed when a person is displayed as "an object"[18] against the right to be treated with dignity. For fictional media, some type of content can qualify as such under specific conditions, too.[19]

---

14 *Cole/Etteldorf/Ullrich*, Cross-border Dissemination of Online Content, esp. p. 53–168.

15 Charter of Fundamental Rights of the European Union, OJ C 326, 26.10.2012, p. 391–407.

16 The European Convention on Human Rights, as amended by Protocols Nos. 11 and 14, supplemented by Protocols Nos. 1, 4, 6, 7, 12, 13 and 16, available at https://www.echr.coe.int/Documents/Convention_ENG.pdf.

17 On this and the following in detail and with further references, cf. *Cole/Etteldorf/Ullrich*, Cross-border Dissemination of Online Content, p. 53 et seq.

18 Examples include execution videos of terrorist organisations or so-called "snuff videos", which are most commonly disseminated via the Internet.

19 In the case of fictional content, under certain circumstances – although there will regularly be consent of the persons depicted – a violation of human dignity can

Fundamental rights also include the protection of minors on their own behalf, thus laying down the principle that in all actions relating to children, whether taken by public authorities or private institutions, whether in the offline context or in the digital media environment, the child's best interests must be a primary consideration. This high priority of the protection of minors is threatened in the online environment both from the recipient's perspective (in terms of the free accessibility of content harmful for the development of children) and from the victim's perspective (in terms of the dissemination of child pornographic or child sexual abuse content or phenomena such as grooming, which have been proliferating in the online environment). These fundamental rights thus suggest that a strict(er) and clear(er) regulation of the online sector is needed, both in terms of obligations for providers and enforcement possibilities for supervisory authorities. On the other hand, the fundamental right of freedom of expression as well as the freedom of the media demand special attention in the regulation of content, concerning both the handling of user-created content and the free consumption of information originating from different parts of the spectrums.

This finding also applies to the commercial interests of the actors involved in the cross-border dissemination of online content. Regulations that impose obligations on platforms, that, for example, may result in liability in the event of non-compliance, can interfere with the freedom to conduct a business, because they may make certain business models unfeasible or subject to major alignment. This, as well as the potentially affected right to property, are enshrined in the CFR, ECHR (or Protocol) and national constitutional law. The legal framework at sub-constitutional level has to be interpreted in the light of these fundamental rights. Its design also needs to be in line with these rights. This is all the more true considering that fundamental rights, such as human dignity or freedom of expression, can also give rise to active duties to protect on the part of states, including competent state bodies that are also bound by fundamental rights.[20]

---

be constructed on the side of the recipient (through an unintentional identification with the situation depicted) or also on the side of the persons depicted, who may not have been able to give effective consent – whether due to mental, physical or age-related incapacity to consent.

20 Cf. the jurisdiction of the European Court of Human Rights (ECtHR), in particular for Art. 8 ECHR (judgement of 27.10.1994, no. 18535/91, para. 31; judgement of 12.11.2013, no. 5786/08, para. 78), Art. 10 ECHR (judgement of 22.4.2013, no. 48876/08, para. 134; judgement of 17.9.2009, no. 13936/02, para. 100 et seq.;

The fundamental freedoms laid down in the Treaty on the Functioning of the European Union (TFEU)[21] are a significant element in the realisation of the EU's internal market, which includes the digital sector, aptly named the "Digital Single Market" by the Commission. Above all, the free movement of goods, the freedom of establishment and the freedom to provide services aim at keeping markets open and giving legal certainty to commercial operators in those markets. In principle, businesses should be able to distribute their goods and services freely throughout the EU and establish themselves where-ever they wish to do so without being subject to discrimination or restrictions in the receiving state. In the context of cross-border dissemination of online content, this does not only concern media companies, which can invoke these freedoms, but also the actors involved in the dissemination of content, i.e. in particular the ISS. Derogations from fundamental freedoms, whether at national or EU level, must be justified by an objective of general interest, and the measures taken to reach this objective have to be proportionate. This also applies to the COO which has been included in varying degrees in the legislative framework. Although the COO is not a mandatory consequence of the existence of fundamental freedoms, it is another expression of the idea of ensuring a free and fair internal market enshrined therein.

The justification of interferences with fundamental rights and fundamental freedoms essentially entails the necessary balancing of conflicting interests, those other interests themselves potentially being protected by fundamental rights or freedoms. The greater and more drastic the threat to one legal interest is, the easier it is to justify strong interferences by referring to other legal interests. It is therefore a necessary consequence of a carefully differentiated proportionality assessment that certain market participants are subject to different and stronger obligations than other market participants. In the context of the dissemination of online content, for example, content intermediaries play a different role than other platforms and are subject to higher risks for the fundamental rights addressed above. Because of the relevance of such platforms for the dissemination and availability of media and communication content more generally, it is justified to pay specific attention to them when reforming the horizontally applicable framework for information society services.

---

judgement of 29.02.2000, no. 39293/98; judgement of 16.03.2000, no. 23144/93) and Art. 11 ECHR (judgement of 16.3.2000, no. 23144/93, para. 42).

21 Consolidated version of the Treaty on the Functioning of the European Union, OJ C 326, 26.10.2012, p. 47–390.

Finally, the values on which the EU is founded and which the Member States have agreed upon and committed themselves to uphold are also relevant regarding the legal framework for the cross-border dissemination of online content. Art. 2 of the Treaty on European Union (TEU)[22] establishes as foundational values of the Union the respect of human dignity, freedom, democracy, equality, the rule of law and respect of human rights, including the rights of minorities. The close connection with the fundamental-rights-protecting framework is evident. These values are common to all Member States, i.e. in a society in which pluralism, non-discrimination, tolerance, justice, solidarity and equality between women and men prevail. These fundamental values are therefore of direct relevance to the current and future legal framework of the EU concerning the online sector. But they are also important for the legal framework of the Member States: on the one hand, through the validity of the principle of loyalty – in this case to the Union (Art. 4 para. 3 subpara. 2 TEU) – and, on the other hand, as a substantive prerequisite in the accession procedure under Art. 49 TEU and the non-compliance procedure under Art. 7 TEU.[23] Thus – and in light of this fact that both the threats and the benefits of access to information and communication opportunities in the online sector, human dignity, democracy, the rule of law and protection against discrimination are key factors – the EU values serve not only as benchmarks for a minimum level of regulation but also as common denominators for the EU and all Member States in light of exercising their competencies.

II. On the Allocation of Competences

Besides the guiding principles for establishing a framework for the online sector, the question of which actor can act in which way in creating the

---

22 Consolidated version of the Treaty on European Union, OJ C 326, 26.10.2012, p. 13–390.
23 While the mechanisms of Art. 7 TEU (preventive and sanctions) are to be used only in cases of systemic threats or breaches of EU values, in the context of judicial tools like the infringement procedures (Art. 258–259 TFEU) and preliminary references (Art. 267 TFEU) EU values can play a role as well. Cf. on this and further mechanisms to monitor and prevent breaches of EU values in Member States on EU level, in particular regarding the European Commission's rule of law framework and the set-up of annual dialogues on the rule of law, *Diaz Crego/ Manko/van Ballegooij (EPRS study)*, Protecting EU common values within the Member States, p. 19 et seq.

regulation is determined by the allocation of competences to the European Union by the Member States in this multi-level system. Specifically, concerning the dissemination of online content, a variety of factors are decisive that result from the tension between regulating the media sector as an economic market and the significance of the media in democratic societies that goes beyond their role as market participants. Thus we have a dual function of the media as both a cultural asset and an economic asset. However, the various ways in which media and individual media contents or user-generated content, which is relevant to the formation of public opinion in particular, are distributed are just as relevant. In addition, there is the advancing convergence of the media, which is reflected not only in the secondary legal framework – further explained under III. below – but also impacts the use of competences, depending on whether "media" are regarded to be moving closer to regular market players or services that are not actually media are being regarded through the lens of their comparability to media in terms of their function. In the following, this study will only outline the essential framework conditions for the allocation of competences that are relevant to the scope of the study. An extensive analysis of this question can be found in a recent study co-authored by authors of this study.[24]

To begin with, according to the principle of limited conferral of powers (Art. 5 TFEU), all competences not conferred to the Union by the Treaties remain with the Member States. Where powers to act have been allocated to the Union, it acts only within the limits of the powers conferred to it by the Member States in the Treaties to attain the objectives set out therein. The categories of competences are: exclusive (Art. 3 TFEU), shared (Art. 4 TFEU) and the power to support, coordinate or supplement the actions of the Member States (Art. 6 TFEU). The nature of each competence also determines the respective powers to act of both the Union and the Member States.

This applies also regarding legislative measures in the field of dissemination of online content. However, it is not possible to define a specific area of law which would cover all aspects relevant in this context in the sense of one single competence basis. Rather, various matters are involved here. Different objectives can be pursued with legislation, and its addressees and substantive rules are likely not uniform. This is reflected in the variety of legal bases in the TFEU that potentially are connected to this field of regu-

---

24 Cf. *Cole/Ukrow/Etteldorf*, On the Allocation of Competences between the European Union and its Member States in the Media Sector.

lation: namely Art. 28, 30, 34, 35 (free movement of goods), Art. 45–62 (free movement of persons, services and capital), Art. 101–109 (competition policy), Art. 114 (technological harmonisation or the use of similar technological standards, for instance, in products needed to operate the Internet), Art. 165 (education), Art. 166 (vocational training), Art. 167 (culture), Art. 173 (industry) and Art. 207 (common commercial policy). Considering the context of this study, in particular three competence areas of the EU are foremost relevant and will be highlighted in the following: the internal market competence of the EU, the EU competition law regime and the EU's (limited) cultural competences.

Exclusive competences, under which only the EU can take legislative actions, exist in particular for "the establishing of the competition rules necessary for the functioning of the internal market", which is laid down specifically in Art. 101 et seq. TFEU. Competition law focuses on market power and on counteracting or preventing anti-competitive behaviour; therefore market power that has a dimension of inhibiting competition in the EU market overall is addressed by regulation on that level. However, this economic focus does not mean that competition law aspects are not also relevant in the area of content dissemination. On the contrary, market power, even more so when it amounts to market dominance, especially in the online sector, often equates to having power over opinion-forming of the population. One of many examples of this is the market-leading search engine, which is the gatekeeper for the findability and visibility of content – an aspect that the Regulation on promoting fairness and transparency for business users of online intermediation services (Platform-to-Business (P2B) Regulation)[25], for example, takes into account with its economic focus.[26]

Therefore, the competition regime is generally suitable for achieving the goal of a diverse content offer not as a direct but as a side effect in light of, for example, ensuring media pluralism.[27] At the same time, competition

---

25 Regulation (EU) 2019/1150 of the European Parliament and of the Council of 20 June 2019 on promoting fairness and transparency for business users of online intermediation services, OJ L 186, 11.7.2019, p. 57–79.

26 Cf. on this in particular *Cole/Ukrow/Etteldorf*, On the Allocation of Competences between the European Union and its Member States in the Media Sector, p. 142 et seq.; *Cole/Etteldorf*, in: Cappello (ed.), Media pluralism and competition issues, p. 32, 33.

27 Cf. *Cole*, Europarechtliche Rahmenbedingungen für die Pluralismussicherung im Rundfunk, p. 93, 104 et seq.; *Jungheim*, Medienordnung und Wettbewerbsrecht im Zeitalter der Digitalisierung und Globalisierung, p. 249 et seq.

law not being directed at reaching media pluralism as such is not sufficient to substitute for targeted actions that are not based on the competition law competence. On the basis of competences under competition law, undertakings with significant market power in particular can therefore be subjected to special conditions. The exclusive competence of the EU includes the control of a ban on cartels (i.e. the prohibition of concerted practices by colluding in an anti-competitive manner), of the abuse of a dominant market position, of mergers and of State aid.[28] However, the economic focus of this competence basis may equally require – if it is also applied "horizontally" in an area in which cultural or, in particular, media policy aspects play a role – to provide in turn for special rules for indirectly affected areas, as is the case, for example, in the context of state aid law[29] or in the framework of the Merger Regulation[30].

Although the functioning of the internal market as a goal is a prerequisite for any matter that is allocated exclusively to the EU, the shaping of the internal market (Art. 114 TFEU) itself does not fall under the exclusive competence of the EU. According to Art. 4 para. 2 TFEU, it is instead a shared competence where both the Union and the Member States have the possibility of adopting legally binding acts. In such areas Member States can only take action to the extent that the Union has not yet taken action. Pursuant to Art. 114 (1) TFEU, the European Parliament and the Council are empowered to adopt measures for the approximation of the laws and regulations of the Member States which pursue the establishment and functioning of the internal market. This functional definition of the scope of application is very broad and has led in the legislative practice of the EU, especially in recent times, to a large number of legal acts – and further proposals by the Commission – being mainly based on Art. 114.

However, Art. 114 TFEU is by no means a universal competence that can be used for all measures within the internal market or to regulate companies operating within it. Rather, this provision must be interpreted as focussing on the removal or prevention of obstacles to the free movement of goods and services in the internal market or noticeable competition im-

---

28 Cf. on this *Ukrow*, in: UFITA, 83 (1), 2019, 279, 279 et seq.
29 According to Art. 107 para. 3 lit. d TFEU, state aid to promote culture may be considered to be compatible with the internal market.
30 According to Art. 21 para. 4 of the Merger Regulation (Council Regulation (EC) No 139/2004 of 20 January 2004 on the control of concentrations between undertakings, OJ L 24, 29.1.2004, p. 1–22), Member States may provide for special rules in the field of merger control, inter alia, to safeguard media pluralism.

pairments.[31] This means that the EU legislator must follow the purpose of improving the conditions for the establishment and functioning of the internal market, because if a "mere finding of disparities between national rules and of the abstract risk of obstacles to the exercise of fundamental freedoms or of distortions of competition liable to result therefrom were sufficient to justify the choice of Art. 100a [TEC, now: Art. 114 TFEU] as a legal basis, judicial review of compliance with the proper legal basis might be rendered nugatory."[32] This strict understanding of the provision also corresponds to the fundamental idea of the principle of conferral of powers, subsidiarity and proportionality, which the EU legislator must observe separately when exercising its competences. In particular, the principle of subsidiarity, enshrined in Art. 5(3) TEU, obliges the EU to carry out a subsidiarity test for all its "acts" and in this way complements the requirements arising from the relevant competence provision in Art. 4, 5 and 6 TFEU.[33] This test includes the assessment that, first, the EU shall act only if and insofar as the objectives of the envisaged action cannot be sufficiently achieved by the Member States and, second, in the sense of an efficiency or added value criterion, that the regulatory objectives can be better achieved at Union level by reason of the scale or effects of the envisaged measures.[34] The subsidiarity principle is of such relevance that in a legislative procedure, already at the outset, the parliaments of the Member States are informed and have a number of possible ways to react in case they are of the opinion that the principle was disregarded.

As regards the competence of the EU in the cultural sector, there are significant limitations set out in the TFEU which have to be taken into account. According to Art. 6 lit. c), only support, coordination and complementary measures can be taken by the EU in the field of culture, which is therefore fundamentally and intrinsically the responsibility of the Member States. Culture in that sense includes a variety of media-related aspects like areas of intellectual and creative human activity, which undisputedly include art, literature and music, but also the audiovisual sector as well as

---

31 CJEU, C-300/89, *Titandioxyd*, para. 23; C-376/98, *Advertising and sponsorship of tobacco products-I*, para. 110.

32 CJEU, C-376/98, *Germany v. Parliament and Council*, para. 84.

33 Cf. *Bast/von Bogdandy*, in: Grabitz/Hilf/Nettesheim, Art. 5 TEU, para. 50 et seq.; *Weber*, in: Blanke/Mangiameli, Art. 5 TEU, para. 7.

34 In more detail and with further references: *Cole/Ukrow/Etteldorf*, On the Allocation of Competences between the European Union and its Member States in the Media Sector, p. 53 et seq.

media-specific aspects of the protection of pluralism.[35] Furthermore, Art. 167 para. 1–3 TFEU enable, but to a very limited extent, an active cultural policy of the EU. Thus, the EU should contribute to the development of the cultures of the Member States and promote cooperation between them, supporting and supplementing activities of the Member States where necessary, amongst others in the field of artistic and literary creation, "including in the audiovisual sector". In principle, the EU is free to choose which instruments it uses for support and coordination, which may also include the enactment of binding legislation in the form of Regulations or Directives. However, it is limited to the extent that the basic power to regulate must remain with the Member States. The EU may not counteract, unify or replace the policies of the Member States. Harmonisation of national legislation is therefore explicitly excluded. Art. 167 para. 4 TFEU serves as a horizontal or "cross-cutting" cultural clause, requesting the Union to take cultural aspects into account whenever acting under other provisions of the Treaties, bearing in mind that such other measures, for example based on its economic competence, can affect matters of culture and that a weighing of interests might therefore become necessary. This does not amount to a rule according to which anything concerning culture would be excluded from EU action. Rather, the EU's basic competence order remains unaffected, and Art. 167 para. 5 TFEU determines the (narrowly allocated) instruments and procedures available to the EU in this field[36], serving as a negative clause preventing the EU from a recourse to the general titles of competence under the approximation of laws, particularly in the area of the internal market (Art. 114 TFEU), while taking action in the cultural sector.

To summarise the competence framework in light of the focus of the present study, it has to be stressed that the EU has a number of different legal bases at its disposal, which empower it to adopt both legally binding acts and non-binding support and coordination measures, for instance combined with self- and co-regulatory mechanisms. For the adoption of

---

35 Cf. *Cole/Ukrow/Etteldorf*, On the Allocation of Competences between the European Union and its Member States in the Media Sector, p. 45; already at a very early stage of the debate about this question cf. *Schwartz*, in: AfP 24 (1) 1993, 409, 417 with further references.

36 Only recommendations adopted by the Council on a proposal from the Commission, as well as support measures adopted by the European Parliament and the Council in accordance with the ordinary legislative procedure and after consulting the Committee of the Regions, but excluding any harmonisation of the laws and regulations of the Member States, can be considered.

rules and in particular for a reform of the ECD by way of a horizontal approach to create a legal framework for a broad range of internet players, the most likely legal base is the creation and better functioning of the internal market (Art. 114 TFEU). When exercising this shared competence, the principles of limited conferral of powers, subsidiarity and proportionality must be observed, which are capable of curtailing EU action. With regard to rules for the cross-border dissemination of online content, the limited competences of the EU in the area of media regulation must also be considered, which result on the one hand from the absence of explicit competences at EU level and, on the other hand, from the cultural clause, which requests consideration of Member States' cultural policies before EU action is taken. In addition, the imposition of special rules on platforms with significant market power may be based on competition aspects.

III. The Network of Sectoral Regulation

The starting point for the network of sectoral rules that apply in the area of online content dissemination is the horizontal framework of ECD. Adopted in the year 2000, the ECD was intended to create for the first time a framework for Internet commerce by eliminating legal uncertainties for cross-border online services and ensuring the free movement of ISS between the EU Member States. In order to do so, the ECD lays down some basic rules for ISS by following a minimum harmonisation approach based on the COO principle. Besides general rules concerning information obligations, the establishment of service providers, commercial communications, electronic contracts, codes of conduct, out-of-court dispute settlements, court actions and (a very basic rule on) cooperation between Member States, the liability (exemption) regime provided by the ECD is (until today) a core element of the Digital Single Market. Art. 12 to 15 set out conditions under which ISS (specifically access, caching and host providers) are not liable for third-party content which is accessed, transmitted or stored on their platforms. In addition, the principle that no general monitoring obligation may be imposed on these providers is established. These rules apply in principle to all providers that qualify as such ISS, unless the ECD itself or sectoral law, by which it is supplemented or superseded in many areas, provides otherwise.

In the two decades since creation of the ECD, the dissemination of online content is actually addressed by a broad and complex network of sectoral rules. These include, on the one hand, media-specific rules such as the provisions of the Audiovisual Media Services Directive (AVMSD)[37] as the core of European "media regulation". On the other hand, it concerns more general rules which are directed at regulating certain aspects of the online economy, but which are particularly relevant for the dissemination of media content because of their scope, such as the P2B Regulation. In between, there are a number of sectoral rulesets of importance such as the Directive on copyright and related rights in the Digital Single Market (DSM Directive, DSMD)[38], which concerns certain forms of dissemination and is directed at achieving an appropriate financial participation in the exploitation of works from a copyright law perspective, or the proposed Regulation on preventing the dissemination of terrorist content online (TERREG)[39], which concerns certain type of content that is supposed to be suppressed and takes a criminal law and fundamental rights protection perspective.[40]

The AVMSD is an essential part of the relevant legal framework for the dissemination of online content because, despite the approach of minimum harmonization pursued therein, a number of fundamental rules apply to online platforms. It covers audiovisual media services within the meaning of Art. 1 para. 1 lit. a AVMSD (including both services (linear and non-linear) in the meaning of Art. 56 and 57 TFEU when they fulfil the criteria of the AVMS-definition and audiovisual commercial communications) and – since the revision of the reform of the AVMSD in 2018[41] – video-sharing platforms (VSP(s)) within the meaning of Art. 1 para. 1

---

37 Directive 2010/13/EU of the European Parliament and of the Council of 10 March 2010 on the coordination of certain provisions laid down by law, regulation or administrative action in Member States concerning the provision of audiovisual media services, OJ L 95, 15.4.2010, p. 1–24.

38 Directive (EU) 2019/790 of the European Parliament and of the Council of 17 April 2019 on copyright and related rights in the Digital Single Market and amending Directives 96/9/EC and 2001/29/EC, PE/51/2019/REV/1, OJ L 130, 17.5.2019, p. 92–125.

39 Proposal for a Regulation of the European Parliament and of the Council on preventing the dissemination of terrorist content online. A contribution from the European Commission to the Leaders' meeting in Salzburg on 19–20 September 2018, COM/2018/640 final.

40 A detailed analysis of the sectoral regulation relevant in the context of dissemination of online content is provided in the study *Cole/Etteldorf/Ullrich*, Cross-border Dissemination of Online Content, p. 91 et seq. An overview of the interconnection between these different provisions can also be found in *Dreyer et al.*: The European Communication (Dis)Order, p. 24 et seq.

41 Directive (EU) 2018/1808 of the European Parliament and of the Council of 14 November 2018 amending Directive 2010/13/EU on the coordination of cer-

lit. aa AVMSD. Thereby, for the online sector, the definition of audiovisual media services covers, for example, streaming offers or media libraries of traditional broadcasters as well as on-demand offers of other providers. However, individual channels or profiles on platforms such as YouTube or Twitch can already fall under this term if they are designed in the way that Art. 1 para. 1 lit. a AVMSD describes and fulfil those criteria. The very broad definition[42] of VSPs includes – irrespective of their size and content provided – a wide range of actors in the online environment providing us-er-generated audiovisual content. Therefore, it does not only apply to the "obvious" example of providers such as YouTube but potentially also to electronic versions of newspapers and magazines or social network services.[43]

For all of these online actors the AVMSD sets out minimum standards that audiovisual content must comply with. This primarily concerns the protection of minors, the protection against violence, hatred and terrorist content and the content of audiovisual commercial communication (Art. 6, 6a, 9 AVMSD). With regard to VSPs, the implementation of these requirements at national level leaves a wide scope for choosing the form of the rules with recourse to mechanisms of self-regulation and co-regulation. At the same time, the design of the measures to be foreseen in these rules, namely concerning technical systems, is already specified in the AVMSD.

---

tain provisions laid down by law, regulation or administrative action in Member States concerning the provision of audiovisual media services (Audiovisual Media Services Directive) in view of changing market realities, OJ L 303, 28.11.2018, p. 69–92. An unofficial consolidated version of the AVMSD provided by the EMR is available at https://emr-sb.de/gb/synopsis-avms/.

42 According to Art. 1 para. 1 lit. aa AVMSD, video-sharing platform service means a service as defined by Art. 56 and 57 TFEU, where the principal purpose of the ser-vice or of a dissociable section thereof or an essential functionality of the service is devoted to providing programmes, user-generated videos, or both, to the gener-al public, for which the video-sharing platform provider does not have editorial responsibility, in order to inform, entertain or educate by means of electronic communications networks within the meaning of lit. a of Art. 2 of Directive 2002/21/EC, whereby the organisation of such providing is determined by the video-sharing platform provider, including by automatic means or algorithms in particular by displaying, tagging and sequencing

43 This question depends on the criterion of the "essential functionality" of the re-spective offer, which is the condition for it to qualify as VSP. In this regard, the Commission provides guidance in its Communication from the Commission Guidelines on the practical application of the essential functionality criterion of the definition of a 'video-sharing platform service' under the Audiovisual Media Services Directive, 2020/C 223/02, C/2020/4322, OJ C 223, 7.7.2020, p. 3–9.

Appropriate mechanisms include relevant provisions in the terms of use, the provision of technical systems for labelling advertising by uploaders or reporting and flagging procedures.

Furthermore, the 2018 AVMSD reform introduced provisions that will impact other types of platform providers. Although it does not directly address them by defining them as being within the scope of the Directive, relevant provisions will affect the way these providers offer their services indirectly. In particular, Art. 7a AVMSD authorises Member States to take measures to ensure in their dissemination the appropriate prominence of audiovisual media services of general interest. Art. 7b AVMSD goes a step further and demands that Member States take appropriate and proportionate measures to ensure that audiovisual media services are not, without the explicit consent of the media service providers concerned, overlaid for commercial purposes or modified.[44] This will lead or has already led[45] to provisions for "content intermediaries" at national level, and it is to be expected that there will be a reliance on instruments of self- and co-regulation as foreseen in Art. 4a AVMSD.

Concerning the supervision of the sector, in view of the division of competences between EU and Member States, it is left to the latter to decide on the structures and allocate the powers to a competent body. This allows the Member States to choose the appropriate instruments according to their legal traditions and established structures and to adopt, in particular, the form of their competent independent regulatory bodies in order to be able to carry out their work in implementing the AVMSD impartially and transparently. However, with the 2018 revision of the Directive a number of more detailed requirements about supervision and cooperation between competent bodies in the Member States are established. The expectations towards an independent regulatory authority or body are formulated[46] as well as the procedures for cooperation between individual regulators and

---

44 Cf. on Art. 7b, for example, *Cole*, Die Neuregelung des Artikel 7b Richtlinie 2010/13/EU (AVMD-RL).

45 Cf. on this for example the new provisions of the German Interstate Treaty on the Media (in particular §§ 80 and 84). An (unofficial) English translation of these provisions – then based on the Technical Regulation Information System (TRIS) notification of the draft version of the Treaty, which for the relevant provisions in §§ 80 and 84 is identical to the final version – is available at https://ec.europa.eu/growth/tools-databases/tris/de/search/?trisaction=search.detail&year=2020&num=26.

46 See the newly formulated Art. 30 and the accompanying Recital 94. On the previous situation when the existence of such regulatory authorities was implicitly ex-

within the network of all the main national regulators for the oversight of audiovisual media services. The pre-existing European Regulatory Group for Audiovisual Media (ERGA) is now formally established by the AVMSD and tasked with providing technical expertise, giving its opinion to the Commission and facilitating cooperation among the authorities or bodies and between them and the Commission.[47]

Although copyright law is not exclusively oriented to media content, it is obviously highly relevant for any type of protected content disseminated online. The relevant EU Directives and Regulations, especially the Directive on the harmonisation of certain aspects of copyright and related rights in the information society (Infosoc Directive)[48] and the Directive on the enforcement of intellectual property rights (Enforcement Directive)[49], have been of significant relevance to the online sector since their adoption in 2001 and 2004 because of the prevalence of cross-border dissemination of works protected by intellectual property law. The focus is on the question of the unauthorised public availability of protected works and the responsibility of intermediary services for such situations. A major change in the application of copyright rules in the online sector will come with the DSMD which is currently being implemented by Member States. The deadline for transposition into national law is 7 June 2021. The DSMD defines a new category of "online content-sharing service provider" (OCSSP) as platforms on which users can post large amounts of content that is made publicly available, and the main purpose of which must be to store and publish content uploaded by users. For these providers, a completely

---

pected without specific requirements being set, see for example ERGA's statement on the independence of NRAs in the audiovisual sector, ERGA(2014)03, October 2014, available at https://ec.europa.eu/digital-single-market/en/avmsd-au diovisual-regulators, and ERGA, Report on the independence of NRAs. Cf. also *Cole et al.*, AVMS-RADAR, p. 40 et seq.

47 See Art. 30b and the accompanying Recitals 56–58; for further details also the ERGA Statement of Purpose, http://erga-online.eu/wp-content/uploads/2019/06/ER GA-2019-02_Statement-of-Purpose-adopted.pdf, and for details about the functioning of the Group the Rules of Procedure, last amended on 10.12.2019, http://erga-online.eu/wp-content/uploads/2020/04/ERGA-Rules-of-Procedure-10-12-201 9-ver-1.pdf.

48 Directive 2001/29/EC of the European Parliament and of the Council of 22 May 2001 on the harmonisation of certain aspects of copyright and related rights in the information society, OJ L 167, 22.6.2001, p. 10–19.

49 Directive 2004/48/EC of the European Parliament and of the Council of 29 April 2004 on the enforcement of intellectual property rights, OJ L 157, 30.4.2004, p. 45–86.

new set of obligations will impose a significantly higher level of accountability while at the same time installing a deviation from the liability privilege laid down in Art. 14 ECD. Based on the premise that the platform
provider of the new category as described above must generally license
content uploaded by users, the providers can only escape direct liability for
illegal uploads under certain criteria: according to Art. 17 DSMD they
must have made sufficient efforts ("all efforts") to obtain authorisation
from rights holders, they must have made every effort to ensure that legally protected content is as inaccessible as possible ("in accordance with high
industry standards of professional diligence") and they must, as previously
under Art. 14 ECD, remove content expeditiously after becoming aware of
it and prevent similar infringements of rights in respect of the work in the
future (notice and takedown as well as stay-down measures).[50] With this
new provision special rules for a certain category of illegal content online
for certain types of ISS are introduced, clearly adjusting the setting as it existed under the ECD.

A different type of illegal content is addressed by the Proposal for a
TERREG. After lengthy negotiations in the legislative procedures, an
agreement was reached in the trilogue in December 2020.[51] The TERREG
aims to improve the effectiveness of the current measures for the detection,
identification and removal of terrorist content on online platforms. It addresses hosting service providers which offer their services within the
Union, regardless of their place of establishment or their size. A number of
obligations to prevent the misuse of their services for the dissemination of
terrorist content are to be introduced. These include, inter alia, the introduction of a removal order which can be issued as an administrative or judicial decision by a competent authority in a Member State, obliging the
provider to remove the content or disable access to it within one hour.
Furthermore, the Regulation requires hosting service providers, where appropriate, to take proactive measures proportionate to the level of risk and

---

50 Cf. on the fundamental rights dimension *Geiger/Jütte*, Platform liability under Article 17 of the Copyright in the Digital Single Market Directive, with extensive
references to studies concerning the DSMD and national transposition proposals,

51 Cf. the press release of the EU Commission of 10.12.2020, https://ec.europa.eu/co
mmission/presscorner/detail/en/ip_20_2372. In the meanwhile the LIBE Committee approved the text provisionally on 11.1.2021 (https://oeil.secure.europarl.e
uropa.eu/oeil/popups/ficheprocedure.do?lang=en&reference=2018/0331(COD))
and forwarded an according note to the Council (27.1.2021), https://eur-lex.europ
a.eu/legal-content/EN/TXT/PDF/?uri=CONSIL:ST_5634_2021_INIT&qid=161269
2237149&from=EN.

to remove terrorist material from their services, including by deploying automated detection tools. The rules are accompanied by the obligation to establish complaint mechanisms in order to ensure the protection of the freedom of expression, as well as general provisions on the establishment of competent authorities to act against terrorist content and the cross-border cooperation between them.

The P2B-Regulation creates information and transparency obligations for online intermediation services and search engines that are relevant for the visibility of content and products. The purpose of this Regulation is to contribute to the proper functioning of the internal market by laying down rules to ensure that business users of online intermediation services and corporate website users in relation to online search engines are granted appropriate transparency, fairness and effective redress possibilities. Core elements of the Regulation are, in particular, the obligation to set up an internal system for handling complaints from commercial users and information and transparency obligations including the disclosure of the main determining parameters for the ranking of an online intermediation service and the reasons for the relative weighting of these parameters. In addition, it must be made clear which data collected by the platform may also be used by the participating companies and which data will remain reserved for exclusive use by the provider of the platform. These transparency obligations do not only have significance for the online sector in general but can also be especially relevant for the visibility and findability of media content against the backdrop of the protection of media or information pluralism. The Commission has the power to issue guidelines about the ranking transparency requirements and has announced to "provide sector specific guidance, if and where appropriate".[52]

Data protection law also plays a major role in the context of regulating digital services[53] and in particular concerning online content dissemination. Not only is data and its exploitation for profit (e.g. via personalised advertising) the basis of the business models of a number of online platforms, but (personal) data often also determines, via algorithmic systems,

---

52 Cf. Targeted online survey on the ranking transparency guidelines in the framework of the EU regulation on platform-to-business relations, https://ec.europa.eu/digital-single-market/en/news/targeted-online-survey-ranking-transparency-guidelines-framework-eu-regulation-platform.

53 The European Parliament considers regulations regarding the use of personal data by platforms to be of particular importance with regard to the Digital Services Act. Cf. Report with recommendations to the Commission on the Digital Services Act: Improving the functioning of the Single Market (2020/2018(INL)).

to whom which content is displayed, recommended and presented. It can also gain importance in the context of law enforcement when it comes to information obligations of platform providers, which require the existence of data and the lawfulness of its disclosure.[54] The main legal bases are provided by the General Data Protection Regulation (GDPR)[55], the Law Enforcement Directive[56] and the Directive on privacy and electronic communications (ePrivacy Directive)[57]. The latter plays a decisive role in the area of electronic communications, i.e. in particular with regard to the storage of data on user terminals ("cookies" and the tracking of users' behaviour) and advertising by means of electronic communications. The data protection framework overall contains provisions on when the processing of personal data is permitted and for what purposes; it regulates the conditions for its transfer to third parties and defines rights for data subjects. The GDPR – and the same would apply if a reform of the ePrivacy Directive takes place along the lines of the Proposal for a Regulation by the Com-

---

54 The original efforts to harmonise retention of communications data in the Directive 2006/24/EC were annulled by the CJEU, C-293/12, *Digital Rights Ireland*. The e-Privacy Directive of 2002, as last amended in 2009, is supposed to be replaced by an e-Privacy Regulation (Proposal for a Regulation of the European Parliament and of the Council concerning the respect for private life and the protection of personal data in electronic communications and repealing Directive 2002/58/EC, COM/2017/010 final – 2017/03 (COD)). In February 2021, a final agreement has been found among Member States in the Council (https://eur-lex.e uropa.eu/legal-content/EN/TXT/PDF/?uri=CONSIL:ST_6087_2021_INIT&from= EN) so that negotiations in the trialogue can now take place. Relevant in this context is also the Interim Regulation on the processing of personal and other data for the purpose of combatting child sexual abuse (COM(2020) 568 final).

55 Regulation (EU) 2016/679 of the European Parliament and of the Council of 27 April 2016 on the protection of natural persons with regard to the processing of personal data and on the free movement of such data, and repealing Directive 95/46/EC (General Data Protection Regulation), OJ L 119, 4.5.2016, p. 1–88.

56 The Directive (EU) 2016/680 on the protection of natural persons with regard to the processing of personal data by competent authorities for the purposes of the prevention, investigation, detection or prosecution of criminal offences or the execution of criminal penalties (OJ L 119, 4.5.2016, p. 89–131) can also play a role as regards law enforcement due to its rules to the exchange of personal data by national police and criminal justice authorities.

57 Directive 2002/58/EC of the European Parliament and of the Council of 12 July 2002 concerning the processing of personal data and the protection of privacy in the electronic communications sector (Directive on privacy and electronic communications), OJ L 201, 31.7.2002 p. 37–47, as amended by Directive 2009/136/EU.

mission[58] – is based on the market location principle, pursues a strict harmonisation approach[59] and contains specific rules for the design of supervision with the establishment of a differentiated system of cooperation, including the possibility of joint decision-taking in cross-border situations.

In addition, there are instruments that deliberately leave to the Member States room for manoeuvre and the possibility of exceptions for the pursuit of media and cultural policy objectives at the national level, which enable supplementary rules concerning content dissemination.

This secondary law framework is supplemented by a series of measures encouraging self-regulation in EU coordination and support measures. Besides several recommendations in the field of the protection of minors and human dignity[60] there are measures in the area of tackling illegal content online. The latter include the Code of conduct on countering illegal hate speech online[61] and the Commission's Communication on Tackling Illegal Content Online[62] as well as the Recommendation on Tackling Illegal Content Online[63]. Relevant are also the measures addressing online disinformation, resulting mainly in the Code of Practice to address the spread

---

58 Proposal for a Regulation of the European Parliament and of the Council concerning the respect for private life and the protection of personal data in electronic communications and repealing Directive 2002/58/EC (Regulation on Privacy and Electronic Communications), COM/2017/010 final – 2017/03 (COD), https://eur-lex.europa.eu/legal-content/EN/TXT/?uri=CELEX%3A52017PC0010.

59 Nevertheless, even within the framework of this strict harmonisation, there are numerous opening clauses and room for manoeuvre for the Member States. These include, in particular, exceptions in the area of the so-called "media privilege" in Art. 85 GDPR, according to which the Member States are required to adopt rules for data processing for journalistic purposes.

60 See for a more detailed overview as well *Lievens*, Protecting Children in the Digital Era: The Use of Alternative Regulatory Instruments, p. 112 et seq.

61 Available at https://ec.europa.eu/info/policies/justice-and-fundamental-rights/com batting-discrimination/racism-and-xenophobia/countering-illegal-hate-speech-onl ine_en or http://ec.europa.eu/justice/fundamental-rights/files/hate_speech_code_ of_conduct_en.pdf.

62 Communication from the Commission to the European Parliament, the Council, the European Economic and Social Committee and the Committee of Regions, Tackling Illegal Content Online. Towards an enhanced responsibility of online platforms, COM/2017/0555 final, available at https://eur-lex.europa.eu/legal-conte nt/EN/TXT/?uri=CELEX%3A52017DC0555.

63 Commission Recommendation (EU) 2018/334 of 1 March 2018 on measures to effectively tackle illegal content online, C/2018/1177, available at https://eur-lex.e uropa.eu/legal-content/GA/TXT/?uri=CELEX:32018H0334.

of online disinformation and fake news[64]. These measures lay down a set of guidelines and principles for online platforms aiming to facilitate and intensify the implementation of good practices for preventing, detecting, removing and disabling access to illegal content or online disinformation. Core elements in both fields are transparency and reporting rules as well as cooperation provisions. However, coordination and support measures are legally non-binding, and, regarding the codes of conduct, which the signatories voluntarily committed to, there are no enforcement mechanisms or sanctions so far besides the publication of the assessment by the Commission on compliance and progress of the rules.

64　EU Code of Practice on Disinformation, available at https://ec.europa.eu/digital-si ngle-market/en/news/code-practice-disinformation. Further, non-content-specific measures encouraging self-regulation include: the Memorandum of Understanding on online advertising and intellectual property rights, available at https://ec.e uropa.eu/docsroom/documents/30226; the Memorandum of Understanding on the Sale of Counterfeit Goods via the Internet, available at http://ec.europa.eu/Do csRoom/documents/18023/attachments/1/translations/; the EU Product Safety Pledge, available at https://ec.europa.eu/info/sites/info/files/voluntary_commitme nt_document_4signatures3-web.pdf; the EU Internet Forum, available at https://e c.europa.eu/commission/presscorner/detail/en/IP_15_6243.

C. Problems Identified regarding the Cross-Border Dissemination of Online Content

Based on an analysis of the development of the online sector as well as the set-up of the regulatory framework applicable to providers involved in cross-border dissemination of online content as presented above, a number of shortcomings and problems can be identified.[65] These issues concern three areas in particular: the lack of legally binding regulations in certain areas, the question of continued coherence, or even validity, of existing rules and the enforcement of the norms, especially in cross-border situations which includes the question of supervisory structures.

The issue of a lack of binding rules concerns, on the one hand, areas for which no regulation exists at all, although some form of regulatory response could – and likely should – address threats to fundamental rights and values in the EU. On the other hand, some rules are laid down in non-binding texts and therefore cannot be enforced in a legally binding manner. In addition, some of the "targeted measures", as characterised by the Commission,[66] address the specific issues but cannot take into account the possible multiplication of risks – or even the initial generation of them – by the fact that some intermediaries are of systemic relevance due to their size and popularity.

Although there is a variety of rules addressing certain types of illegal content as mentioned above and imposing obligations on (sometimes reduced to specific types of) online intermediaries when such content is disseminated via their services, there is no overarching approach at EU level. This is mainly due to the limited competences of the EU when it comes to regulating content. Media law in general is and remains a competence of the Member States; thus the EU competence is triggered only in the context of the distribution of content when addressing the economic dimension of the single market of the providers involved in this dissemination. It has also repeatedly been acknowledged by the CJEU that differing stan-

---

65 See extensively for a detailed analysis the study *Cole/Etteldorf/Ullrich*, Cross-border Dissemination of Online Content, *passim*, and for a summary of the problems to be addressed in a reform in particular p. 221 et seq.

66 Commission staff working document, impact assessment accompanying the DSA Proposal, SWD(2020) 348 final, 15.12.2020, Part 1/2, p. 7.

dards between the Member States in regulating content is possible and does not constitute a contradiction with EU law, because in this field no full harmonisation is possible.[67] An illustrative example is the protection of minors, for which there are regularly specific rules in all Member States but no EU-wide harmonised (binding) rules applicable to online providers. For areas like this there is a need – in particular in cross-border situations – for general rules or minimum standards that are not linked to the type of illegality of the content, as this categorisation is left to the national level or other provisions in EU law, but to the totality of providers or offers. So far, the ECD contains such rules only sporadically, for example with regard to information obligations. By contrast, mechanisms of pure self-regulation, which also include commitments on the terms of use of platforms or association standards organised solely by the private sector, have proven ineffective in countering existing threats to fundamental rights and values in the EU.[68] They are not capable of addressing the issue with a democratically legitimised control, nor can such "norms" be enforced from outside of the providers or associations. This flaw can even apply to mechanisms of co-regulation if they do not have provisions about supervision, enforceability and, if necessary, sanctions. Therefore, such approaches need a robust system ensuring effective and fundamental rights-respecting enforcement means.

The second issue is about the question whether the existing legal framework can still claim to be valid (and thus flexible enough) in light of the developments of the past years and future evolution of the online environment. Also, there is a question of consistency of the rules which were not all prepared at the same time or in accordance with each other but – as has been shown – to partly address sector-specific or pressing issues without always keeping a bird's eye view of the existing framework. Especially the continued relevance of the ECD in its current shape has rightly been put into question. The difficulties in applying a ruleset designed two decades ago for a completely different Internet environment have become obvious. The actors have changed, and the role of platforms in the dissemination of online content, thereby influencing the public sphere, has become domi-

---

67 Cf. e.g. CJEU, C-244/06, *Dynamic Medien*; more recently C-555/19, *Fussl Modestraße Mayr*; further details in *Cole*, Zum Gestaltungsspielraum der EU-Mitgliedstaaten bei Einschränkungen der Dienstleistungsfreiheit, and *Cole*, in: AfP, 52 (1), 2021, 1, 1 et seq.

68 Recently also: *Smith*, Enforcement and cooperation between Member States, p. 11.

nant. A general issue is therefore already the categorisation of specific ISS[69], to which the liability regime applies in different levels; thus, this regime has turned out to be no longer reflective of the reality of intermediaries which fulfil these and combined functions today. Furthermore, there are in particular three key aspects in this regard. First, the principal idea for setting up a liability framework granting privileges to intermediaries was based on the idea that they fulfil the condition of neutrality. This observation cannot be upheld as a rule and poses problems in that it contradicts the approach of having more active platforms when it comes to monitoring for illegal content. Second, the precise determination of the notion of "actual knowledge" (triggering the need to act expeditiously) as a requirement for the liability privilege is difficult to apply and difficult to prove, because there are no formalised notice requirements from which actual knowledge could "automatically" be derived. There has also been a certain reluctance in voluntary establishment of efforts to identify illegal content – often referred to as "Good Samaritan" efforts – as it is perceived to endanger the liability privilege. Third, there is a tension between Art. 14 and 15 ECD, which, on the one hand, allow for specific preventive injunctions directed at service providers against infringements but prohibit, on the other hand, imposing on them what is characterised as general monitoring obligations.

These issues are also closely related to the coherence of the ECD with other (sectoral) rules. As described in the previous chapter, a trend towards greater responsibility expectations, especially for platform operators, going beyond soft law instruments can be observed. Overlaps with the horizontal rules of the ECD are unavoidable.[70] These newly created other secondary rulesets must be considered when aligning the existing ECD or creating a new framework. They are also evidentiary of the need for special rules concerning certain providers of ISS addressing specific objectives or particularities. If this presents itself as an issue of coherence already at EU level, it is in addition an issue of fragmentation with regard to the added layer of national level of legislation. The unabated occurrence and rise of illegal content and activity promulgated through platforms have led to the adoption

---

69 For the preceding problem of whether a provider qualifies as an ISS at all, cf. an overview of CJEU case law recently in *Chapius-Doppler/Delhomme*, in: European Papers, 5 (1), 2020411, 411 et seq.

70 Cf. on this most recently the Opinion of Advocate General Saugmandsgaard Øe, Joined Cases C-682/18 and C-683/18 – *YouTube and Cyando*, where the gap between the currently applicable copyright framework and the DSMD was highlighted in the context of a communication to the public by intermediaries.

of national rules in some Member States addressing this phenomenon based on their legislative competence. The possible result of a fragmentation of an otherwise cross-border market, such as the dissemination of online content, can lead to legal uncertainties for providers operating on a supranational level as well as to problems in enforcement of the national laws.[71] Thus, in order to avoid a further fragmentation of the rules applicable to different types of online service providers and having to introduce new categories of service providers depending on the further development of the online sector, a beneficial outcome can be expected from a newly designed, horizontally applicable framework concerning all types of "information society services" or however they would be addressed. In this context, it is particularly important to consider and closely examine the purposes pursued by special rules in the Member States. Provisions that fall within the remit of the Member States, whether due to a lack of legislative competence of the EU or because opening clauses in sectoral law permit or even require such specific rules by the Member States, should not be seen as targets of such a "defragmentation".

The problems outlined carry over into the enforcement of existing provisions, especially in cross-border situations. The enforcement issue is closely linked to the question of supervisory structures. Fundamental rights requirements and a value-based approach trigger the need for effective law enforcement when it comes to combating illegal or harmful content. This is above all directed at independent national regulatory authorities, which, in connection with the dissemination of online content, are in the current set-up the only competent entities – besides courts if confronted with proceedings concerning such content – which are able to defend the endangered rights and values. It is only these authorities that have the necessary independence which is guaranteed by law, because considered against the background of the protection of freedom of expression not only media but also regulatory bodies overseeing the media need to be independent of the state while bound by fundamental rights protection, unlike in the case of private undertakings.[72]

---

71 Cf. *Montagnani/Trapova*, in: JIL, 22 (7), 2019, 3, 3 et seq, arguing that intermediaries are no longer subject to a conditional liability but instead fall within the ambit of an organisational liability regime.

72 This must be considered in particular against the background of the risks discussed under the heading of "overblocking" and the associated chilling effects on freedom of expression. The threat is seen in transferring the responsibility to private undertakings to decide on the legality of content within the framework of content moderation. Cf. on this *Penney*, in: IPR, 6 (2), 2017; *Quintel/Ullrich*, "Self-

The ECD itself contains only very basic and minimum rules regarding supervision. The Member States are supposed to set up appropriate bodies for this purpose, and general rules are laid down on cooperation between each other, such as complying with requests for information and setting up contact points but without the establishment of concrete cooperation procedures. However, the ECD relies on the COO principle for ISS and thereby on the approach that – with only limited exceptions – there is one Member State that uses its jurisdiction power where necessary vis-à-vis established providers on their territory. It allows for exceptional derogations in case of problems concerning certain overarching goals and enforcement measures. This procedure, which resembles exceptional derogation procedures of the AVMSD, is not only complex in its design but has turned out to be difficult to apply in practice and to be burdensome and lengthy; thus, it has been rarely used irrespective of the fact that Member States or their competent authorities have in the past been pointing out enforcement shortcomings. Therefore this procedure alone has not proven to be a sufficient approach to reconcile legitimate protection interests with the fundamental principle of COO. This poses challenges for regulators who are set up according to other legal bases but are regularly (or mainly) tasked with monitoring content creators rather than content intermediaries.

In addition, there are problems regarding liability privileges, which must also be taken into account in the context of law enforcement and, above all, evaluated by the regulatory bodies before taking action. Questions of classification of a provider as an ISS and, more specifically, as falling under one of the ECD-categories of ISS, but also the necessary assessment of the applicability of a liability exemption, including the prohibition of general monitoring obligations, and the inconsistent application or interpretation of liability exemptions in the Member States do not only limit the possibilities of the regulatory bodies but can also lead to a reluctance on their side to carry out supervisory tasks concerning online content dissemination. This is also underpinned, for example, by the statistics of the Internal Market Information System (IMI)[73], which is intended, inter alia, to facilitate the exchange of information between competent authorities in a given sector. It includes (as a pilot project since 2013) the

Regulation of Fundamental Rights? The EU Code of Conduct on Hate Speech, related initiatives and beyond", in: Petkova/Ojanen (eds.), 182, 182 et seq.

73 For further information cf. https://ec.europa.eu/internal_market/imi-net/library/index_en.htm.

ECD and inter alia enables authorities to enter requests for measures (i.e. to ask another Member States' authorities to take specific measures against an online service provider, for example, if general information requirements are not respected on its websites) and notify measures intended to be taken against online service providers that are based in another Member State. This possibility has hardly been used[74], which is another indicator for the difficulties in cross-border cooperation under the current shape of the ECD.

---

74 The statistics from 2013 to the third quarter of 2019 show a total of 139 requests and 105 notifications.

D. The Commission Proposals for a DSA and a DMA

I. On the Digital Services Act Proposal

The DSA – as mentioned in the act and the accompanying Explanatory Memorandum – is intended to govern the responsibilities of digital services in the future, which act as intermediaries between recipients on the one hand and the providers of goods, services and content on the other. To this end, a horizontal setting is envisaged, containing rules for all relevant services and creating a harmonised cross-sectoral framework of rights, obligations, responsibilities, procedures and rules on jurisdiction throughout the EU, without the intention to replace sector-specific provisions, e.g. from audiovisual media services, electronic communications services, copyright and consumer protection law.

Following the aim to contribute to the proper functioning of the internal market for intermediary services and therefore set out uniform rules for a safe, predictable and trusted online environment, where fundamental rights enshrined in the Charter are effectively protected (Art. 1 para. 2 DSA Proposal), 74 provisions, detailed in 106 Recitals, propose new obligations for intermediary services.

However, these new obligations are initially prefaced by the liability privileges already known from the ECD, which will not be replaced by the DSA Proposal but merely amended, in particular by transferring the provisions on liability into the new legal act (Art. 3 to 5 and 7 DSA Proposal). The previous Art. 12 to 15 ECD are imported almost word by word, so that the technical terms (mere conduit, caching and hosting) are now also included in the DSA Proposal. However, the existing ECD system of liability exemption is supplemented by a provision on "voluntary own-initiative investigations and legal compliance" (Art. 6), which is aimed to address fears that providers might refrain from taking voluntary measures, for example to combat illegal online content, for fear of losing their privileges in the context of liability, which largely presupposes passivity and lack of knowledge. The rules on liability exemptions are further supplemented by provisions on orders to act against illegal content (Art. 8) and to provide information (Art. 9), the relevant requirements and legal bases which derive from national law and which are issued by the relevant national judicial or administrative authorities. The inclusion of these provisions shall not only clarify the obligation to follow such orders but lead to at least an alignment of the orders across the Member States in formal terms by specifying a minimum content they need to contain.

Irrespective of the question of whether providers can invoke a liability exemption in individual cases and of the fact that no general monitoring obligations can be imposed on them, the DSA Proposal introduces a set of general "due diligence" obligations that apply to (all) providers of intermediary services as a new layer.

The nature and scope of the obligations depend on both the type and size of the platform addressed. The DSA Proposal covers "intermediary services" as a generic term for "mere conduit", "caching" and "hosting" services but subdivides them both in the context of the exemption from liability (here again into caching, mere conduit and hosting as in the ECD) and in the context of the imposition of obligations (hosting providers, online platforms, very large online platforms (VLOPs)) while providing for facilitation for micro and small enterprises. In the context of the territorial scope of application, the Proposal is based on the principle of market location, i.e. the rules would apply to any intermediary service provided to recipients of the service that have their place of establishment or residence in the Union, irrespective of the place of establishment of the provider of this service (Art. 1 para. 3). Offering of a service in the Union means that there is a "substantial connection to the Union" which is concretised in Art. 2 lit. d and concerns, in particular, having an establishment in the Union or a significant number of users or by the targeting of activities towards the internal market.

The new obligations include labelling obligations for illegal goods, services and content, the establishment of complaints systems for users and transparency requirements. But the DSA also intends to improve the enforcement of the law online and proposes in particular new supervisory structures that should also function in cross-border cases. The DSA Proposal suggests that certain obligations should be applicable to all intermediary services, which includes the obligations to establish a single point of contact allowing for direct communication by electronic means with the respective supervisory body (Art. 10). Where applicable, the way providers apply content moderation has to be disclosed in the services terms and conditions of the service (Art. 12), and there are transparency reporting obligations on a regular basis (Art. 13). In addition, there is an obligation to designate a legal representative in one of the Member States for providers without establishment in the EU which offer their services in the Union (Art. 11).

Additional provisions are applicable to providers of hosting services, including online platforms, which are defined in Art. 2 lit. h as providers of a hosting service which, at the request of a recipient of the service, stores and disseminates to the public information, unless that activity is a minor and purely ancillary feature of another service and, for objective and technical reasons, cannot be used without that other service and unless the integration of the feature into the other service is not a means to circumvent the applicability of the proposed Regulation. These additional obligations cover the installation of easily usable notice and action mechanisms enabling users to submit sufficiently precise and adequately substantiated notices on illegal content (Art. 14). They are combined with concretised information obligations vis-à-vis recipients of the services whose content has been removed or if access to their content has been disabled (Art. 15). In both cases, the DSA Proposal is concerned with the creation of minimum standards that determine how notice mechanisms should be designed and what information must be provided to content producers, especially for the purposes of effectiveness and transparency.

A further layer of obligations is proposed for online platforms in Articles 17 to 24 excluding micro or small enterprises. This includes the provision of effective, user-friendly and easily accessible internal complaint-handling systems associated with information obligations regarding complaints that have been submitted (Art. 17) and the implementation of out-of-court dispute settlement procedures to resolve disputes relating to decisions on complaints taken by online platforms (Art. 18). Complaints from trusted flaggers – a status which can be given to entities under certain qualifying conditions on Member State level –should be given priority in the complaints mechanisms according to the DSA Proposal (Art. 19), whereby mechanisms to protect against abuse through the repeated flagging of actually lawful content are not only implemented in relation to trusted flaggers but also in relation to the use of complaints mechanisms as a whole (Art. 20). Furthermore, the section for online platforms includes a requirement to inform competent enforcement authorities in the event they become aware of any information giving rise to a suspicion of serious criminal offences involving a threat to the life or safety of persons (Art. 21) as well as the obligation to receive, store, make reasonable efforts to assess the reliability of and publish specific information on the traders using the respective service the online platform provides for when this service includes allowing consumers to conclude distance contracts with traders (Art. 22).

In addition to transparency and labelling obligations for online advertising (Art. 24), online platforms are also obliged to publish reports on their activities relating to the removal and the disabling of information considered to be illegal content or contrary to their terms and conditions (Art. 23). In contrast to the reporting obligations under Art. 13 of the DSA Proposal, Art. 23 provides for greater concretisation, especially in terms of the content of such reports, whereby the focus is on the level of detail of the information and the Commission is enabled to adopt implementing acts to lay down templates concerning the form, content and other details. In addition, the reporting obligation here also covers the publication, at least once every six months, of information on the average monthly active recipients of the service in each Member State. This allows monitoring for the purpose of assessing whether an online platform is a very large online platform (VLOP). These VLOPs are addressed in a separate section of the DSA Proposal with obligations beyond the ones just described to manage systemic risks emanating from them.

According to the description laid down in Art. 25 para. 1 of the DSA Proposal, VLOPs are online platforms which provide their services to a number of average monthly active recipients of the service in the Union equal to or higher than 45 million, which has to be calculated in accordance with the methodology to be laid down in delegated acts of the Commission. VLOPs shall be obliged to conduct assessments of the systemic risks, such as the dissemination of illegal content through their services, taking into account how different systems (e.g. content moderation, recommender systems, advertising tools) established on their platform pose risks (Art. 26). In a second step the Proposal obliges the VLOPs to also take reasonable and effective measures aimed at mitigating those risks (Art. 27). This is not only to be monitored at EU level by a board in cooperation with the Commission but also through the power to issue guidelines on what constitutes appropriate risk mitigation measures to be established by the Commission in cooperation with national authorities. The DSA Proposal further obliges VLOPs to submit themselves to external and independent audits performed by qualified and independent organisations (Art. 28) and, in case of a negative audit report, to take account of any operational recommendations addressed to them by the auditors via the adoption of an audit implementation report within one month. There are also specific obligations proposed in case VLOPs use recommender systems (Art. 29) or display online advertising on their online interface (Art. 30). The section dedicated to VLOPs closes with provisions about information requirements, in particular in light of cooperation with supervisory authorities. VLOPs are obliged to provide access to data that are necessary to monitor and assess compliance within a specified period of time (Art. 31) and to appoint one or more compliance officers to ensure compliance with the proposed rules, these officers serving also as link to cooperation with supervision (Art. 32); furthermore they are subject to specific, additional transparency reporting obligations (Art. 33). Regarding the latter, these transparency obligations are more restrictive in terms of time (to be published every six months) than the reporting obligations of intermediary services (Art. 13) and online platforms (Art. 23). They are extended to include reporting on the results of the risk assessment as well as the related risk mitigation measures identified and implemented pursuant (Art. 26 and 27) and on the audit and audit implementation report (Art. 28).

In the context of these due diligence obligations contained in the DSA Proposal there are several mechanisms of self-regulation introduced. According to these rules, the Commission shall support and promote the development, implementation and also updating of voluntary industry standards, in particular regarding certain technical mechanisms of the proposed Regulation such as the electronic submission of notices or the auditing procedures vis-à-vis VLOPs (Art. 34).[75] It shall encourage and facilitate the drawing up of codes of conduct at Union level in order to contribute to the proper application of the proposed Regulation (Art. 35), in particular in the field of online advertising (Art. 36). In addition the Commission shall encourage and facilitate the participation of VLOPs and, where appropriate, other online platforms in the drawing up, testing and application of so-called "crisis protocols" for addressing crisis situations strictly limited to extraordinary circumstances affecting public security or public health (Art. 37).

Finally, the DSA Proposal contains a complex system of supervision that divides powers among several involved actors and establishes both general cooperation mechanisms and concrete and procedure-dependent ones at several junctures. Supervision is to remain essentially with the Member States' supervisory bodies, some of which are already established in various sectors, for which the DSA Proposal is now intended to provide a horizontal framework. However, the Proposal also provides for its own mechanisms as well as numerous challenges to this assignment of supervision at Member State level. For example, it introduces Digital Services Coordinators (DSCs) that must be given their own regulatory powers at national

---

75 E.g. the electronic submission of notices (Art. 14), the auditing of VLOPs (Art. 28) or the interoperability of ad repositories (Art. 30 para. 2).

level, with the minimum requirements already set by the DSA Proposal (Art. 41). These DSCs are central to supervisory activities and serve both as coordinators of different supervisory authorities at the national level and for cooperation at the supranational level within the newly created European Board for Digital Services (EBDS) and as a focal point for DSCs in other Member States and the European Commission.

The DSCs also shall be a central point for receiving complaints from citizens about violations of the proposed rules by intermediaries (Art. 43) and are required to publish annual reports on their activities (Art. 44). In this regard, the procedure of cross-border cooperation proposed in Art. 45 should also be particularly emphasised. This provides for the possibility, under certain conditions, for a DSC in a Member State or the EBDS to request the DSC of the provider's place of establishment to take action in case of suspected violations of the proposed rules of the DSA, subject to certain deadlines. In case of disagreement on the appropriate course of action among the DSCs concerned, participation and evaluation by the Commission is also foreseen.

The rules on supervision in Art. 38 to 49 are, however, modified by Art. 50 et seq. of the DSA Proposal with regard to the regulation of VLOPs. Within this framework, the Commission is placed as the centre of supervisory activity, although supervision of VLOPs is not per se transferred from the DSCs of the place of establishment in its entirety to the Commission. Rather, special procedures with strong participation and final decision-making powers of the Commission are provided for. This applies, on the one hand, to the enhanced supervision procedure (Art. 50) when it comes to the violation of the special rules for VLOPs, which provides for coordination between the Commission, EBDS and DSC before a DSC decision is finally enforced. On the other hand it applies to the intervention possibilities attributed to the Commission by Art. 51 of the DSA Proposal, within the framework of which it can react, for example, to what it considers to be a lack of action on the part of a competent DSC. In these cases, the Commission is entrusted with several investigatory powers, such as requests for information (Art. 52), interviews (Art. 53) and on-site inspections (Art. 54), and it can adopt interim measures (Art. 55), make binding commitments proposed by VLOPs (Art. 56) and monitor their compliance with the Regulation (Art. 57). In case of violations, the Commission can adopt non-compliance decisions (Art. 58), issue fines (Art. 59) and periodic penalty payments (Art. 60), whereas providers are granted procedural guarantees (Art. 63 and 64).

The DSA Proposal provides for several layers of cooperation mechanisms interconnecting the different levels of supervision (national regulatory authorities, DSCs and the Commission), the main forum for which is the EBDS. This advisory group, composed of the DSCs and chaired by the Commission, is established to contribute to achieving a common Union perspective on the consistent application of the proposed Regulation and to cooperation on the supranational level regarding appropriate investigation and enforcement measures, in particular by drafting relevant templates and codes of conduct and analysing emerging general trends in the development of digital services in the Union. Furthermore, different cooperation mechanisms concerning concrete investigations, procedures and decisions can be found throughout numerous provisions of the DSA Proposal linking DSCs between each other and with the Commission. The exchange of information plays a decisive role, which is why Art. 67 proposes an information sharing system to be established and maintained by the Commission.

II. On the Digital Markets Act Proposal

Unlike the DSA, the Commission's Proposal for a DMA aims to create "contestable and fair markets" in the digital sector, thus primarily addressing competition aspects. In doing so, the aim is also to open up growth opportunities for small and new players and to ensure that companies and consumers do not have to accept unfair conditions dictated by established providers and such with strong market power. In order to ensure this, certain providers with a large economic and therefore also social influence, thus posing a potential systemic risk, should be subject to clear and, above all, stricter rules than hitherto. This includes both active obligations to act and duties to refrain from certain practices for gatekeeper platforms.

Relying on the market location principle, the DMA Proposal addresses core platform services (which are, inter alia, online intermediation services, search engines, social networks and VSPs) provided or offered by gatekeepers to business users established in the Union or to end users established or located in the Union, irrespective of the place of establishment or residence of the gatekeepers (Art. 1 para 2). The status of a gatekeeper is, according to the DMA Proposal, designated (and may be reviewed regularly) by the Commission if the criteria laid down in Chapter II are met, either based on quantitative criteria (through a presumption subject to counter-demonstration) or following a case-by-case assessment in a market investigation (Art. 3). Criteria that may play a role in the Commission's assessment are, for example, the size, including turnover and market capitalisation, the number of business users, entry barriers derived from network effects and data driven advantages, scale and scope effects the provider benefits from (including with regard to data) or business user or end user lock-in.

For these core platform services designated as gatekeepers, the DMA Proposal contains a list of practices that are assumed to limit contestability of the market and that are therefore unfair. In order to effectively counter such practices, the draft distinguishes between self-executing obligations (Art. 5) and obligations that are susceptible to further specification (Art. 6), the latter meaning that the provider has to conduct a self-assessment how to imply the rules for its service in an appropriate manner. For this purpose, Art. 7 proposes a framework for a possible dialogue between the designated gatekeeper and the Commission in relation to measures that the gatekeeper implements or intends to implement based on its self-assessment.

The obligations to act and to refrain from action contained in the provisions are manifold. In particular, gatekeepers are to refrain from merging personal data from the central services with data from other services and from preventing their business customers from complaining to supervisory authorities. Gatekeepers shall no longer prevent users from uninstalling pre-installed software or apps or from accessing services they may have purchased outside the gatekeeper platform. Gatekeepers shall not use data obtained from their business users to compete with those business users. They shall also not make the use of their services by end users and business users conditional on registration with another service of the same gatekeeper. On the other hand, they must allow business customers to offer their services and products through third party intermediary services at different prices and to advertise their offers and conclude contracts with their customers outside the gatekeeper's platform. Gatekeepers must provide businesses advertising on their platform with access to the gatekeeper's performance measurement tools and to the information (e.g. on prices) necessary to enable advertisers and publishers to conduct their own independent review of their advertising hosted by the gatekeeper. This also includes data generated by the business customer's use of the platform. These rules apply regardless of whether the relevant practice of the designated gatekeeper is of a contractual, commercial, technical or any other nature (according to the anti-circumvention rule in Art. 11).

To keep some flexibility, the Proposal empowers the Commission to adopt delegated acts to update the obligations where, based on a market investigation, it has identified the need for new obligations addressing practices that limit the contestability of core platform services or are unfair in the same way as the practices already addressed in the Proposal. However, according to Art. 8 and 9, under certain conditions obligations for an individual core platform service may also be suspended in exceptional circumstances or an exemption can be granted on grounds of public interest. Enabling in another way to react flexibly to developments, gatekeepers are obliged to notify the Commission of any intended concentration within the meaning of the EU Merger Regulation (Art. 12) – meaning in advance of the obligations under that Regulation, i.e. already at the stage of the plans for such a concentration – and to submit any techniques for profiling of consumers that the gatekeeper applies to or across its core platform services to an independent audit (Art. 13).

To ensure the appropriate and up-to-date adoption of the rules, the DMA Proposal entrusts the Commission with several powers to carry out market investigations, in particular on the designation of a core platform service as a gatekeeper (Art. 15), on investigation of systematic non-compliance (Art. 16) and of new core platform services and new practices (Art. 17) as well as with regulatory and enforcement powers. The powers, very similar as in the DSA Proposal, include the request of information (Art. 19), the conducting of interviews and taking statements (Art. 20), on-site inspections (Art. 21) on the investigatory level, the adoption of interim measures (Art. 22), the making binding of commitments of the gatekeepers (Art. 23), monitoring (Art. 24) and finally the issuing of non-compliance decisions (Art. 25) as well as the imposing of fines (Art. 26) or periodic penalty payments under certain conditions (Art. 27). The penalty cap is higher (10% of total turnover in the preceding financial year) compared to the DSA Proposal and the respective provisions (Art. 26 to 29 DMA Proposal) are more concrete regarding the different treatment of violations of different provisions. Art. 35 clarifies that the CJEU shall have unlimited jurisdiction in respect of fines and penalty payments.

The Commission performs the central function of supervision for the DMA in a nearly solitary manner. The DMA Proposal – in order to ensure that the adoption of implementing acts by the Commission is subject to the control of Member States as required by Regulation (EU) No 182/2011[76] – provides for the establishment of the Digital Markets Advisory Committee. This Committee is composed of representatives of Member States and shall give opinions on certain individual decisions of the Commission, but it is not equipped with regulatory powers. Besides that, the DMA Proposal provides for a possibility for three or more Member States to request the Commission to open a market investigation pursuant to regarding the designation of (new) gatekeepers (Art. 33). Furthermore, the Commission is empowered to adopt implementing (Art. 36) and delegated (Art. 37) acts.

---

76 Regulation (EU) No 182/2011 of the European Parliament and of the Council of 16 February 2011 laying down the rules and general principles concerning mechanisms for control by Member States of the Commission's exercise of implementing powers, OJ L 55, 28.2.2011, p. 13–18.

E. Legislative Options at EU Level

In this chapter of the study the different legislative options at EU level for reforming the framework applicable to online content dissemination will be presented. Based on the summarised findings of the reform needs presented in chapter C. and the overview of the Commission Proposals for a DSA and DMA in chapter D., this part will focus on the six most relevant issues. In doing so, for each of those issues there is, first, a presentation of the status quo and the reasons why and in what way an update of the applicable provisions is needed ("1. Starting Point"). Subsequently, the relevant parts of the actual Proposal for the DSA are explained and analysed, where necessary with brief mentions of the provisions in the proposed DMA ("2. DSA Approach"). In the final section of each part, our detailed assessment of the proposed rules follows and an evaluation of what further changes or different approaches than in the current state of the Proposals should be achieved ("3. Assessment").

I. Regulatory Approaches

1. Starting Point

On the basis of allocated competences, fundamental rights and values, the EU has a wide range of regulatory options using mainly the achievement of a functioning (digital) single market as legal basis. The starting point for any regulatory approach in the area of dissemination of online content must therefore, on the one hand, take into account the actual realities of the online environment and, on the other hand, reflect legal requirements – including those arising from fundamental rights and values – as well as the existing sector-specific legal framework. The way in which content is distributed online, via which platforms, using which means of presentation, selection or prioritization, and how it is ultimately consumed by recipients is diverse. This is not about a single snapshot in time. The online environment is subject to constant change, new technical possibilities and also trends in consumer preference. This means, on the one hand, new opportunities and, on the other, new entrance gates for the threats to the preservation of European values, the protection of fundamental rights and public interests in this environment.

This is particularly true in the media sector and is the reason why sector-specific law is adapted to new circumstances at regular intervals in order to continue to meet the objective of regulation on the basis of taking into account the interests of all players involved. Recent examples include the reforms of the AVMSD and the DSMD, which now also address VSPs and OCSSPs with their provisions and respond to the influence of such platforms on the online media environment as well as to the risks arising in the context of content that can be classified as illegal under this sectoral law. Any legislative approach must keep pace with these aspects. Only a future-oriented and flexible design that provides sufficient room for possible reactions both at the legislative (whether EU or national) and regulatory level is adequate for this purpose. This applies in particular to the choice of the appropriate legal instrument, the material scope of application of a potential legal instrument, the room for manoeuvre it leaves for problem- and sector-oriented rules, also against the background of specific objectives, and to the questions of the content neutrality of horizontal rules.

a. Legal Instrument

The question of the appropriate legal instrument is generally determined by the specifications of the legal basis which is chosen and which covers the scope of possible action for the EU. As described above (B.II.), there are several possible options for binding and non-binding legislative acts which have the establishment and functioning of the internal market as their objective.

For binding legislative acts there is a choice, in principle, between Regulations and Directives if the legal bases only generally refer to measures. The main difference lies in the legal nature of the two legal instruments: Whereas a Regulation is directly applicable in all Member States and therefore in principle also takes precedence over national law in its scope of application, Directives must be implemented by the Member States in national law. The Regulation thus also takes precedence over the Directive or rather its national transposition if there is an overlap. This also results in different advantages and disadvantages of the two legal instruments.

Regulations first of all have the advantage that they enable harmonisation to a high degree, since their directly binding nature and priority character give them a strong impact. In addition, the rules originate from a single legislator and are (initially) found in a single set of provisions, which provides for more legal certainty. This is particularly useful in sectoral law when a high degree of harmonisation is intended and the Member States can agree on joint standards. But also with regard to a horizontal legal framework, a Regulation has advantages at first glance: it can be used to establish a basic framework that is directly applicable, and sectoral law can then, to the extent necessary, provide for possibilities of deviation and exceptions. Also, and in particular when it comes to regulations for areas that regularly have a cross-border nature and when its impacts are not limited to just one Member State, a Regulation initially seems to make sense to address the problems. A prominent example that relied on both these aspects to justify the choice of this instrument is the GDPR, which sets extensively harmonised rules in an area that has an overarching fundamental rights basis and necessitated sectoral rules only to a certain extent (e.g. data protection in electronic communications, employee data protection, data processing rules for certain institutions and bodies) and which regularly concerns cross-border (data processing) activities.

However, opting for a Regulation brings significant disadvantages besides the advantages, too. Apart from the principal limitations of choosing Regulations as the most limiting instrument in view of Member States' legislative and administrative powers, there are a number of more specific issues. If, as is the case here, the proposed new legislative act has to be incorporated into a network of existing sectoral rulesets both at EU and national level – Member States retain important competences because of the interconnection with the regulation of media and are also entitled to a number of derogations and powers of deviation under sectoral law –, the question of the degree of intended harmonisation of a horizontal legal framework needs to be carefully assessed. Three principles need to be taken into account in doing so: in effect, Regulations have (in principle and in terms of collision)[77] precedence over (overlapping) Directives as well as national law within its scope of application; more recent law takes (in principle)[78] precedence over preceding law; more specific law takes precedence

---

77 A general hierarchy cannot be derived from the EU Treaties. However, unlike Directives, Regulations are directly applicable. When a Regulation is adopted, it also implicitly repeals conflicting provisions of an earlier Directive if there is an overlap. The reverse is not true when a Directive is issued. See *Nettesheim*, in: EuR, 41 (6), 2006, 737, 765 with further references.

78 However, functional questions of decision-making authority take precedence here over this fundamental rule. Cf. on this *Nettesheim*, in: EuR, 41 (6), 2006, 737, 738, 767.

over general law. In order to avoid legal uncertainty, a newly adopted legal instrument must address clearly all these points. This is already proving difficult in the area of cross-border dissemination of online content, for which a complex set of interrelating rules not only of a media-specific but also of a more general economic nature exists due to the diversity of actors involved as well as of distribution channels and reception possibilities. Furthermore, the clear prohibition of harmonisation by the EU in the field of culture (Art. 167 para. 5 TFEU[79]) must also be carefully taken into account. This need becomes even more relevant if a ruleset is not limited to a (horizontal) regulation of a multitude of online actors with some basic elements of a framework – as was the case for the ECD, in which problems in the relationship to sectoral EU and national law had become apparent – but contains very specific and extensive rules.

Most importantly, however, the subsidiarity principle is a potential blocking reason for a Regulation. Depending on the specific rules chosen, it may be difficult to justify the need for such a high level of harmonisation, risking a potential conflict with sectoral rules by arguing that the aims can only be achieved in a better way at Union level. Protocol (No. 2) on the application of the principles of subsidiarity and proportionality[80] – unlike the predecessor to the Treaty of Amsterdam[81] – no longer contains any reference to Directives having a precedence of choice compared with regulations. This change is due to the more precise provisions on the

---

79 Cf. on Art. 167 para. 5 TFEU, which allows the European Parliament and the Council to adopt incentive measures in the area of the culture clause according to Art. 167 TFEU but clearly excludes any harmonisation of the laws and regulations of the Member States, *Ukrow/Ress*, in: Grabitz/Hilf/Nettesheim, Art. 167 TFEU.

80 Consolidated version of the Treaty on the Functioning of the European Union – Protocol (No. 2) on the application of the principles of subsidiarity and proportionality, OJ C 115, 9.5.2008, p. 206–209.

81 Treaty of Amsterdam amending the Treaty on European Union, the Treaties establishing the European Communities and certain related acts – Protocol annexed to the Treaty of the European Community – Protocol on the application of the principles of subsidiarity and proportionality, OJ C 340, 10.11.1997, p. 105. Point 6 stated, "The form of Community action shall be as simple as possible, consistent with satisfactory achievement of the objective of the measure and the need for effective enforcement. The Community shall legislate only to the extent necessary. Other things being equal, Directives should be preferred to Regulations and framework Directives to detailed measures. Directives as provided for in Art. 189 of the Treaty, while binding upon each Member State to which they are addressed as to the result to be achieved, shall leave to the national authorities the choice of form and methods."

choice of the form of legislative acts in the Treaty of Lisbon, but it still leaves the assessment in place that the far less intrusive character of Directives should be taken into account for setting up new rules by the competent EU institutions, because the idea of subsidiarity will often limit the areas in which regulations should be chosen.[82] Furthermore, the principle of proportionality requires that any Regulation may only have impact on fundamental rights – in the context of the present study above all the right to freedom of expression and information – to the extent that is strictly necessary in order to achieve the envisaged objectives.

Directives, on the other hand, have the advantage that they are more open to other legislative sources associated with a regulatory matter, both at national or Union level. In this respect, it is not the degree of harmonisation that is decisive. This can be seen for the examples of the AVMSD with its continued minimum harmonisation approach and the multitude of legal bases in copyright law that continue to take the form of Directives despite the very advanced harmonisation. This shows that Directives are also suitable for ensuring a sufficient degree of legal certainty and effectiveness from the perspective of EU law. They regularly leave more room for specifications, which is decisive especially in the area of creating a cross-sectoral framework for the online sector, taking into account the specifics of content dissemination with its impacts on fundamental rights. Finally, with the adoption of a Directive, the interrelation of different (sectoral and horizontal) rules needs to be (re)assessed separately, always taking into account the different areas of application and objectives, and is not, as in the case of a Regulation, already determined by the general EU law rules. This applies in particular to the question of updating the legal framework for the dissemination of online content, as this is already partially addressed by an existing network of (mainly) Directives.

These observations do not allow the conclusion that a Regulation is entirely and independently of the concrete scope of regulation excluded as an appropriate legal instrument in the area of establishing a framework for digital services. But it does mean that with such a choice even greater attention must be paid to compatibility with the existing EU competence framework and that the coherence with other EU law, the material scope of application (see on this also E.I.1.c) and its intended regulatory framework (e.g. in the sense of establishing a precise aim and objective of the

---

82 In this regard *Lopatka*, in: European View, 18 (spring), 2019, 26, 26 et seq.; *Ukrow*, Die Vorschläge der EU-Kommission für einen Digital Services Act und einen Digital Markets Act, p. 11.

legal instrument chosen, on this E.I.1.d.) must be delineated even more precisely.

With regard to non-legally binding instruments of regulation, it should be noted that these only take sufficient account of interests protected by fundamental rights on the basis of an orientation towards EU values if their actual implementation and enforcement can also be guaranteed. Self-regulatory instruments – although they have proven to be beneficial for the development of best practices and the establishment of cooperation and dialogue – have not proven to be effective in the area discussed here, as they lack both accessibility for control based on democratic principles and enforceability. This is in particular true regarding a lack of availability of more reliable data needed to assess compliance, which has become evident especially in the past couple of years.[83] In the area of online content dissemination, which is particularly sensitive in light of freedom of expression because of the deletion or blocking of content at issue, there is a need for proportionate protection mechanisms. Although it is not per se unimaginable that systems are in place that allow for a balanced approach to the treatment of content disseminated via platforms on their own behalf, it is not possible to guarantee in an accountable manner that such systems are implemented and practically enforced without external, in particular some form of regulatory oversight initiated by the State but organised independently. Instruments of co-regulation, however, are capable of fulfilling these criteria if there are effective monitoring mechanisms and sanctions implemented that in sum ensure effective enforcement.[84] Relying alone on some form of negative reputational impact for services with their

---

83 For example, the evaluation problems resulting from the EU Code of Practice on Disinformation have been expressed by the ERGA in its report of the activities carried out to assist the Commission in the intermediate monitoring of the Code of Practice on Disinformation as follows: "The platforms were not in a position to meet a request from ERGA to provide access to the overall database of advertising, even on a limited basis, during the monitoring period. This was a significant constraint on the monitoring process and emerging conclusions." ERGA, Report of the activities carried out to assist the European Commission in the intermediate monitoring of the Code of practice on disinformation, June 2019, available at http://erga-online.eu/wp-content/uploads/2019/06/ERGA-2019-06_Report-interm ediate-monitoring-Code-of-Practice-on-disinformation.pdf.

84 In the area of hate speech, the non-binding measures were only selectively applied by some services. Cf. Commission staff working document, impact assessment accompanying the DSA proposal, SWD(2020) 348 final, 15.12.2020, Part 1/2, https://ec.europa.eu/transparency/regdoc/rep/10102/2020/EN/SWD-2020 -348-F1-EN-MAIN-PART-1.PDF, para. 107.

users if content dissemination is organised in an unsatisfactory manner is evidently not enough considering the risks both for freedom of expression and the rights of others that could be infringed by the content in question.

However, the practicability of co-regulation instruments depends to a large extent on the type of rules envisaged. Such mechanisms have the advantage of typically offering a high degree of flexibility as they are not subject to a lengthy legislative process and can therefore be created and (more importantly also) adapted in a swift manner. They offer the added advantage of having been developed regularly with the participation of the addressees of the rules, which allows for aspects of implementation – including technical issues – to be taken into account in the creation of the rules from a practical application perspective. Including the subjects of rules in the setting up of these will likely lead to a greater willingness of implementing them in a meaningful way, as the actors (co-)developed the rules themselves.[85] That is why co-regulatory solutions are particularly suitable in the sectoral area of content creation and dissemination.[86] This is the case, for example, when the establishment of standards is intended to counteract a certain identified risk (such as in the area of hate speech or online disinformation) or to address a certain group of addressees (such as journalistic standards in media law).

Limitations for co-regulatory instruments exist as well. It is hardly a suitable approach for the creation of an overarching horizontal legal framework with general rules or minimum standards for actors in the online environment, not at least because of the diversity of actors and interests. The integration of a large variety of such actors, for example by way of a voluntary self-commitment, could be practically unfeasible and could counteract the cooperation within such an instrument (for example, for the development of best practices or the exchange of information). Instead, co-regulatory instruments can and should be used to expand on the legislative base by complementing the fundamental rules with solutions in specific areas to be developed and applied in a co-regulatory setting. This has been done, for example, with the AVMSD. Especially in the area of the dissemination

---

85 Cf. on this also the EU Commission's Communication on Online Platforms and the Digital Single Market Opportunities and Challenges for Europe, COM/ 2016/0288 final, available at https://eur-lex.europa.eu/legal-content/EN/TXT/?uri= CELEX:52016DC0288#footnoteref21, stating that the traditional top-down legislation reaches its limits in the platform economy.

86 See on the advantages and disadvantages of self- and co-regulation in detail and with further references *Cole/Etteldorf/Ullrich*, Cross-border Dissemination of Online Content, p. 241 et seq.

of online content there are several points of application, such as the harmonisation of reporting and takedown mechanisms or the transparency of decision-making processes of both automated algorithmic and human content review systems[87] that can be usefully supplemented by such mechanisms.

b. Content Neutrality of Horizontal Approaches

The diversity of platforms and the sectoral legislation call for the continuation of a horizontal approach containing general rules for all relevant internet actors. In this context, two characteristics in particular have to be taken into account with regard to the online dissemination of content: the volume of its (re)distribution and its unpredictability.

Content spreads at very high velocity and breadth on the internet, and, once online, it is difficult to trace it back to its origin or to contain it. In addition, it often does not remain in its original format and spreads across different networks: for example, a livestream of a terrorist propaganda activity might be found shortly afterwards as a video hosted on a VSP available on demand, image excerpts from it might be shared via social networks, an audio recording could appear in a podcast library or a text contribution might be created on an information platform. With the advanced development of technology, this transformation of content can be done with a few simple steps or can even be set up automatically. This also leads to the continuous emergence of new forms of content that are distinct from traditional categories of content and therefore require, from a regulatory perspective, a more flexible approach that is open to further development. Incidentally, this also corresponds to the realities within online platforms, which regularly do not (or do no longer) distinguish between content genres (even if they have a focus on one) but rather enable the dissemination of different formats – whether video, audio, text, image or mixed forms.

The type of the content does not change the threat it poses to fundamental rights or democratic decision-making processes. Unequal treatment of content therefore can only be justified under certain circumstances, for example if sectoral law targets "only" content of high risk, even though it is

---

87 Cf. on this in particular *Quintel/Ullrich*, "Self-Regulation of Fundamental Rights? The EU Code of Conduct on Hate Speech, Related Initiatives and Beyond", in: Petkova/Ojanen (eds.), 182, 193–195.

not the only type of content that can result in the risk being realised. Certainly, a content-neutral approach is required for the basic rules by taking a horizontal approach ensuring that the rules are open enough for the dynamic nature of the online environment. This applies at least as far as general rules are concerned. Where, in addition, specific rules should apply to certain forms of content, because such content has a particular risk potential or is of particular importance in the democratic decision-making process – as is the case, for example, for audiovisual media[88] –, this can be done either by sectoral law or by adding within a general framework certain obligations that go beyond the minimum requirements applicable for all types of content (on such a graduated approach see below, E.III. and E.V.).

Closely related to the issue of content neutrality is the question of what type of content triggers certain obligations on the part of content intermediaries that go beyond the minimum level. This concerns the definition of illegality of content. Usually, a distinction is made between illegal content and in principle legal but harmful content which therefore needs to be addressed, too.[89] What has to be classified as illegal content can be defined at Union level and/or national level, whereby the latter in turn can also be instructed by opening clauses in secondary legislative acts to do so. Content that is qualified as illegal on EU level is in particular child pornography[90], content that infringes copyright, racist and xenophobic hate

---

88 Cf. in particular the case law of the ECtHR, which grants the audiovisual sector (in this case in the context of ensuring pluralism) a special impact, judgements in cases no. 38433/09, *Centro Europa 7 S.R.L. and di Stefano v. Italie [GC]*, para. 134; no.48876/08, *Animal Defenders International v. United Kingdom*, para. 101.

89 Cf. for example *Madiega* (EPRS study), Reform of the EU liability regime for online intermediaries, p. 10.

90 Directive 2011/93/EU of the European Parliament and of the Council of 13 December 2011 on combating the sexual abuse and sexual exploitation of children and child pornography, and replacing Council Framework Decision 2004/68/JHA, OJ L 335, 17.12.2011, p. 1–14, contains some minimum harmonisation regarding the distribution, dissemination or transmission of child pornography.

speech[91] and terrorist[92] content.[93] In a broader context, infringing actions not fully harmonised at the Union level, trademark violations, counterfeiting and parallel distribution of products, trade secret violations, consumer protection violations, privacy, libel and defamation law violations, data protection violations and what is referred to as "revenge porn" may also be considered as illegal.[94] On the other hand, there is harmful but not illegal content, including regularly in particular disinformation campaigns, cyberbullying, instigation to self-harm, but also phenomena such as conspiracy theories or extreme selfies.[95] There is also a wide range of other problematic content that is not illegal per se but only harmful to a specific group of persons (such as for minors), the dissemination of which is therefore only permissible if certain conditions are met, or that is not harmful per se but can become so in combination with other conditions; such types of content or practices could be advertising that is not labelled as such or (unintentional) disinformation which may be subjected to limiting rules if it, e.g., takes place in connection with elections.

---

91 Council Framework Decision 2008/913/JHA of 28 November 2008 on combating certain forms and expressions of racism and xenophobia by means of criminal law, OJ L 328, 6.12.2008, p. 55–58.

92 According to Directive 2017/541 of the European Parliament and of the Council of 15 March 2017 on combating terrorism, OJ L 88, 31.3.2017, p. 6–21, the public provocation to commit a terrorist offence is illegal and is defined (Art. 5) as "the distribution, or otherwise making available by any means, whether online or offline, of a message to the public, with the intent to incite the commission of [terrorist offences], where such conduct, directly or indirectly, such as by the glorification of terrorist acts, advocates the commission of terrorist offences, thereby causing a danger that one or more such offences may be committed". The TERREG Proposal addresses within its required proactive measures (Art. 6) the 'dissemination of terrorist content': inciting or advocating, including by glorifying, the commission of terrorist offences, thereby causing a danger that such acts be committed; encouraging the contribution to terrorist offences; promoting the activities of a terrorist group, in particular by encouraging the participation in or support to a terrorist group within the meaning of Art. 2 para. 3 of Directive (EU) 2017/541; instructing on methods or techniques for the purpose of committing terrorist offences.

93 Cf. on this in general *de Streel et al.*, Online Platforms' Moderation of Illegal Content Online, p. 17 et seq.

94 On these categories cf. *van Hoboken et al.*, Hosting intermediary services and illegal content online, p. 20 et seq.

95 See also the Commission's view in its Impact assessment accompanying the DSA Proposal, SWD(2020) 348 final, https://eur-lex.europa.eu/legal-content/EN/TXT/HTML/?uri=CELEX:52020SC0348&rid=1.

The broadness of the examples listed already shows that the specific definition of the illegality or harmfulness of content within a single regulatory instrument, for example by some sort of enumeration as a kind of "one-size-fits-all"-approach, is not possible. Such an approach, especially in a horizontal legal framework, would not be flexible enough. This applies at least insofar as the general approach is concerned and not the possible introduction of specific obligations for certain types of illegal content.[96] Essentially, the factors already mentioned under the heading of content neutrality also apply here: due to the diversity of content and its rapid development, a permanent categorisation would be difficult, and in addition there is a lack of complete data on how much and what type of illegal content is disseminated online, which would be necessary as a basis for further legislative measures. Therefore, the definition of illegality can only be left to sectoral law in Union law as well as national law. If it would be approached differently, discretion given to the Member States deliberately by secondary legislation or action in competence areas which anyway remain with the Member States would be disregarded.

However, this does not mean that a simple reference overall to Union or national law would suffice at this point. In order to avoid legal uncertainties, a clear distinction should be made between what is illegal in the sense of the horizontal legal framework (and thus results in additional obligations imposed on platforms dealing with this content) and what is legal and therefore not covered by the obligations. Differently, the distinction between what is illegal and harmful should not be upheld in the way it is done so far. Already now, as demonstrated above, harmful content that is not "per se" illegal is regarded to be addressed by rules concerning online platforms.[97] It is therefore not so much the question of illegality but (the potential) of negative impact which is why a new regulatory framework

---

96 Different in light of the relevant obligations of service providers: *Schulte-Nölke et al.*, The legal framework for e-commerce in the Internal Market, p. 39, suggesting that the question what kind of content should be removed by the host-providers should be addressed to ensure an adequate and transparent take-down procedure. This would also be a possibility, but it would not contradict the fundamentally neutral approach proposed here. Categorisation would then be required within the framework of the obligations (see E.V.). An example of this would be transparency obligations also with regard to disinformation, insofar as this is recorded by a platform, even if this content would otherwise not fall under the definition of illegal content and thus under the other obligations.

97 For an overview of several other harms (referring to harmful threats, economic harms, harms to national security, emotional harm, harm to young people, harms to justice and democracy, and criminal harms) to be considered opting

should not rule out the consideration of harmful content in defining obligations by intermediaries. For this type of content, a connecting factor in the law of the EU or the Member States is possible, too, such as, e.g., the co-regulatory instruments resulting from the new rules on VSPs under the AVMSD.[98] Such rules should, however, also be within the scope of effective enforcement. Thus, the issue here will be less about classification and more about creating a legally sound delineation approach. In this context it should be clarified that the way in which content is presented or communicated can also constitute illegality, which is of high importance especially in connection with the protection of minors online.

c. Material Scope, Sectoral Exceptions and Discretion

As described above (B.II. and E.I.1.), although a legislative instrument to shape the internal market is mainly or fundamentally driven by economic considerations and policy, it can have considerable impact on other sectors which are already regulated at the Member State and EU level. This is in particular true regarding the dissemination of online content with a wide range of sectoral legislation accompanied by a set of coordination and support measures in several media-related fields. Although there is a continued need for horizontally applicable rules which allow for sector-specific approaches to be upheld, the sector-specific perspective, through which the regulation of ISS must also be viewed despite their common features as "intermediation services", makes full harmonisation within a single set of rules impossible. For this reason, the horizontal approach, which has to be retained in principle, calls for a detailed examination of existing legislative approaches and the establishment of sectoral exceptions and margins of

---

harm-based approach cf. *Woods/Perrin*, Online harm reduction – a statutory duty of care and regulator, p. 35 et seq., 42. The authors opt here for regulating illegal and harmful content but in a risk-based regulation not treating all qualifying services the same and being implemented in a sector where there is already indicative evidence of harms.

98 For the purposes of the implementation of the measures referred to in para. 1 and 3 of Art. 28b AVMSD (rules on protection of minors, against hate speech and regarding commercial communication), Art. 28b para. 4 AVMSD states that Member States shall encourage the use of co-regulation as provided for in Art. 4a para. 1. If the rules issued in this sense were not included in the definition of illegal content, this would counteract the AVMSD and the partial alignment of rules on VSP to classic audiovisual media services intended here.

discretion for the Member States when exercising their competencies regarding, for example, cultural policy or safeguarding pluralism while taking into account the impact on the freedom of expression.

It is, therefore, of vital importance that the future regulation will have a legal structure that is coherent with the already existing rules that touch upon issues relevant for the Digital Single Market but address them from different perspectives.[99] This means that not only the existing rules in the ECD need to be revised or replaced, but a new assessment must also be made as to which sectoral rules should continue to take precedence over the general rules of the ECD and where there must be (additional) sectoral exceptions in the light of competence limitations of the EU.

This applies first and foremost to the secondary legal framework at the EU level, where recent reforms (in particular Art. 17 of the DSMD[100] and also the proposed rules of the TERREG[101]) already indicate potential conflicts with the existing framework in the ECD. As outlined in the summary of the applicable legal framework (B.III.), particularly relevant for this study are the provisions of the AVMSD, the relevant copyright Directives, the TERREG Proposal, the P2B-Regulation and the rules of data protection law as they lay down rules for (certain) ISS.

As far as the AVMSD is concerned, it should be noted, first of all, that its rules aim to establish certain measures to permit and ensure the transition from national markets to a common programme production and distribution market and aim to guarantee conditions of fair competition without prejudicing public interest roles of audiovisual media services.[102] In order to achieve this, providers of audiovisual media services, on-demand audiovisual media services and with the reform of 2018 also VSPs are subject to a basic set of rules that apply as minimum standards in all Member States. These may conflict with rules of the ECD or a future legal instrument, in

---

99 Cf. *Schulte-Nölke et al.*, The legal framework for e-commerce in the Internal Market, p. 35.

100 In this regard e.g. *Smith*, Enforcement and cooperation between Member States, p. 24, pointing out that an effective transmission of the rules would require some kind of ex ante filtering system through the use of algorithms, though this in turn seems to be prohibited as 'general monitoring' and would also have the effect of moving platforms from passive to active in CJEU case law. Cf. on case law CJEU C-18/18, *Eva Glawischnig-Piesczek*.

101 Cf. on this *de Streel et al.*, Online Platforms' Moderation of Illegal Content Online, p. 26 et seq.; *Kuczerawy*, Intermediary Liability and Freedom of Expression in the EU: from Concepts to Safeguards, p. 109 et seq.

102 Recital 2 of Directive 2010/13/EU.

particular in the area of online offers of these providers. To a large extent the rules serve the interests of the recipients (e.g., advertising rules or protection of the general public and minors) and are therefore the result of a balancing between their interests and those of the providers. These rules therefore sufficiently take into account the interests in a specific area. For that reason they should take precedence over general rules as a matter of principle, so as not to counteract the development of AVMSD and its merits that have surfaced so far. This could be achieved either by excluding providers addressed by the AVMSD from the general horizontal legal framework or by giving AVMSD rules precedence as lex specialis. The former, however, would mean that general rules (in particular the liability privileges and, where applicable, other general obligations imposed on platforms) would also not apply in their entirety to AVMSD providers. As the AVMSD does not aim at full harmonisation and does not pursue the same objective as a horizontal legal framework, the second option seems more appropriate. The scope needs to be evaluated carefully; nonetheless, it has to take into account every rule (especially concerning obligations for platforms) in the new instrument in comparison with the rules of the AVMSD. A clarification, at least in the Recitals, may be useful here. In this context, the lex specialis-lex generalis correlation can only refer to the coordinated area[103] and prevents rules in the general legal framework from contradicting the more specific law.

Similar considerations apply in copyright law. Against the backdrop of massive violations concerning copyright-protected works on the Internet, even an exclusion of the liability rules for copyright infringements is being advocated by some.[104] An orientation towards the US-American model may be justified here by the fact that – unlike in other areas such as hate speech or disinformation – there are already advanced technologies for detecting content that infringes copyright; in addition, the standards for copyright are comparable. However, since this approach would be infringement-based and not provider-based, special rules for small providers or certain types of providers (e.g. not-for-profit) might be necessary to ensure proportionality. This present study proposes an approach that initially

---

103 Cf. in the context of rules on commercial communication not falling in the specific (no provision on this specific issue in its specific objections) but general (audiovisual commercial communication) scope of the AVMSD recently CJEU, C-555/19, *Fussl Modestraße Mayr*, para. 43 et seq. Cf. on this case as well *Cole*, Zum Gestaltungsspielraum der EU-Mitgliedstaaten bei Einschränkungen der Dienstleistungsfreiheit, p. 6 et seq.

104 Cf. *Sartor*, New aspects and challenges in consumer protection, p. 31.

applies (at the level of the scope) to all providers regardless of their size or thematic focus; establishing a priority ratio is more appropriate here as well.

This suggested approach also applies to the TERREG Proposal and the P2B Regulation. Here, too, conflicts are conceivable both with exemptions from liability or the exclusion of general monitoring obligations (if these are retained) and obligations arising from a new legal instrument (if these should be imposed). As these are regulations, a clarification rule is all the more important against the background of collision rules of EU law (see above at E.I.1.).

Data protection law does contain rules in particular on the lawfulness of data processing operations and thus pursues a different objective than the regulation of digital services in general. However, in particular with regard to the protection of data subjects intended by fundamental rights, it must be remembered that obligations for providers (for example, transparency obligations, information requirements) may conflict with obligations under data protection law. Provisions on personalised advertising may also conflict with provisions of the ePrivacy Directive, which is set to be replaced by a Regulation in the future, too. That is why defining the priority relation is of particular significance here. When the GDPR was enacted, it was also intended to harmonise and defragment as much as possible and to bundle rules within one legal instrument. This should not be contradicted.

The future regulation will also impact on the EU consumer protection acquis. The Unfair Commercial Practices Directive (UCPD) requires that traders act with professional diligence and refrain from misleading conduct.[105] The exact link between these requirements and the liability exemptions provided by the ECD has been unclear in the past.[106] Only the 2019 Omnibus Directive clarified that online marketplaces will be considered as traders in their own right.[107] They therefore need to comply with obligations imposed through the UCPD and with new transparency obligations

---

105 Directive 2005/29/EC of the European Parliament and of the Council of 11 May 2005 concerning unfair business-to-consumer commercial practices in the internal market and amending Council Directive 84/450/EEC, Directives 97/7/EC, 98/27/EC and 2002/65/EC of the European Parliament and of the Council and Regulation (EC) No 2006/2004 of the European Parliament and of the Council, OJ L 149, 11.6.2005, p. 22–39, Art. 5 para. 2, Art. 6 and 7.

106 *Ullrich*, in: MJ, 26 (4), 2019, 558, 575 – 577.

107 Directive (EU) 2019/2161 of the European Parliament and of the Council of 27 November 2019 amending Council Directive 93/13/EEC and Directives 98/6/EC, 2005/29/EC and 2011/83/EU of the European Parliament and of the

spelled out through the Omnibus Directive[108] regardless of the exemptions provided for in the ECD. In this wider context there is also a link between future and new responsibilities of these actors with regards to product and food safety provisions. This will receive further relevance with the ongoing review of the General Product Safety Directive.[109]

The need to create coherence applies further with respect to those rules of secondary law that deliberately give Member States room to manoeuvre or a discretion in order to allow basing national rules on the own legal (constitutional) traditions. In the media sector, this is of utmost relevance. It must be ensured that such scope for design by Member States, which in some cases allows for deviations and in others for supplementing the general rules, is not overridden by overarching provisions. These powers are usually the result of negotiations between the EU institutions, taking into account, above all, Member States' interests and a balancing of different interests. National provisions created on the basis of such rights are part of the coordinated scope of the sectoral legislation.

Finally, coherence must be ensured where the EU has no legislative competence, so that existing Member State schemes to pursue objectives at the national level based on the actual circumstances in a national territory are, and must remain, possible. This concretely means that measures taken at (EU or) national level in order to promote cultural and linguistic diversity and to ensure pluralism must still be excluded from a harmonisation approach. In other words, such harmonisation may not create any blocking effects for that type of Member State law.

The fact that tensions in this regard are possible can be documented by the example of the notification procedure for the German Interstate Media Treaty. That new regulatory framework for broadcasters and online media, but also for platforms, recently introduced in particular transparency obligations for so-called media intermediaries. In its comments during the notification procedure, the Commission stated that it identified "potential legal overlaps" between the P2B Regulation and this new media-oriented

---

Council as regards the better enforcement and modernisation of Union consumer protection rules, OJ L 328, 18.12.2019, p. 7–28, Art. 3, 4.

108 Ibid., Art. 6a.

109 European Commission, Combined Evaluation Roadmap/Inception Impact Assessment – Revision of Directive 2001/95/EC on General Product Safety – Ref. Ares(2020)3256809.

legislation at national level.[110] While the Interstate Media Treaty pursues primarily cultural policy and namely pluralism goals, the P2B Regulation is geared to economic factors, in particular the relationship "business to platform". Since the obligations for service providers of the P2B-Regulation as described above can also have a reflexive effect on promoting pluralism in the media sector, this leads to the question of whether the Regulation has a suspensory effect or otherwise limits the regulatory approaches of Member States with regard to providers already covered by the regulation and transparency requirements applied to them.[111] In this context, it should be emphasised that, unlike the AVMSD, the P2B Regulation does not contain any explicit power to derogate from the coordinated field of the EU legislative act for introducing stricter rules at national level for providers under the jurisdiction of a given Member State. Nor does it reference, as is the case for the ECD, any additional power to restrict such providers. In that sense, the ECD ensures through Art. 2 para. 6 that it does not affect measures taken at Union or national level (in respect of Union law) in order to promote cultural and linguistic diversity and to ensure the safeguarding of pluralism. Not least against this background, the provision of Art. 2 para. 6 ECD should be retained at least for clarification purposes. It may also be necessary to explicitly foresee additional derogation options, for example in the interest of effective protection of minors.

d. Defining Objectives of a Regulatory Approach

Finally, with regard to the general regulatory approach of a new or reformed legal instrument, the question may still arise as to whether it is necessary to include an objective in the rules. The ECD regulates such an objective in Art. 1 para. 1 by formulating: "This Directive seeks to contribute to the proper functioning of the internal market by ensuring the free movement of information society services between the Member States". In addition, other acts on secondary law level also provide for comparable descriptions of the aim or describe the topic of the specific legis-

---

110 European Commission, notification 2020/26/D, 27.04.2020, C(2020) 2823 final, https://dokumente.landtag.rlp.de/landtag/vorlagen/6754-V-17.pdf (hereinafter own translations), p. 9.

111 Cf. on this question *Cole/Ukrow/Etteldorf*, On the Allocation of Competences between the European Union and its Member States in the Media Sector, p. 27, 144.

lative act (such as the P2B Regulation, Art. 1), or both (such as the GDPR, Art. 1).

This is an approach that should be followed in particular against the background of ensuring coherence.[112] For a horizontal general legal framework that has points of contact and tension with numerous other rules this is especially the case. In that way, also potential tensions that have not yet been identified or that only arise as a result of further technological developments in the digital sector (e.g. new transmission methods for content that fall within the scope of an existing ruleset) can be interpreted in light of the aim, as well as those that are created as a result of the introduction of new sectoral rules at EU or national level. In this context, the definition of an objective can serve as an important tool when assessing the relationship between different legal acts with regards to the conflict of laws principles of EU law, which are also applied differently in some cases in the case law of the CJEU.[113] The description of the objective or aim must be based on the rules adopted, but also on the legal basis chosen, i.e. it would have to be formulated in the context of new rules for the online sector with regard to the protection of the internal market in light of the role and responsibility of platforms.

2. DSA Approach

For the DSA Proposal the Commission opted for the legal basis of Art. 114 TFEU, which provides for the creation of measures to ensure the establishment or functioning of the Internal Market. Regarding the necessary harmonisation and its level, the Commission takes the view that obstacles to economic activity result from differences in the way national laws are emerging, as exemplified by some Member States that have legislated or intend to do so on issues such as the removal of illegal content online, diligence obligations, notice and action procedures, and transparency of platform providers.[114]

Art. 114 TFEU leaves the choice of legislative act between Regulations and Directives. The choice of Regulation is explained in the DSA Proposal with the aim to ensure a consistent level of protection throughout the

---

112 In this regard *Ukrow*, Die Vorschläge der EU-Kommission für einen Digital Services Act und einen Digital Markets Act, p. 9.

113 Cf. on this *Nettesheim*, in: EuR, 41 (6), 2006, 737, 767.

114 Point 2 of the Explanatory Memorandum to the DSA Proposal.

Union, to prevent divergences hampering the free provision of the relevant services within the internal market, to guarantee the uniform protection of rights and introduce uniform obligations for business and consumers across the internal market. Furthermore the Commission relies on a Regulation as being necessary to provide legal certainty and transparency for economic operators and consumers alike. This type of instrument would facilitate consistent monitoring of the rights and obligations, ensuring equivalent sanctions in all Member States as well as effective cooperation between the supervisory authorities of different Member States and at Union level.

Concerning the principle of subsidiarity, the Commission explains in the accompanying document on the DSA Proposal that the Internet is "by its nature cross-border, the legislative efforts at national level referred to above hamper the provision and reception of services throughout the Union and are ineffective in ensuring the safety and uniform protection of the rights of Union citizens and businesses online".[115] In its Impact Assessment, the Commission further states that "a patchy framework of national rules jeopardises an effective exercise of the freedom of establishment and the freedom to provide services in the EU", thus concluding that intervention at national level cannot solve this problem. In the view of the Commission this situation can only be overcome by rules at Union level because it assumes that only Union level action provides predictability and legal certainty and reduces compliance costs across the Union while fostering the equal protection of all Union citizens and ensuring a coherent approach applicable to providers of intermediary services operating in all Member States.[116]

As regards content neutrality of the approach, the DSA Proposal does not contain a restriction of certain forms of content. Rather it relies in several places on the neutral term "content" ("content moderation", "illegal content", etc.). In the context of the question which content is subject to the obligations suggested in the DSA, the Proposal chooses to rely on the concept of a broad definition of illegal content referring to Union or national law. According to this formal definition as listed in Art. 2 lit. g), illegal content means "any information, which, in itself or by its reference to

---

115 Commission staff working document, impact assessment accompanying the DSA Proposal, SWD(2020) 348 final, 15.12.2020, Part 1/2, https://ec.europa.eu/t ransparency/regdoc/rep/10102/2020/EN/SWD-2020-348-F1-EN-MAIN-PART-1.P DF.
116 Point 2 of the Explanatory Memorandum.

an activity, including the sale of products or provision of services is not in compliance with Union law or the law of a Member State, irrespective of the precise subject matter or nature of that law". Recital 12 states that this concept should be understood to refer to information, irrespective of its form, that under the applicable law is either itself illegal, such as illegal hate speech or terrorist content and unlawful discriminatory content, or relates to activities in connection with content that are illegal, such as the sharing of images depicting child sexual abuse, unlawful non-consensual sharing of private images, online stalking, the sale of non-compliant or counterfeit products, the non-authorised use of copyright-protected material or activities involving infringements of consumer protection law.

In the Explanatory Memorandum the Commission highlights that the results of the stakeholder consultation showed a general agreement that 'harmful' content, which is not "yet" or at least not necessarily also illegal, should not be defined in or by the DSA and should not be subject to removal obligations, as this is a sensitive area with potentially serious implications for the protection of freedom of expression. The term "harmful" itself is not at all used in the proposed substantive provisions themselves, in particular not in connection with the definition of illegal content, but only in the Recitals (5, 52 and 68) when describing the risks posed by platforms through the increasing distribution of illegal or otherwise harmful content.

As regards the material scope of application in light of ensuring consistency, Art. 1 para. 5 DSA Proposal states that the Regulation is without prejudice to the rules laid down by the ECD,[117] the AVMSD, Union law on copyright and related rights, the TERREG Proposal, the P2B Regulation, Union law on the protection of personal data, in particular the GDPR and ePrivacy Directive, as well as other secondary legislation[118]. It is to be noted that, although there is no difference in the formulation of the substantive provision in Art. 1 para. 5 of the Proposal concerning these different elements of secondary law, the Recital about the relation to the AVMSD, TERREG Proposal and ECD (Recital 9) differs from the one on

---

117 As the Proposal only amends the rules of the ECD without replacing it. The liability exemptions are transferred to the new Proposal.

118 Namely Regulation (EU) 2019/1148; Union law on consumer protection and product safety, including Regulation (EU) 2017/2394; the proposal for a Regulation on European Production and Preservation Orders for electronic evidence in criminal matters and for a Directive laying down harmonised rules on the appointment of legal representatives for the purpose of gathering evidence in criminal proceedings (e-evidence once adopted).

copyright law (Recital 11) and the other legislation mentioned (Recital 10). Recital 9 states that the DSA should complement, yet not affect, the application of rules resulting from other acts of Union law regulating certain aspects of the provision of intermediary services, in particular the ECD, with the exception of those changes introduced by the DSA, the AVMSD and the TERREG Proposal. Therefore, the DSA leaves those other acts, which are to be considered lex specialis in relation to the generally applicable framework, unaffected. However, according to Recital 9 the proposed rules of the DSA shall "apply in respect of issues that are not or not fully addressed by those other acts as well as issues on which those other acts leave Member States the possibility of adopting certain measures at national level".

Recital 11 clarifies in simple terms that the DSA Proposal is without prejudice to the rules of Union law on copyright and related rights that establish "specific rules and procedures" which should stay in place. Regarding the remaining rules, Recital 10 only mentions that "for reasons of clarity" it is specified that the DSA Proposal is without prejudice to all of those, while adding in comparison to the substantive provision that this also applies rules of Union law on working conditions.

Concerning the aims, under Art. 1's heading "subject matter and scope" the Proposal declares in para. 2 as aims of the Regulation to contribute to the proper functioning of the internal market for intermediary services and to set out uniform rules for a safe, predictable and trusted online environment, where fundamental rights enshrined in the Charter are effectively protected.

Briefly, to complement the information on the DSA Proposal, it can be pointed out that the DMA is also proposed in form of a Regulation. Its subject matter – in comparison to the DSA even more briefly described – is to lay down harmonised rules ensuring contestable and fair markets in the digital sector across the Union where gatekeepers are present (Art. 1 para. 1). Although being based on Art. 114 TFEU, too, it resembles competition law rules, but it has not been mentioned as Proposal according to the legal basis of Art. 103 TFEU to concretise the antitrust provisions in Art. 101 and 102 TFEU, as is, e.g., the case for the Merger Regulation 1/2003.[119] The Commission reiterates – again: based on the internal market clause – that adequate solutions can only be found on Union level, not least because of a possible fragmentation of the regulatory landscape at na-

---

119 Cf. on this *Ukrow*, Die Vorschläge der EU-Kommission für einen Digital Services Act und einen Digital Markets Act, Impulse aus dem EMR, p. 11.

tional level. In light of the cross-border nature of the platform economy and the systemic importance of gatekeeper platforms for the internal market, such a reliance on national laws would be insufficient in view of the Commission. Regarding the principle of subsidiarity, the Commission relies in its Explanatory Memorandum on the fact that, on the one hand, digital players typically operate across several Member States if not on an EU-wide basis, which is in particular the case for core platform services provided or offered by gatekeepers, and, on the other hand, even those Member States that have not yet adopted legislation to address unfairness and reduced contestability of core platform services provided or offered by gatekeepers are increasingly considering national measures to that effect, which would eventually lead to a fragmentation across the European Union.[120]

3. Assessment

As already considered above, both the aspects of the subsidiarity principle according to Art. 5 para. 3 TEU and the necessary coherence of different legal instruments at EU and national level tend to speak in favour of the adoption of a Directive. This is all the more true when looking specifically at the scope of the Commission's Proposals, taking into account the legal basis on which they are based.

The Proposal introduces a variety of different obligations for providers which, as mentioned above, may conflict with a number of rules under secondary law and national law. This applies to existing rules already identified as potentially conflicting by the DSA Proposal, but it applies also to new ones. Assuming that – without this being explicitly laid down, but as a result of rules on how to deal with conflicting laws on EU level – these more specific rules would take precedence over the more general provisions of the DSA because of their protection objective, the directly binding nature of the Proposal as a Regulation would nonetheless give rise to legal uncertainty. As the delineation between falling under the more general

---

120 Due to the close relation with rules in competition law, there is less of an issue with choosing the instrument of a Regulation, as the secondary framework in competition law is completely structured by Regulations (and communications of the Commission) and the Commission has a long-standing experience also in the application of these rules; cf. again *Ukrow*, Die Vorschläge der EU-Kommission für einen Digital Services Act und einen Digital Markets Act, p. 12 fn. 28.

Regulation or under specific Directive's provisions requires an interpretation in every case, this can pose issues for entities and practitioners: it is necessary to know which norms apply and for which actions there may be sanctions. Where this is not clear, even a Regulation does not increase legal certainty; on the contrary it can actually turn into the opposite as Member State solutions with a clarifying effect would not be possible.

Both Proposals for the DSA and the DMA are based on Art. 114 TFEU; thereby they have a very broad legal basis that is not very specified in terms of what can be based on that provision. It also concerns a subject matter that falls within the category of shared competences between EU and Member States. All of that speaks in favour of choosing a type of instrument that is less restricting for Member State actions within their retained competence at least if the scope of the proposed legislative act is so wide as is the case with the proposed DSA. Although recourse to Art. 114 TFEU as a legal basis is possible if the aim of a legal instrument is to prevent the emergence of future obstacles to trade as a result of divergences in national laws, the emergence of such obstacles must be likely and the measure in question must be designed to prevent them.[121] Several of the proposed rules, in particular in the area of content moderation, are situated on the verge of regulating economic aspects of the internal market while affecting matters of media and communication policy. The latter regulatory competence, however, clearly remains in the sphere of the Member States. Fully harmonising "media law" on EU level would thus contradict the division of competences as laid down in primary law, which is why a certain degree of fragmentation between applicable rules across the internal market is inherent in the systematics of competence allocation. In that regard the passages in the Explanatory Memorandum concerning the principle of subsidiarity are under-developed and do not reflect sufficiently the need to argue why the proposed DSA actually is a necessity in form of a Regulation notwithstanding that principle. Advocating for primacy of creating legislation at Union level cannot be based solely on the fact that the internet is cross-border by nature and therefore uniform rules should apply in the internal market.[122] If that were the case, any reference to the internal market could be used to justify a maximum harmonisation approach. Should the proposed piece of legislation go ahead as Regulation and should the scope of application of it be retained more or less as it currently stands – thereby

---

121 CJEU, C-482/17, *Czech Republic v. Parliament and Council*, para. 35.
122 *Ukrow*, Die Vorschläge der EU-Kommission für einen Digital Services Act und einen Digital Markets Act, p. 9.

clearly departing from the much more limited scope of the ECD, notabene that being "only" a Directive, in addition –, then other ways need to be included that safeguard Member State powers and existing sectoral rules. The subsidiarity principle is usually only seen as a guiding factor in the political negotiations at an early stage in that the Commission integrates the Member State perspective in the preparing of a Proposal.[123] However, it is a legally binding principle that includes procedural safeguards by the Member State parliaments in case it has not been fully taken into account. Therefore, integrating more specifically the Member State perspective will be important, because currently a specific derogation/exception power is lacking and the definition of the objective is not detailed enough to make clear that the scope still leaves open room for manoeuvre for the Member States within their field of competence.

The fact that the Proposal refers to the main legislative acts in relation to the dissemination of online content and assigns them with priority as lex specialis is to be welcomed. In particular, the fact that the provisions of the (recently adapted but still to be fully transposed) AVMSD and its platform rules (for VSPs) remain unaffected by the DSA Proposal is important. The priority "in the coordinated area" is the least to be aimed for in light of the intentions of the 2018 reform and the further development of the AVMSD in its application in practice. In addition, the more general references in Art. 1 para. 5 lit. c) of the DSA Proposal could be formulated more precisely at least in the accompanying Recital to avoid any misunderstanding as to the extent of their priority and the exactly applicably pieces of secondary legislation. Therefore, instead of general references such as "Union law on copyright and related rights", an enumeration of the targeted acts would be preferable.[124]

One important clarification is necessary concerning Recital 9 that accompanies Art. 1 para. 5 of the DSA Proposal. The way it is put now could create uncertainty in relation to the AVMSD and its priority as it may dilute the understanding of the coordinated field. The last sentence states that the DSA applies in "respect of issues that are not or *not fully addressed* by those other acts as well as issues on which those other acts *leave Member*

---

123 Cf. on this in general and the principle of subsidiarity, its significance and practical handling, *Constantin*, in: CYELP 4, 2008, 151, 167 et seq.

124 The EU copyright legislation covers 11 Directives and two Regulations and is complemented by three Directives on protection of topographies of semiconductor products. Cf. for an overview: The EU copyright legislation, https://ec.europa.eu/digital-single-market/en/eu-copyright-legislation.

States the possibility of adopting certain measures at national level" (emphasis added). As such a clarification is only made with regard to the ECD, the AVMSD and the TERREG, but not for the exceptions concerning other secondary legislation, it could give the impression that a deviation from the general principles of an exception is intended. With regard to the first half-sentence, it is not clear whether this wording only explains the relationship of lex specialis established in the previous sentence or whether it is intended to imply a deviation from these principles. An exemption ("without prejudice"), as proposed in Art. 1 para. 5, can anyway only refer to the area coordinated by the respective other legislative act. There would be no need for further clarification in this respect, so that either the first half-sentence should be deleted from the Recitals or the terminology should be adapted ("coordinated" instead of "addressed") in order to ensure consistency with other provisions using this term.[125]

The second half-sentence with its wording "possibility of adopting certain measures" (by the Member States based on authorisations in the applicable EU legislation) has a lack of clarity. It is unclear whether it merely refers to general powers of derogation (such as Art. 4 para. 1 AVMSD in relation to the adoption of stricter rules in the coordinated field of that directive), to specific powers of derogation (such as Art. 28b para. 6 AVMSD regarding measures that are more detailed or stricter than the measures foreseen for VSPs in the AVMSD), to rules that allow Member States to adopt rules on national level (such as Art. 7a AVMSD regarding measures to ensure the appropriate prominence of audiovisual media services of general interest) or finally to rules that leave Member States room for manoeuvre in the implementation of a specific objective (such as Art. 7b AVMSD regarding measures to ensure that audiovisual media services are not overlaid for commercial purposes or modified). As the speciality character of the AVMSD exists without specific mention anyway, as has been shown above at E.I.1.c, a further clarification in the Recitals is not actually necessary and only risks to contradict the lex specialis relationship. The half-sentence should therefore be deleted or specified to the effect that it refers only to the possibility of Member States to generally impose (for some secondary acts) measures that are more detailed or stricter than the measures coordinated by the respective legislative act. It should be considered to explicitly underline instead that the lex specialis rule of the AVMSD also ac-

---

125 See, e.g., Art. 4 para. 1 AVMSD, on which the CJEU already adjudicated concerning "coordinated field" repeatedly, most recently CJEU, C-555/19, *Fussl Modestraße Mayr*, para. 43 et seq, with further references.

counts for those Member State laws that were enacted making use of the discretionary powers granted to them.

In addition, as explained above, it is very important to explicitly underline that also the general rules of the proposed DSA do not – as is the case for existing secondary law – affect measures taken at Union or national level in order to promote cultural and linguistic diversity or to safeguard pluralism. This applies in particular as the minor changes to the ECD uphold its unequivocal rule of Art. 2 para. 6 ECD, which clarifies Member States' margins. As the ECD is much more limited in its scope than the proposed DSA, such a clarification is even more necessary. With such a clarifying statement, especially if the instrument of a Regulation is retained, there is a possible suspensory effect as in the context of the P2B Regulation which contains economy-driven transparency rules with indirect effects on media pluralism aspects and can therefore conflict with national provisions that are directly aiming to ensure media pluralism. In general, it should be reassessed whether an inclusion of the remaining ECD rules in a new overarching DSA in form of a Directive could be advantageous to leaving a few basic norms in the ECD (thereby indeed allowing the Member States to leave untouched their current transpositions) and transplanting the liability exemption rules into the DSA in form of a Regulation, which currently has been proposed in order to supposedly remove differences in Member States application of those rules.

With regard to the objective or aim of the DSA, the proposed Regulation mentions the intention under subject matter and scope. The aims are primarily of an economic nature and in view of consumer protection by ensuring an internal market for intermediaries. Read together with Art. 1 para. 4 and Recital 6 of the Proposal, which implicitly state that the object is precisely not content regulation, this description of the aim can be used as a sufficient basis in interpretation to clarify possible tensions with other aims or other pieces of legislation. For reasons of clarification, however, the definition of an objective should also be included in the title of the respective provision or even addressed in a separate norm. Should the suggestion to clarify in a separate clause that there is a "cultural exception", meaning that a provision explicitly confirms Member States' prerogative for provisions addressing pluralism besides the DSA rules, not be maintained and should the instruments finally be a Regulation, it is even more important to specify in the objectives that the aim is not to supersede Member State laws enacted for other reasons than the objectives of the DSA.

II. The Country-of-Origin Principle

1. Starting Point

The COO principle has been a core element of the internal market; therefore it also underlies the ECD as a core piece of secondary internal market legislation for the online environment. Art. 3 para. 1 ECD obliges Member States to ensure that ISS which are established under their jurisdiction, the country of origin, comply with the rules of that Member State for their activities throughout the EU. In turn the internal market principle precludes Member States from restricting the freedom to provide ISS established in another Member State on the basis of their domestic (destination) law. Thus, in principle, ISS are only required to comply with the law of one Member State and are, in principle, free to provide their services in other Member States. This approach was justified at the time of the creation of the ECD by the EU's objective to create a legal certainty with some rules in a harmonised regulatory framework for the then still emerging electronic commerce services while protecting against the possible negative outcome of legislative forum shopping and fragmentation of rules.[126]

The principle extends to the internal market of the EU as the ECD has no extraterritorial scope,[127] which means that content originating from ISS outside the EU that target EU consumers does not fall within the scope of that Directive and can therefore be dealt with by each Member State according to their national laws.[128] The COO principle underlies not only the ECD but also other relevant legislative acts of the EU. In the area of online content dissemination, this includes above all the AVMSD.[129] Notwithstanding certain differences in the way the COO was included in

---

126 *Rowland/Kohl/Charlesworth*, Information Technology Law, p. 268–269; *Cole/Etteldorf/Ullrich*, Cross-border dissemination of Online Content, p. 92 et seq.

127 Recital 58 of the ECD.

128 Member States are therefore free to take action concerning content supplied from providers based outside the EU, unless this is incompatible with rules of international law (e.g. the rules of the World Trade Organization (WTO) or the Organisation for Economic Co-operation and Development (OECD)) or other legal instruments.

129 However, the AVMSD applies to VSP providers from third countries outside the EU with a market attachment to the EU, which can follow from a subsidiary or parent of the service provider established in the EU; cf. Recital 44 of Directive (EU) 2018/1808.

both Directives, taking the two together illustrates that the COO has been one of the core principles of EU's "online content regulation".

However, in its scope of application[130] there are possibilities to derogate from the CCO approach by restricting the free movement of ISS in particular where Member States deem it necessary (and proportionate) for reasons of, inter alia, public policy, which includes the protection of minors, the fight against incitement to hatred and violations of human dignity (Art. 3 para. 4 ECD). To this end, the ECD lays down basic features of a cooperation mechanism: Member States are requested to coordinate with the country-of-origin Member States and first ask that state to apply the enforcement measures aimed for; the destination Member State may only act if the origin Member State did not act on requests made or when the action taken was insufficient; the Commission has to be notified of any derogative measures taken by a destination Member States and is held to examine any derogation action with an option to request that a Member State stop these measures should they be deemed disproportionate. A similar[131] approach is also contained in Art. 3 AVMSD.

a. Key Issues for Assessment

In order to assess legislative options at EU level regarding the approach to the COO principle, the (practical) implications of this principle shall be presented.

On the one hand, the COO principle is a consequence of establishing an internal market based on the use of the fundamental freedoms. The appli-

---

130 In addition, Art. 3 para. 3 ECD refers to a number of areas (specified in the Annex of the Directive) which are outside of the scope of the coordinated field altogether and therefore the COO does not apply to them. These include intellectual property rights, electronic money transfers, contractual obligations concerning consumer contracts, real estate contracts and unsolicited mail. See on this for example, *Savin*, EU Internet Law, p. 55 et seq.

131 While Art. 3 para. 4 of Directive 2010/13/EU still contained a special provision for taking (not only in the case of linear services temporary) measures against non-linear offers, which almost identically adopted the wording of the corresponding possibility of deviation from the COO as in the ECD (Art. 3 para. 4), Art. 3 para. 4 with the reform by Directive (EU) 2018/1808 has given way to a uniform regulation of derogation for linear and non-linear services under Art. 3 para. 2 and 3, which is why the exact synchronisation between AVMSD and ECD on this matter ceased. Cf. on this in detail *Cole/Etteldorf/Ullrich*, Cross-border Dissemination of Online Content, p. 110 et seq.

cation of the principle creates legal certainty for providers, as they basically only have to comply with the legal systems of a single Member State (chosen by them) and only have to deal with that State or its competent regulatory bodies in procedural terms even if they provide their services in other Member States, too. This is an idea that is also at the heart of the freedom to provide services enshrined in Art. 56 et seq. TFEU as one of the cornerstones of the internal market. Consequently providers offering cross-border services (i.e. offering or disseminating content) should be shielded against a double (regulatory) burden.[132] In this context it has often been discussed whether – and, if so, to what extent – the freedom to provide services mandates the implementation of the COO in any context.[133] Art. 56 et seq. TFEU, however, are primarily intended to dismantle barriers to market access but do not specify how equivalence has to be established for service providers. Member States are (only) obliged to examine whether equivalence and recognition exists, i.e. whether (equivalent and recognisable) control measures already carried out in the country of origin may not be carried out again. However, this does not mean that the legal situation of the country of origin takes precedence in principle. It merely obliges the Member State to take account of it. The freedom to provide services therefore does not necessarily require the application of COO principle.[134] However, restrictions of the freedom to provide services must be justified, which must also be taken into account when assessing a legislative approach on how to deal with differences between Member States: it can either mean to include in a secondary act, based on the COO, derogation possibilities for Member States or it can be solved by relying completely or for specific aspects on the market location principle. In addition to the justifications expressly provided for by the TFEU – public security, public order and public health – other restrictive measures may also be justified if they are necessary in order to pursue an objective in the public interest and if they are applied in an appropriate manner that does not go beyond what is necessary in order to achieve the objective (proportionality test).[135]

---

132 CJEU, judgement of 15.3.2001, C-165/98, para. 24.
133 Cf. on this in detail *Waldheim*, Dienstleistungsfreiheit und Herkunftsland-prinzip; *Albath/Giesel*, in: EuZW 9 (2), 2006, 38, 39 et seq.; *Hörnle*, in: International and Comparative Law Quarterly, 54 (1), 2005, 89, 89–126.
134 Cf. on this, e.g., CJEU, C-55/94, *Gebhard .v Consiglio dell'Ordine degli Avvocati e Procuratori di Milano*.
135 CJEU, C-19/92, *Kraus v. Land Baden-Württemberg*, para. 32; C-272/94, *Guiot*, para. 11.

Securing the basic idea of COO and the freedom to provide services is very relevant economically. This is particularly essential in the online sector, since the offered services are regularly cross-border in nature without the provider necessarily having to actively orient the service to a specific Member State market. This applies to media content, too. The principle is therefore particularly important not only for large and internationally oriented ISS but also for SMEs and start-ups, which regularly would have more difficulties to obtain detailed information about the legal requirements in all Member States, let alone to comply with them. This aspect is of specific relevance in the context of the proportionality test and must find its way into the legislative approach, especially when incorporating (elements of) the market location principle.

Finally, in particular in the area of dissemination of online content, the alignment of the ECD with the AVMSD is of importance. In regulatory practice, the fact that similar rules have been established for both Directives leads to similar procedures for similar circumstances, which are the result of the convergence of the media and the multitude of new distribution channels.

However, the application of the COO (not only regarding the provisions of the ECD) has caused problems in practice, especially in efforts to enforce the law. This concerns in particular the complex procedure of enforcement measures directed at providers located in another EU Member State. While the application of the COO principle is in theory distinct from the question of jurisdiction over a provider, in practice they are closely intertwined. For the enforcement of the rules of the ECD itself, requests for redress or information usually have to be addressed to the competent authority of the country of origin. The low level of response within the IMI System mentioned above (C.) speaks for a reluctant and difficult handling within the cooperation[136] of supervisory authorities.[137] Under the

---

136 The IMI System including the ECD as a pilot project should be used for the implementation of the derogation procedure foreseen by Art. 3 of the ECD, too. Cf. on this Art. 29 para. 3 Regulation 1024/2012 of the European Parliament and of the Council of 25 October 2012 on administrative cooperation through the Internal Market Information System and repealing Commission Decision 2008/49/EC (the IMI Regulation), OJ L 316/1, as amended by Directives 2013/55, 2014/60, 2014/67 and Regulations 2016/1191, 2016/1628 and 2018/1724.

137 Cf. on this also Commission staff working document, impact assessment accompanying the DSA Proposal, SWD(2020) 348 final, 15.12.2020, Part 1/2, para. 116.

COO, Member State authorities are required to direct their requests towards the EU jurisdiction where the entity has its seat of establishment, even if a branch or subsidiary entity may exist in their own country.[138] This does not only come with high administrative burdens and therefore a perceived lack of effectiveness in enforcement but can create a conflict of law rule by virtue of pointing towards the law of place of establishment of the ISS provider.[139] More important are the problems with the power to derogate as foreseen in the Directive. The fact that the power to derogate has so far been hardly used[140] is probably also due to the complexity of the procedure envisaged.[141]

A closely related factor that is commonly understood as a risk under the COO principle is the making use of "forum shopping" by providers.[142] The ratio of the COO principle can make certain states more attractive as host countries due to a perceived lighter regulatory framework. This can lead to economic imbalances, since Member States may be inclined to enact provider-friendly rules in their territory, in particular when there are only a limited set of harmonised areas and by choosing to the least restrictive alternative in areas with a wide room for manoeuvre. By choosing their place of establishment, on the other hand, providers can avoid a possibly stricter legal framework in a Member State although (also) directing their offer to another Member State. This possibility is particularly attractive for content intermediaries, as they are regularly not bound to a specific location with their offer and frequently offer their services throughout the entire internal market and beyond. Against this background, the back-

---

138 Administrative Court of Berlin, judgement of 20.7.2017, case 6 L 162.17, para. 33–39. In this case Berlin authorities were refused an order for disclosure of information made to the local subsidiary of *AirBnB* on the grounds that this request would need to be directed at the company's EU seat of establishment in Ireland. See also: *Ullrich*, Unlawful Content Online: Towards a New Regulatory Framework for Online Platforms, pp. 101 – 102.

139 *Büllesbach et al. (eds.)*, Concise European IT Law, p. 306.

140 *Savin*, EU Internet Law, p. 59. The intention of these derogations was clarified in: CJEU, judgement of 25.10.2011, C-509/09 and C-161/10, *eDate Advertising GmbH v. X and Olivier Martinez, Robert Martinez v. MGN Limited*.

141 *Cole/Etteldorf/Ullrich*, Cross-border Dissemination of Online Content, p. 174; *Rowland/Kohl/Charlesworth*, Information Technology Law, p. 270.

142 Cf. on this for the AVMSD rules *Harrison/Woods*, Jurisdiction, forum shopping and the 'race to the bottom'; *Vlassis*, in: Politique européenne 56 (2), 2017, 102, 116 et seq.; for enforcement against copyright infringements cf. *Matulionyte*, in: JIPITEC, 6 (2), 2015, 132, 132 et seq.

stop mechanisms on the power to derogate and the prohibition of circumvention (for the AVMSD only) are of particular importance.

Finally, a risk of inconsistency concerning comparable content must also be taken into account, as the COO principle only applies to domestic EU providers. The logical consequence of tying the advantage of the COO for providers to the guarantee of compliance with the joint minimum standards and the regulatory framework of a Member State is that it can only be legitimately applied in an inner-EU context. For providers from third countries the Member States can in principle lay down different and, in particular, stricter rules, even if they regularly offer the same or similar services.[143] This is particularly important in the area of intermediaries, as US providers dominate the market here, even though many of them operate for the European market from a branch within the EU.

b. Options: COO Principle or Market Location Principle

Taking into account the aforementioned aspects, the question arises as to how the problems identified can be addressed. In principle, two options can be considered: the full retention of the COO principle or the introduction of the market location principle. In addition, mixed forms are conceivable, which either supplement the COO principle with market location elements or only apply the market location principle to certain providers.[144] The question of jurisdiction must be reconciled with the preferred option in each case, especially in relation to cross-border situations (see for the enforcement aspect E.VI).

In this context, it should first be noted that the previous selective convergence of ECD and AVMSD against the background of the media-related online environment does not imperatively require the retention of the COO principle. Rather, more recent legal instruments that also or primarily have effects in the online environment, such as the TERREG Proposal (Art. 1 para. 2), the P2B Regulation (Art. 1 para. 2) and also the GDPR (Art. 3 para. 2), provide for the establishment of the market location prin-

---

143 For example the German Netzwerkdurchsetzungsgesetz (Network Enforcement Act), which is currently being further amended (for further information in English cf. https://www.bmjv.de/DE/Themen/FokusThemen/NetzDG/NetzDG_EN _node.html). Critical on the compatibility with EU law in light of the COO principle *Spindler*, in: JIPITEC, 8 (2), 2017, 166, 166 et seq.

144 With regard to the territorial scope. For questions of the personal scope of application see E.III.

ciple as far as the territorial scope of application is concerned and refrain from applying special rules only to EU domestic companies. The incorporation of the market location principle is particularly suitable if the legal instrument has a high level of harmonisation for a certain area, and it leaves little room for manoeuvre, derogations and exemptions for the Member States. This is often the case when the instrument chosen is a Regulation. The advantages and disadvantages of relying on the market location principle, be it as an entirely new ruleset or by adopting only certain elements of it, therefore also depend on the degree to which the law in the area of the concerned online services will be harmonised, which will certainly go beyond the establishment of the minimum standards set in the ECD.[145]

Irrespective of the question of the degree of harmonisation, however, the establishment of the market location principle for certain providers seems appropriate. This applies to third country providers, provided that a connecting factor can be found between their offers (see E.II.1.c. below) and the internal market. In that way a fragmentation through diverging national laws for similar questions could be avoided and the application of joint standards would be ensured not only by one (origin) State. This is particularly true in light of the objective of strengthening the internal market by supporting European companies in order to create a level playing field vis-à-vis undertakings from third countries. Until recently a stricter regulation of online intermediaries, or actually a dedicated regulation of online intermediaries at all, was the exception rather than the rule in Member States with the consequence of a beneficial situation of such undertakings. At the very least, if there is no overall turn towards the market location principle for such providers, the possibility to rely on the market location principle for content originating or disseminated by non-domestic providers in certain clearly defined cases must be established in a horizontal EU legislative act.

In other respects, however, the fundamental validity of the COO should remain untouched due to its importance for questions of legal certainty and the aforementioned implications for small and niche providers in particular. Nevertheless, against the background of the problems described above adjustments are urgently needed. This includes on the one hand a better, stronger and (statutorily) organised cooperation between Member States on the level of regulatory bodies to make the procedure more effi-

---

145 *Cole/Etteldorf/Ullrich*, Cross-border Dissemination of Online Content, p. 232.

cient and rapid in particular in cross-border cases (see on this E.VI.).[146] On the other hand, it necessitates the update of the legal foundation[147] with regard to derogation possibilities, the establishment of a prohibition of circumvention, further clarifications especially in the area of urgent cases of derogation power as well as the concretisation of terms such as the criteria of necessity and urgency (Art. 3 ECD). Such a newly found procedural set-up could serve as a blueprint for possible future clarifications of the COO/market-destination distinction also for other parts of the legal framework concerning content, in particular the AVMSD.

Finally, however, it should be noted that the establishment of a market location principle in the sense of a uniform regulation based on the models of the GDPR or the P2B Regulation, i.e. also for EU domestic providers, is not per se opposed by considerations of the freedom to provide services. They are – above all in order to justify restrictions of Art. 56 et seq. TFEU in a proportionate manner – however to be evaluated similarly according to the criteria just mentioned and must therefore contain protection mechanisms for smaller providers at various levels and provide for clear rules and streamlined procedures.

c. Key Points for Design

In order to reach more clarity about the possibilities of Member States to derogate from the COO principle and connected to that less hesitation on the part of regulatory authorities to act in high-risk cases in using the exceptional possibilities, these should be explicitly stated and framed precisely: besides the streamlining of the procedure for derogation itself (see on this E.VI.) this concerns the possibility for Member States of resorting – in urgent cases directly – to measures against (domestic) technical "carriers",

---

146 Already in *Cole/Etteldorf/Ullrich*, Cross-border Dissemination of Online Content, p. 221 et seq.; as well in this regard *De Streel/Husovec*, The e-commerce Directive as the cornerstone of the Internal Market, p. 37, 39 et seq.; *de Streel/Broughton Micova*, Digital Services Act: Deepening the internal market and clarifying responsibilities for digital services, p. 12.

147 *de Streel/Broughton Micova*, Digital Services Act: Deepening the internal market and clarifying responsibilities for digital services, p. 12, opt beyond that for an assessment of the exceptions to the internal market clause, contained in the Annex of the ECD, in particular regarding consumer protection rules, which means that the exception relating to contractual obligations for consumer contracts may no longer be justified.

in particular Internet Access Providers (IAPs), instead of (foreign) content providers or host providers when responding to illegal content, without this being a violation of the COO per se.

Further, the reasons for deviations based on a threat to public interests need to be maintained, but they should be reassessed.[148] In particular, it should be assessed whether the general interest objectives contained so far are sufficient to take account of existing problems. This is especially relevant with respect to the most recent amendments in the last AVMSD reform concerning matters that are also included in the ECD (and which were in the previous version aligned with each other). Regarding the definition of incitement to hatred, the expansion of this provision in the AVMSD ("incitement to violence or hatred directed against a group of persons or a member of a group based on any of the grounds referred to in Art. 21 of the Charter") should also be reflected for intermediaries (at the moment the formulation in the ECD only relates to "incitement to hatred on grounds of race, sex, religion or nationality"). Accordingly, the possibility to derogate in light of the protection of minors could also be concretised in line with Art. 6a AVMSD.[149] This would also take into account the broad understanding of the term "protection of minors", which goes beyond protecting against illegal content, a necessary clarification in light of the risks posed in the online environment. In light of current threats by terrorist propaganda online, a further alignment with Art. 6 para. 1 lit. b AVMSD should also be made – possibly within the framework of the emergency derogation power –, which provides this possibility also concerning public provocation to commit a terrorist offence as set out in Art. 5 of Directive (EU) 2017/541 (and which again the AVMSD refers to in Art. 6 para. 1 lit. b). Moreover, establishing a derogation power for threats to democratic elections should be considered in the light of disinformation campaigns. This would leave enforcement options open to

---

148 This is even more true as a general "culture clause" is not included in the DSA Proposal in contrast to, e.g., the ECD. Cf. chapter E.I.1.d and E.I.3.

149 The provision reads: "Member States shall take appropriate measures to ensure that audiovisual media services provided by media service providers under their jurisdiction which may impair the physical, mental or moral development of minors are only made available in such a way as to ensure that minors will not normally hear or see them. Such measures may include selecting the time of the broadcast, age verification tools or other technical measures. They shall be proportionate to the potential harm of the programme. The most harmful content, such as gratuitous violence and pornography, shall be subject to the strictest measures."

Member States if special rules are created at national level for this purpose or if further EU legislation would be enacted. This is especially true since these dangers are primarily limited to one national territory and therefore enforcement interests and assessment possibilities do not exist or might not be that urgent in/for other states.[150]

In addition, the concepts of necessity and urgency of a measure should potentially be enriched with criteria or defined in more detail in order to avoid uncertainty or reluctance to use the provision. With regard to necessity, it should be made clear that no examination of particular seriousness beyond the violation of Member State law in the areas mentioned needs to take place, at least where serious threats are concerned, such as in the case of violation of criminal law. Otherwise, there would also no longer be a graduation compared to the particularly urgent cases. With regard to urgency, the particular seriousness of an infringement, on the other hand, could at least be included as an example, as such instances pose the risk of a greater harm if they are not reacted to swiftly.

Against the background of the threats to forum shopping described above, a ban on circumvention should be introduced, which can also be modelled along the AVMSD (Art. 3 para. 4 lit. b.[151] This would be more difficult to prove in light of the often general roll-out of a service across Europe, but for niche service providers such a specific targeting and relocation of establishment to circumvent could be shown in practice.

With regard to the connecting criteria for the market location principle, existing rules such as the GDPR (relying inter alia on "the offering of goods or services to data subjects in the Union") or the Proposals for TERREG (relying on a "substantial connection to the Union", Recital 11) or the Proposal for an E-Evidence Directive[152] (relying on "offering services in the Union") can be used as a reference. The GDPR is particularly suitable as a point of reference, since in that legislative act the recipient (data subject), like in the area of cross-border distribution of online con-

---

150 In principle, this would also not raise any concerns against the background of the freedom to provide services, since there is scope here in particular for shaping cultural policy as an objective of general public interest; cf., e.g., CJEU, C-353/89, *Commission v. Netherlands*.

151 See on the AVMSD circumvention provision *Cole*, AVMSD Jurisdiction Criteria concerning Audiovisual Media Service Providers after the 2018 Reform, p. 28 et seq., with further references.

152 Proposal for a Directive laying down harmonised rules on the appointment of legal representatives for the purpose of gathering evidence in criminal proceedings, COM/2018/226 final – 2018/0107 (COD).

tent to consumers, is at the centre of the risk situation. In addition to specifications in the Recitals, the supervisory authorities entrusted with monitoring a consistent compliance with the GDPR and united in the European Data Protection Board (EDPB) have already developed guidance on this.[153] Regarding the criterion "offering of goods or services" in Art. 3 para. 2 lit. a) GDPR, the EDPB in particular relies on case law of the CJEU[154] on Art. 15 para. 1 lit. c) of the Council Regulation (EC) 44/2001 on jurisdiction and the recognition and enforcement of judgments (now Art. 17 para. 1 lit. c) of Regulation (EU) No 1215/2012), which relies on the criterion of directing activities to another Member State. Based on this, the EDPB develops further examples in which a sufficient connection within the meaning of Art. 3 para. 2 lit. a GDPR can be assumed, thus emphasising that the cumulation of several criteria can also lead to a corresponding assessment.[155]

---

153 Guidelines 3/2018 on the territorial scope of the GDPR (Art. 3) – Version for public consultation, adopted on 16 November 2018, https://edpb.europa.eu/our-work-tools/public-consultations/2018/guidelines-32018-territorial-scope-gdpr-art icle-3_de.

154 Joined cases C-585/08 and C-144/09, *Pammer v. Reederei Karl Schlüter GmbH & Co and Hotel Alpenhof v. Heller.*

155 Guidelines 3/2018 (cf. fn. 153), p. 15 et seq.: "The EU or at least one Member State is designated by name with reference to the good or service offered; The data controller or processor pays a search engine operator for an internet referencing service in order to facilitate access to its site by consumers in the Union; or the controller or processor has launched marketing and advertisement campaigns directed at an EU country audience; The international nature of the activity at issue, such as certain tourist activities; The mention of dedicated addresses or phone numbers to be reached from an EU country; The use of a top-level domain name other than that of the third country in which the controller or processor is established, for example ".de", or the use of neutral top-level domain names such as ".eu"; The description of travel instructions from one or more other EU Member States to the place where the service is provided; The mention of an international clientele composed of customers domiciled in various EU Member States, in particular by presentation of accounts written by such customers; The use of a language or a currency other than that generally used in the trader's country, especially a language or currency of one or more EU Member States; The data controller offers the delivery of goods in EU Member States."

2. DSA Approach

According to Art. 1 para. 3 of the Proposal, the DSA shall apply to intermediary services provided to recipients of the service that have their place of establishment or residence in the Union, irrespective of the place of establishment of the providers of those services. Art. 2 lit. d specifies the offering of services in the sense that this means enabling legal or natural persons in one or more Member States to use the services of the provider of ISS which has a substantial connection to the Union. Such a substantial connection is deemed to exist where the provider has an establishment in the Union. In the absence of such an establishment, the assessment of a substantial connection is based on specific factual criteria, whereby the Proposal lists as examples that the service has a significant number of users in one or more Member States or that it targets its activities towards one or more Member States.

For these listed exemplary evaluation criteria, Recital 8 provides some further details. The targeting of activities towards one or more Member States can be determined on the basis of all relevant circumstances, including factors such as: the use of a language or a currency generally used in that Member State; the possibility of ordering products or services; using a national top level domain; the availability of an application in the relevant national application store; the provision of local advertising or advertising in the language used in that Member State; the handling of customer relations such as by providing customer service in the language generally used in that Member State. A substantial connection should also be assumed where a service provider directs its activities to one or more Member State as set out in Art. 17 para. 1 lit. c of Regulation (EU) 1215/2012 of the European Parliament and of the Council. However, Recital 8 states that mere technical accessibility of a website from the Union cannot, for that reason alone, be considered as establishing a substantial connection to the Union.

Furthermore, Recital 33 clarifies in particular the relation to the COO principle which would continue to be enshrined in the ECD regarding orders of judicial or administrative authorities to act against illegal content. Such orders are subject to the rules set out in Art. 3 ECD only if the conditions of that Article are met. However, orders which relate to specific items of illegal content and information (as it is regularly the case) addressed to providers in other Member States do not in principle restrict those providers' freedom to provide their services across borders. Therefore, the rules set out in Art. 3 ECD, including those regarding the need to justify measures derogating from the competence of the Member State where the service provider is established on certain specified grounds and regarding the notification of such measures, do not apply in respect of those orders.

The DMA Proposal follows a market location approach, too. According to Art. 1 para. 2 it shall apply to core platform services provided or offered by gatekeepers to business users established in the Union or end users established or located in the Union, irrespective of the place of establishment or residence of the gatekeepers. Unlike in the DSA, however, there is no need for a "substantial connection" as a connecting factor for the internal market regime, because the connection is already apparent from the definition of the providers covered (which need to have a significant impact on the internal market, Art. 3 para. 1 lit. a).

3. Assessment

The DSA Proposal does not include for EU domestic providers a reference to the COO principle or an explicit market access clause, thereby leaving the guarantee of the cross-border flow of ISS, which can only be exceptionally stopped, to the ECD, which – in this regard – will remain unamended. In light of that, an update of the ECD remains appropriate in view of the remaining scope of application, taking into account the criteria outlined under E.I.c, in particular regarding the derogation clause.

Moreover, the Proposal moves towards the market location principle, so that the same requirements apply to EU domestic and EU foreign ISS, thus levelling the playing field. However, the wording in Art. 1 para. 3 ("shall apply to intermediary services provided to recipients of the service that have their place of establishment or residence in the Union") should be aligned with the wording in Art. 2 lit. d) ("to offer services in the Union") in order to avoid the impression that different criteria would have to be applied for the provision of the service to EU citizens than for the offering of services in the Union. The wording of the definition of Art. 2 lit. d) is otherwise only found in Art. 11 of the DSA Proposal, and the impression should be avoided that only this provision requires a "substantial connection", while actually the Regulation as a whole should apply to EU-foreign providers with a "substantial connection", as is otherwise expressed in the Proposal.[156]

---

156 Cf. Recital 76: "In respect of providers that do not have an establishment in the Union but that offer services in the Union and therefore fall within the scope of this Regulation [...]."

Besides that, the requirement of a "substantial connection" takes into account the requirements under international law of a genuine link for regulatory action outside the national territory.[157] The graduated assessment of the existence of such a "substantial connection" is also solved in a reasonable manner: This has to be assumed if there is an establishment in the EU (step 1); if not, an assessment must be made, which must be oriented in particular to the number of users and the orientation of the offer (step 2), which then in turn requires an assessment in the sense of the concretisation in Recital 8 (step 3). With regard to the targeting of activities towards one or more Member States, there are details in Recital 8, which are to be welcomed overall. It should be noted that the wording of the corresponding Recital 13[158] of the Proposal for an e-Evidence Directive[159] has been adopted almost identically (except for the criterion of a top-level domain 'close to the Union') and the criteria also closely resemble Recital 23 GDPR. With regard to the significant number of users in one or more Member States, there is no further detailing. However, such a specification would also be welcome, especially in view of the fact that a significant number would only have to be reached in one Member State, whereby otherwise it would not be clear where the internal market relevance would lie that would justify the applicability of the EU rules in the first place even though seemingly only one Member State is concerned. It would be conceivable here to follow numerical criteria (as in the context of the assessment of a very large platform, which is oriented at the threshold of 10% of consumers within the EU) or a threat-based approach as is known from the European Electronic Communications Code[160].

---

157 Cf. on this *Cole/Ukrow/Etteldorf*, On the Allocation of Competences between the European Union and its Member States in the Media Sector, Chapter E.II.2; also *Ukrow*, Die Vorschläge der EU-Kommission für einen Digital Services Act und einen Digital Markets Act, p. 6.

158 Cf. on the similar approach in the E-Evidence Proposal very critical *Svantesson*, in: JIPITEC, 9 (2), 2018, 113, 120, stating that this "targeting test [...] incorporates all the uncertainties, blemishes and warts typical of a targeting test, and which clearly has the potential to cater for far-reaching jurisdictional claims— thus, having little to do with any truly 'substantial connection'".

159 Cf. Recital 13 of the Proposal for a Directive laying down harmonised rules on the appointment of legal representatives for the purpose of gathering evidence in criminal proceedings, COM/2018/226 final – 2018/0107 (COD).

160 Directive (EU) 2018/1972 of the European Parliament and of the Council of 11 December 2018 establishing the European Electronic Communications Code, OJ L 321, 17.12.2018, p. 36–214.

Furthermore, the DSA Proposal provides for safeguards for certain providers, such as taking into account the size of the platform in the scope of the obligations imposed (on this, see below, E.III. and E.V.), thereby exempting micro and small enterprises as defined in Directive 2003/361/EC from obligations that are usually costly to implement, and introduces cooperation mechanisms for enforcement and clear procedures as well as facilitations such as the designation of a legal representative (on this E.VI).

III. Scope of Application

1. Starting point

The intermediary service providers that are subject to the limited liability regime of the ECD are all ISS as defined by the Technical Standards and Regulations Directive[161]. Setting aside some recent controversies over the application of the ISS definition to collaborative economy platform types,[162] this definition, dating back to 1998, has so far in its generality stood the test of time. While the CJEU clarified some controversies on the applicable scope to electronic platforms involving the provision of services in the transportation or accommodation sector,[163] this definition has permitted an inclusion of new types of information services over the last 20 years. Despite the fact that there have been calls for a replacement of

---

According to Art. 114 EECC, Member States may impose reasonable 'must carry' obligations for the transmission of specified radio and television broadcast where a significant number of end-users of such networks and services use them as their principal means to receive radio and television broadcast channels. However, such obligations shall be imposed only where they are necessary to meet general interest objectives as clearly defined by each Member State, and they shall be proportionate and transparent. In particular (Recital 310) transmissions should be considered only where the lack of such an obligation would cause significant disruption for a significant number of end-users. Cf. on this also CJEU, C87/19, *TV Play Baltic*, in relation to links with Member States cultural policies.

161 Directive (EU) 2015/1535 of the European Parliament and of the Council of 9 September 2015 laying down a procedure for the provision of information in the field of technical regulations and of rules on Information Society services, OJ L 241, 17.9.2015, p. 1–15, Art. 1 para. 1 lit. b.

162 *Cole/Etteldorf/Ullrich*, Cross-border Dissemination of Online Content, p. 171–173.

163 CJEU, C-434/15, *Asociación Profesional Elite Taxi*; C-390/18, *Airbnb Ireland*; C-62/19, *Star Taxi App*.

this general definition it can be considered broad enough for encompass-ing most services offered online. At the same time, the very general formu-lation does not allow by itself to address specific types of ISS reflecting spe-cific circumstances.

Given the breath-taking evolution and diversification in the digital econ-omy, the categorisation of different types of intermediaries according to their functional role has been fraught with difficulties. This categorisation is necessary in order to attribute adequate normative obligations and re-sponsibilities to the variety of actors in the market. In this context, the cat-egorisation of intermediary service providers has been in need of readjust-ment. Falling under the scope of one of the three types of intermediary ser-vice providers defined by the ECD (mere conduit, caching, hosting) trig-gers the conditional liability provisions. Of the three, especially the hosting provider category has been problematic. Various new types of online plat-forms, from social networking and messenger services to content sharing platforms, online marketplaces or collaborative economy platforms, have all sought to benefit from the conditional liability system accorded to host-ing providers. In view of these various new types of platforms and business models, their content management practices and the technologies em-ployed, the application of the neutrality criterion for the availability of the liability protections has met with considerable difficulties. The difficulty in deciding whether the online platforms of today are merely technical and neutral – in the wording of Recital 42 ECD "mere technical, automatic and passive nature" – or active intermediaries has led to widely varying as-sessments and interpretations at Member State level, mainly in the form of diverging court judgements. The guidance by a number of relevant judg-ments of the CJEU has been of limited use in terms of a general approach. The CJEU could only attempt to provide guiding criteria for an assessment on a case to case basis. The currently pending case concerning YouTube deals with exactly this problem in that it addresses a specific type of online content sharing service provider and needs to decide whether its activities make it an "active" platform.[164]

Several approaches have been suggested to remedy this situation. One less intrusive adjustment would see a new DSA clarify the scope of the hosting provider definition by expanding on the meaning of neutral and

---

164 On that aspect Opinion of Advocate General Saugmandsgaard Øe, Joined Cases C-682/18 and C-683/18, *YouTube*, para. 141–168.

active intermediaries.[165] This could be done by incorporating the guidance offered by the CJEU's jurisprudence so far. However, according to this approach the distinction between active and passive intermediaries as the main criterion for the availability of the conditional liability protections would be maintained.[166]

A more far reaching solution would see the hosting provider definition being expanded or replaced, with a view to eschew the differentiation between active and passive intermediaries altogether. This solution would have the advantage of removing ambiguity for the legislator (in case of a transposition need), the competent authorities and, importantly, courts, related to determining the nature and role of technologically complex and multi-layered intermediation practices.[167] This would also provide a better basis for the imposition of positive obligations or responsibilities.[168]

In addition, the scope of application of new provisions for intermediary service providers should take account of the diversity of the different types of hosts that exist today and will emerge over the coming years. First, a definition of hosting providers should be broad and encompassing, limited to a few basic characteristics. This definition could refer simply to hosting providers as ISS whose activity consists of the storage of information provided by a recipient of the service and where that recipient is not acting under the authority or the control of the provider.[169] This solution would discard the active/passive distinction from the scope of the hosting provider protections and could also dispel ongoing unclarity over other intermediation services, like internet registrars, search engines, autocomplete services or online payment services.[170] Secondly, this broad definition should be supplemented by accommodating specific types or sub-categories of hosting providers that have emerged in the past. This would facilitate the allocation of specific duties under sectoral regulations, which

---

165 *Madiega* (EPRS study), Reform of the EU liability regime for online intermediaries, p. 13–14; *De Streel*, in: Blandin, Proceedings of the Workshop on "E-commerce rules, fit for the digital age", p. 10.

166 *Nordemann*, Internal Market for digital services: Responsibilities and duties of care of providers of digital services.

167 *Nölke*, in: Blandin, Proceedings of the Workshop on "E-commerce rules, fit for the digital age", p. 11.

168 *Smith*, Enforcement and Cooperation between Member States, p. 30.

169 On this proposal *Ullrich*, Unlawful Content Online: Towards a New Regulatory Framework for Online Platforms, p. 398.

170 *De Streel/Husovec*, The e-commerce Directive as the cornerstone of the Internal Market, p. 43.

take account of distinct business models and intermediation practices and do not primarily hinge on the premise that the intermediary needs to be passive and merely technical. This sectoral specification could also include, where appropriate, considerations and assessments about the degree of editorial involvement and influence of the intermediary during the intermediation process, which is an important and controversially discussed issue with current content curation and recommender systems.[171] Such an approach would also reinforce the technological neutrality of the new regime.[172]

The new act could either incorporate these categories under its horizontal remit or leave room for the formulation of new hosting provider categories and respective duties in sectoral legislation in the form of lex specialis. The EU has in recent years already established such new categories of intermediaries as presented above: Under the AVMSD, VSPs have been established; the DSMD defines OCSSPs, although the application of the ECD protections for intermediaries is conditional; the Regulation on the marketing and use of explosives precursors[173] and the Omnibus Directive[174] define and establish specific obligations for online marketplaces; the P2B Regulation defines and establishes specific due diligence obligations on online intermediation services and on online search engines (Art. 6– 12). Further categories could be added through vertical, sectoral acts as necessary.

It appears as necessary to create a new category of "content platforms/ intermediaries", which captures providers that act as intermediaries between content producers and users. These content intermediaries should be distinguished from other intermediaries that do not primarily engage in the intermediation of content but operate, for example, e-commerce or sharing services. Content dissemination has become the centrepiece of

---

171 *Cobbe/Singh*, in: EJLT, 10 (3), 2019.
172 European Parliament resolution of 20 October 2020 with recommendations to the Commission on the Digital Services Act: Improving the functioning of the Single Market (2020/2018(INL)), no. 14.
173 Regulation (EU) 2019/1148 of the European Parliament and of the Council of 20 June 2019 on the marketing and use of explosives precursors, amending Regulation (EC) No 1907/2006 and repealing Regulation (EU) No 98/2013, OJ L 186, 11.7.2019, p. 1–20, Art. 9.
174 Directive (EU) 2019/2161 of the European Parliament and of the Council of 27 November 2019 amending Council Directive 93/13/EEC and Directives 98/6/EC, 2005/29/EC and 2011/83/EU of the European Parliament and of the Council as regards the better enforcement and modernisation of Union consumer protection rules, OJ L 328, 18.12.2019, p. 7–28 ('Omnibus Directive').

many intermediaries' business models, which calls for specific regulatory provisions due to the high relevance of this activity in a societal context. The definitions for sub-categories of intermediaries should be subject to regular review. Such a periodic evaluation of the definitions could either take place as part of the legislative act review – thus, however, it would be less flexible – or by competent bodies authorised to do so in giving guidance of how to apply the definition in practice, e.g. by listing criteria which constitute elements of the definition. This would allow for a review of new types of services to see whether they could at all qualify as one of the specific categories and, if so, to indicate which aspects of it result in fulfilling the given criteria.

Furthermore, in the interest of increased transparency for providers, but also for the users of their services, relevant information about services falling under such specific categories should be made available. The intermediaries, for example, would be under an obligation to register within their country of establishment and disclose under which category of intermediary they fall. This registration would be subject to evaluation by the competent supervisory authority or the listing could be organised by an independent body. In addition, these lists of content intermediaries which fall under the definition, should also include an indication of jurisdiction of a specific Member State (or the fact that they are established outside the Union). It should be made publicly available in a comparable way as is foreseen for jurisdiction information concerning audiovisual media services providers in Art. 2 para. 5 lit. b) AVMSD and concerning VSP providers in Art. 28a para. 6 AVMSD.

The scope of application should also provide room to include, on the one side, facilitations for small- and medium-sized companies[175] and, on the other side, heavier obligations for larger players. The differentiation does not necessarily have to be done along the lines of market power evaluating economic factors but ensure that the different impact of providers can also be reflected. Although such differentiation could be done upfront through the horizontal provisions applicable to all intermediary service providers and by limiting the personal scope in excluding certain types ("sizes") of providers, another solution should be aimed for. In the substantive rules there could be exemptions for certain types of providers which fulfil the basic definition and therefore should be bound by the core

---

175 *Smit*, SME focus – Long-term strategy for the European industrial future, in particular p. 37 et seq., who displays the barriers SMEs are facing by undertaking the digital transition, in particular highlighting costs for legal compliance.

elements of the rules, such as treatment of illegal content, but should be liberated from a framework that would be overburdening considering their capabilities compared to more significant market participants. This could concern, e.g., non-profit types of services or allow taking economic disparities into account. The advantage of such a graduated approach or staggered provisions will be further discussed in the section on liability conditions and obligations of intermediary service providers below.

2. DSA Approach

The personal scope of application, as discussed here, is covered by Recitals 5 to 18 and Articles 1 to 5 of the DSA Proposal. These passages define and explain the type of intermediary services to which the future framework would apply. Articles 1 to 2 constitute Chapter I, while Articles 3 to 5, which regulate the criteria for the availability of the liability exemptions for the different types of intermediary services, have been extracted from Articles 12 to 14 ECD to Chapter II of the Proposal.

The DSA leaves largely unchanged the relation between (more specific) intermediary services as under the ECD and the (more general) information society services under the Technical Standards and Regulations Directive.[176] However, Recital 6 provides a clarification that the future DSA would not apply to products or services intermediated through intermediary services. It specifically refers to situations where intermediary services are not free standing in the sense that they are an integral part of another service. This appears to confirm the above-mentioned jurisprudence of the CJEU, notably on collaborative economy platforms, which consequently can be addressed in separate rulesets of the EU or Member States.

Art. 1 para. 4 sets out the (new) extended territorial scope of the DSA. Contrary to the ECD it will also apply to those intermediary services that are not established in the EU but are providing services in the internal market in a way that demonstrates a substantial connection to the EU (Recital 7). With that the reach of the rules would become extraterritorial in the sense that it is the market participation that is decisive and not the location of the provider; therefore "local" (EU) rules would also apply to "foreign" (third country) undertakings. This resembles the approach chosen in the GDPR (Art. 3 para. 2). Recital 8 recalls the familiar methodology and criteria on targeting, which is based on the Brussels I Regulation

---

176 Clearly expressed also in Recital 5.

and international private law rules and has been supported through CJEU case law,[177] to determine the existence of a substantial connection to the EU.[178]

The DSA will not interfere with specific provisions laid down in current and future sectoral provisions. As per Art. 1 para. 5, this would apply to the ECD, the AVMSD, copyright and related rights law, the future TERREG (or as mentioned in the DSA Proposal "TCO") and E-evidence Regulation and Directive, the Regulation on the marketing and use of explosives precursors, the P2B Regulation, the consumer protection and product safety acquis and the GDPR/e-Privacy Directive.

The categorisation of intermediary services providers remains unchanged. The DSA wraps up this categorisation by offering a definition of intermediary services in Art. 2 lit. f, which comprises the three existing categories of mere conduits, caching services and hosting providers and is at the same time limited ("means one of the following ...") to only those three categories. The definitions of these three categories in Articles 3, 4 and 5 DSA hardly vary from those offered in the respective Art. 12 para. 1, 13 para. 1 and 14 para. 1 of the ECD[179]. The DSA thereby now disentangles the definitions of these three categories from the conditional liability exemptions, which was the only place in the ECD where they could be found. Therefore, a hosting service is now plainly defined as a "service that consists of the storage of information provided by, and at the request of, a recipient of the service" in Art. 2 lit. f. Nonetheless, this is a summarised formulation as it is the (continued) basis for the liability exemption rule for hosting providers in Art. 5 DSA. Recital 27 acknowledges the growing diversity of different types of intermediaries, especially those that intervene at an infrastructural level in order to improve the transmission and storage of data in the increasingly complex and busy internet system. The Recital opens the possibility for new services or those so far not in the focus as intermediary services to find refuge under the liability protections: content delivery networks, internet registries, messaging services, digital certificate authorities or Voice over IP services are mentioned, amongst others. The

---

177 CJEU, Joined Cases C-585/08 and C-144/09, *Pammer and Hotel Alpenhof*, para. 83, 84.
178 Cf. similarly Recital 23 GDPR; for the case of "targeting" by on-demand audiovisual media services cf. Recital 38 AVMSD.
179 Art. 5 para. lit. a and b use the term "illegal content" instead of "illegal information" as under Art. 14 para. 1 lit. a and b ECD.

Recital underlines that the liability exemptions only apply if they actually fulfil all criteria of one of the three categories.

However, the DSA introduces a new subcategory of hosting providers in Art. 2 lit. h. Online platforms are defined as those hosting services that store and disseminate information to the public and where that activity constitutes the core activity. Service providers where the information storage and its dissemination to the public are mere ancillary activities that would not be usable without the main service in which they are integrated would not be concerned by this new definition. Recital 13 provides as a clarifying example of such an ancillary public information dissemination service the comments function of an online newspaper, whose main activity relates to the publication of information under its editorial responsibility. However, this exemption would not apply to any bad faith integration of information storage and dissemination into another service that is aimed at avoiding the application of the Regulation. Accordingly, Recital 13 confirms that the creation of the new subcategory of "online platforms" was motivated by their particular characteristics and that it includes namely social networks and online marketplaces within its scope. It is the combination of storage on request of recipients of the service with the dissemination of that information to the public that is the distinctive element. By contrast, the concept of public dissemination would not apply to communication within closed groups with a finite number of pre-determined persons.

The DSA also retains the current conditional exemption from liability for intermediary services of the ECD. The Commission notes in Recital 16 that this system has allowed new intermediary services to emerge and grow and should therefore remain unchanged. At the same time it recognises the diverging interpretations of the horizontal neutrality condition at Member State level and the need to provide clarification of its application along the case law established by the CJEU. Recital 18 reminds of the (unchanged) conditions for the availability of the liability protections for neutrally provided intermediary services that process the information provided by the recipient of the service in a merely technical and automatic way (see similarly formulated the Recital 42 ECD). It further specifies that the exemption would not be available where the intermediary service itself has provided the information or where it was developed under its editorial responsibility. These (unchanged) principles for liability exemptions are also the foundation of the existing Articles 12, 13 and 14 ECD, which have been copied in a nearly identical fashion into Articles 3, 4 and 5 of the new DSA. The important difference to the ECD is that the liability exemptions, by virtue of them being part of a Regulation, would now be directly and equally applicable in Member States..

Recital 20 (in continuation of Recital 44 ECD) further clarifies the neutrality condition by stating that those intermediaries that collaborate with service recipients deliberately in the pursuit of hosting and disseminating illegal content would not be considered as neutral. But the DSA gives no further clarification on the neutrality criterion. Recital 22 merely offers more guidance (considering especially the lack of any further precision in the Recitals of the ECD) on the actual knowledge concept which will be further discussed in the next section of this study.

3. Assessment

The DSA has left the hierarchical relation between intermediary services and ISS largely unchanged. However, given the importance and significance of online intermediaries, it proposes to remove the corresponding passages concerning the liability from the ECD and dedicate an entirely new piece of legislation, the DSA, to their (privileged) liabilities and new responsibilities. Although the new focus on the question of liability is to be welcomed, the simple "transplant" from a Directive to a (proposed) Regulation itself is less so. The DSA would as a Regulation potentially overcome differing national transpositions and understandings of those different categories. But this would only be potentially the case, because the explanations are not of a kind that would remove the possibility of different regulatory approaches by the supervisory authorities or bodies and, subsequently, of different interpretations by national courts, yet with the difference that it is more likely that a speedy clarification by the CJEU in cases of doubt could be achieved, which would then answer the question with authority for all Member States. Although a quicker clarification is likely, this would, however, not change the continuing individual case law on specific issues, which was also previously binding for the Member States under the Directive as the CJEU has the final authority in interpreting EU law. But by retaining the existing categorisation of intermediaries under the ECD into mere conduits, caching and hosting services, the Commission in its Proposal for the DSA resisted calls that advocated for a more differentiated categorisation at the horizontal level in order to clarify the availability of the liability protections for new business models and the conditions under which the liability exemption is precluded.

The Impact Assessment shows that the Commission did consider this argument in detail. It concludes that the hosting provider definition, which it retained, provides sufficient legal certainty in order to ensure its application to new types of services such as online media sharing platforms, social networking sites, various cloud services (such as Infrastructure as a Service (IaaS) and Platform as a Service (PaaS) cloud computing services), collaborative platforms and sharing economy models as well as search and rating and reviews engines.[180] However, the document acknowledges "grey areas" with regards to the application of the intermediary service categories. Content delivery networks, cloud computing services or live streaming providers are specifically mentioned. Domain name registries and "interpersonal communications services" (web-based messaging services such as WhatsApp) are cited as examples.[181] The apparent solution of the DSA is therefore the above-mentioned Recital 27, which can be interpreted as an attempt to provide a degree of certainty regarding new ISS and those whose business models and underlying technologies have been evolving. Whether this offers the legal certainty with regards to innovative new services remains to be seen. The Commission refers to past CJEU jurisprudence on online marketplaces, search engines and social network sites as a confirmation of the adaptability and openness of the ECD's hosting service provider definition.[182] This would imply a future claim on the CJEU to adjudicate in these matters for new types of services. This line of argument also discards the fact that diverging assessments of national courts on the availability of the hosting defence have been ongoing to this day, despite the allegedly clarifying role of the CJEU.[183] Even though this may change if, indeed, at the end the instrument is a Regulation, it would still be proof of the fact that the very general description of hosting services is not as easy to narrow down or apply in specific cases as seems to be suggested in the documents accompanying the Proposal.

Providing at least the categories as separate definition of the new (but actually old) intermediary service provider types, thus disentangling the conditional liability exemptions from the providers themselves, could be bene-

---

180 European Commission, Commission Staff Working Document – Impact Assessment Report, Annexes accompanying the DSA Proposal, SWD(2020) 348 final, Part 2, https://ec.europa.eu/digital-single-market/en/news/impact-assessment-digital-services-act, p. 170–172.

181 Ibid., p. 172–181.

182 Ibid., p. 170–171.

183 *Cole/Etteldorf/Ullrich*, Cross-border Dissemination of Online Content, p. 190–192.

ficial. In principle, this new clarity may go a long way to offering certainty and predictability for new business models insofar a decision about their falling under one of the categories can be made irrespective of the question of liability. Nonetheless, sticking to exactly the same categories seems to leave unanswered the need for a clarification of certain specific types of intermediaries.

For such a specific type, online platforms, the only new sub-category of hosting services was introduced in the DSA. It appears that this additional categorisation of intermediary services is mainly done in view of different due diligence obligations that correspond to the size and nature of the services. This is even more evident for the case of the newly introduced category of "very large online platforms" (VLOP): they are not separately defined in Art. 2, but the criteria for calculating whether an online platform is to be classified as a VLOP are laid down in Art. 25 and Recitals 53 to 55 under the section concerning "Additional Obligations" for VLOPs to "manage systemic risks". Therefore this new "category", which is not a separate category but a sub-category of online platforms, is discussed further below.[184]

The new categorisation of online platforms as content disseminators with added obligations is to be welcomed given that the DSA is meant to address the new risks to individuals and society which result from the increased use of new intermediary services, such as social networks or marketplaces (Recital 1).[185] In this respect the new category is clearly linked to the perceived risks that emanate from the activities of these new different types of intermediaries. In addition, the DSA appears to be in principle open with regards to additional obligations defined by sectoral law, which the DSA complements (Recital 9) or applies to without prejudice (Recital 10). The practical interlinkage between the general obligations set by the DSA and the sectoral acts defined in those Recitals and Art. 1 may still bear potential for debate, especially if they impose potentially conflicting requirements. Nonetheless, the approach of integrating the new DSA into the existing network of secondary law is necessary and aims to respect the need for sectoral solutions besides the overarching rules of the DSA. In

---

184 The powers the Commission assigns to itself in the Proposal (Art. 25 para. 2 and 3) to further detail the methodology for calculation in delegated acts should be critically assessed; cf. on this also *Ukrow*, Die Vorschläge der EU-Kommission für einen Digital Services Act und einen Digital Markets Act, p. 16 et seq.

185 Cf. also *Ukrow*, Die Vorschläge der EU-Kommission für einen Digital Services Act und einen Digital Markets Act, p. 15.

addition, what is still needed is a further clarification towards the continued relevance of Member State law and the possibility of Member States to legislate for aims not covered by the DSA or other sectoral law (see already Chapter E.I.3).[186]

The Commission left untouched the basic condition for the availability of the liability defence for hosting providers – the neutrality requirement. Although this relates to the question of whether a provider actually is more involved in the content dissemination than just by its neutral "forwarding", by being part of the definition of a hosting provider it has been reinforced. The DSA admits the need for providing clarification on the question of neutrality, but the result is not entirely convincing. The demarcation of editorial responsibility for content from automated arrangement, organisation and recommendation appears to go into the direction of the recent Opinion of AG Saugmannsgaard Øe in the joined cases of YouTube/Cyando,[187] a case for which the judgment of the CJEU is still pending. Apart from that, the CJEU guidance that is incorporated in its substance into Recital 18 recites the familiar passages from the 2010 and 2011 cases of Google France[188] and L'Oréal v. eBay[189] on the criteria that determine when an intermediary plays "an active role of such a kind as to give it knowledge of, or control over, the data" stored. The harmonising effect of these judgements, which now date back ten years, has been debated controversially ever since.[190] It is doubtful whether this quite marginal clarification is really future proof, in particular as Recital 18 limits the applications of the passive/active distinction to the finding of editorial responsibility. In this Proposal the intended clarification can therefore be seen as potentially even widening the intermediary liability exemption. In the context of more elaborate due diligence and transparency obligations (see further on these below) this may be regarded as useful in order to address only those providers that play a crucial role with those additional obligations. But, as stated above, this approach still does not address other

---

186 Cf. on this aspect *Ukrow*, Die Vorschläge der EU-Kommission für einen Digital Services Act und einen Digital Markets Act, p. 7 et seq.
187 Opinion of Advocate General Saugmandsgaard Øe, Joined Cases C-682/18 and C-683/18, *Google and Cyando*, para. 160–161.
188 CJEU, C-236/08, *Google France and Google*, para. 120.
189 CJEU, C-324/09, *L'Oréal and Others*, para. 116.
190 *van Eecke*, in: Common Market L. Rev., 48 (5), 2011, 1455, 1455 et seq.; *Stalla-Bourdillon/Thorburn*, "The scandal of intermediary: Acknowledging the both/and dispensation for regulating hybrid actors", in: Petkova/Ojanen (eds.), 140, 156–159.

'active roles' outside editorial responsibility. In the context of the debate over the impact of content curation and recommender systems on platform's knowledge, control and even intent,[191] the proposed text in Art. 5 may be of limited use and continue to provoke diverging court rulings. The Commission chose not to go down a more audacious path of challenging the increasingly blurred distinction of passive and active hosts and put the allocation of new obligations on a wider footing that overcomes this distinction.[192] This is an aspect that should be discussed intensively in the legislative procedure.

Finally, the approach of differentiating obligations to be imposed on online platforms, depending on their impact while not excluding certain types of platforms due to their size entirely from the scope of application, makes the right balance possible. On the one hand, according to Art. 16, micro and small enterprises – and for that purpose relying on the existing Commission Recommendation 2003/361/EC[193] –are excluded from having to fulfil certain obligations; on the other hand, an additional layer of obligations is introduced for larger platforms. These VLOPs are described in Art. 25 and Recitals 53 to 55 and are regarded to constitute especially high risks due to their position on the market, which justifies imposing an increased burden on them. With this approach there is the potential of allowing market development with new entrants and smaller sized alternative providers while acknowledging the actual current structure of the market and addressing the dominant players adequately.

IV. Liability Privilege Regime

1. Starting Point

The current intermediary liability framework under the ECD has focused on harmonising the exemptions for (secondary) liability. Once an interme-

---

191 *Cobbe/Singh*, in: EJLT, 10 (3), 2019; *Lavi*, in: JETLaw, 21 (1), 2018; *Oster*, in: Legal Studies, 35, 2015, 348, 348 et seq.

192 On such a potential expansion e.g. *Stalla-Bourdillon/Thorburn*, "The scandal of intermediary: Acknowledging the both/and dispensation for regulating hybrid actors", in: Petkova/Ojanen (eds.), 140, 156–159.; *Helberger/Pierson/Poell*, in: The Information Society, 34, 2018, 1, 2.

193 Commission Recommendation 2003/361/EC of 6 May 2003 concerning the definition of micro, small and medium-sized enterprises, OJ L 124, 20.5.2003, p. 36.

diary falls outside the liability exemptions, Member States will apply their own national provisions that regulate the liability of intermediaries. However, the original aim of promoting innovation through wide reaching and evenly applied generous liability privileges has met with limited success. In fact, new intermediary service providers have seen the generous exemptions in connection with the neutrality condition as a discouragement from engaging themselves more actively and more openly in preventive efforts to fight illegal content, because they fear they could thus forfeit their liability exemptions. This system has also influenced the approach of enforcement authorities generally, but also specifically when they are concerned with overseeing content dissemination, being in a difficult position when considering addressing such providers.

There are several issues with the current regime of intermediary liability exemptions that would need to be readjusted, and in doing so the liability privilege regime needs to be looked at through an entirely different lens than when it was introduced.

For one, the criteria that determine the liability exemptions for information hosts have been fraught with difficulty in their application. The condition of actual knowledge of illegal content or activity (Art. 14 para. 1 lit. a ECD), which triggers the obligation to remove or disable access to this kind of information, expeditiously has been interpreted differently across the EU.[194] It has become common practice that a notification received by the intermediary could lead to such actual knowledge. However, since notice and action procedures have not been harmonised, the exact scope of sufficiently detailed notice that would trigger actual knowledge in the meaning of the provision has varied across the Member States. Furthermore, the concept of awareness of facts and circumstances that indicate illegal activity has led to largely reactive or concealed practices of online platforms vis-à-vis illegal content. The term "actual knowledge" should therefore be better defined by attaching specific procedures and obligations to it. These procedures could then also provide clarification on the term "expeditious removal".

Secondly, the largely reactive liability exemption conditions of actual knowledge and expeditious removal have led to an uneven enforcement landscape compared to content disseminated through traditional media or other forms of dissemination. Users are therefore exposed to more harms

---

194 *Cole/Etteldorf/Ullrich*, Cross-border Dissemination of Online Content p. 192–194; *Ullrich*, Unlawful Content Online: Towards a New Regulatory Framework for Online Platforms, p. 141–151.

and violation of fundamental rights when accessing content through intermediaries. Achieving a comparable level of user protection online as offline in editorial and other content would necessitate rebalancing the current regime of liability exemptions for content intermediaries. In this context the liability exemption regime should go beyond mere reactive removal obligations. These obligations should clarify the scope of proactive measures along due care requirements or preventive injunctions, which are already an option under the current ECD (Art. 14 para. 3 and its accompanying Recital 42).

Thirdly, the application of these due care and other proactive obligations, such as preventive injunctions by courts or authorities, which are also possible under the ECD, has been hampered by unclarity over whether and when they conflict with the prohibition of a general monitoring obligation of Art. 15 ECD.[195] While the intent of this prohibition is clear and necessary, its meaning should at the very least be clarified in order to allow for an effective and proportional engagement of intermediaries, in particular those disseminating content, in the fight against illegal content.[196] It has also been argued that this provision overall does not serve its purpose any longer and the fundamental rights protected by it can be more effectively safeguarded by other means.[197] In addition, Art. 15 ECD could be read as an over-emphasis of freedom of speech in relation to safeguarding rights of others and more generally objective values, which would not correspond to the need for more equitable balancing of fundamental rights.[198]

---

195 *Cole/Etteldorf/Ullrich*, Cross-border Dissemination of Online Content, p. 194–200.

196 It appears counterproductive to leave it to the CJEU to provide future clarifications on when this rule does not collide with measures to be adopted by providers according to national court orders, such as was done in *UPC Telekabel* (C-314/12) or *Glawischnig* (C-18/18). These rulings due to their nature can only have a limited harmonising effect.

197 *Ullrich*, Unlawful Content Online: Towards a New Regulatory Framework for Online Platforms, p. 398. These other means are notably the safeguards that already exist in legal provisions that govern the specific content and/or illegal activity in question. For example, sectoral rules, like the IPR Enforcement Directive (2004/48/EC, Art. 3) or the Infosoc Directive (2001/29/EC, Art. 8), contain safeguards with regards to injunctions targeted at intermediaries used by third parties for IP infringements.

198 *Smith*, Enforcement and cooperation between Member States, p. 33. In that sense the situation in Europe is entirely different to the approach in the U.S. where the liability privilege for intermediaries was first introduced in view of this diverging constitutional standard of free speech regulation; *Ullrich*, Unlaw-

The current structure of conditional liability privileges should therefore be retained, but its substance should be adjusted. Clarified conditions of actual knowledge and expeditious removal should be supplemented by a graduated system of obligations. The graduated obligations would act as additional conditions for the exemption from liability. Compliance with these obligations would ensure the continued availability of exemptions from liability.

The staggered system of liability exemption conditions would focus on hosting services. It is submitted that, at a basic level, graduated (reactive) obligations already exist with the current distinctions between conduit, caching and hosting services. Within the category of hosting services additional obligations could be allocated to platforms according to their degree of involvement in content dissemination. Given the prominence of harms to public interests and fundamental rights that have been emanating from the practices of online content platforms, an allocation of enhanced obligations would appear to have priority. Specific obligations could be formulated for online content platforms or online marketplaces. Differentiated obligations and responsibilities could also be tied to the severity of harm caused by content, especially the degree of manifest illegality. Other categorisations could take account of the size and economic power of platforms or the degree to which they are involved in the organisation of content through curation or algorithmic recommender and sorting systems.

2. DSA Approach

The liability of information society providers is dealt with in Chapter II, which encompasses Articles 3–9 of the new act. The Proposal leaves the current system of largely reactive conditions for the safe harbour protections unchanged but adds clarifications on the liability conditions with regards to voluntary proactive obligations (Art. 6), the prohibition of general monitoring obligations (Art. 7) and reactive obligations relating to authority orders to act against illegal content (Art. 8) and to disclose information (Art. 9).

Articles 3, 4 and 5 for conduits, caching services and hosts are almost one-to-one renditions of Articles 12, 13 and 14 of the ECD, which in turn would be deleted from there. The main difference in formulation concerns

---

ful Content Online: Towards a New Regulatory Framework for Online Platforms, p. 163–164.

the different type of instrument in which they would be included: the previous formulation concerned an obligation of the Member States to ensure that within the exemptions there would be no liability of the intermediaries, while now these exemptions would be directly granted though the proposed DSA, without putting such an obligation on Member States. In addition, the provision of Art. 14 on hosting services is partly amended in the new Art. 5. The cornerstone conditions of the liability exemptions for hosting service providers, i.e. actual knowledge and expeditious removal, have therefore been carried over into the proposed new act. However, there are some clarifications made. Recital 22 now explains that actual knowledge could be gained through notices, which are submitted by individuals or entities according to the requirements laid down in Art. 14 DSA Proposal concerning "notice and action mechanisms". Recital 22 nevertheless specifies – with language reminiscent of the *L'Oreal v. eBay*[199] ruling of the CJEU – that such notices have to be sufficiently precise and substantiated in order to allow a diligent economic operator to take action against the content in question. Secondly, the Recital specifies that hosting providers may obtain actual knowledge also through investigations conducted on their own initiative. Apart from that, Art. 5 retains the possibility of authorities or courts to issue orders aimed at terminating or preventing an infringement; this has again been done by keeping nearly the same wording as previously, except for the deletion (at this point) of the authorisation addressed to Member States allowing them to establish "procedures governing the removal or disabling of access to information". This makes sense in view of the mandatory notice and action procedures that are now imposed through Art. 14 of the DSA Proposal.

Para. 3 of Art. 5 DSA Proposal now provides an exclusion from the liability exemptions under consumer law for online marketplaces that fail to inform consumers clearly about which party provided a service or product offered to them via their platform.

Art. 6 introduces a 'Good Samaritan' clause that assures the continued availability of the liability exemptions for those providers that conduct "voluntary own-initiative investigations" and take measures that are aimed at detecting, identifying and removing illegal content in order to "comply with the requirements of Union law", which would include the expectations laid down in the DSA.

The prohibition of general monitoring has been carried over virtually unchanged from Art. 15 para. 1 of the ECD to the new Art. 7, again with

---

199 CJEU, C-324/09, *L'Oréal and Others*, para. 122.

the above-mentioned technical change as it is now in a Proposal for a Regulation and in this case in addition with a change of style of the language used. Recital 28 tries to elucidate by stating that monitoring obligations relating to a specific case are allowed, in that sense continuing the explanation of Recital 47 ECD. Recital 28 further states that orders by national authorities that comply with national legislation and the conditions laid down in the proposed DSA are still possible. The Recital also strengthens the intention to steer clear of any general monitoring obligation by instructing that nothing in the proposed act should be construed in such a way. In addition, it refutes any attempts to interpret the new act in a way that imposes a general obligation on providers to take proactive measures with regards to illegal content. Meanwhile the possibilities accorded to the Member States to impose information obligations on providers regarding illegal activities and the identification of users (Art. 15 para. 2 ECD) have been absorbed (and described in much more detail) by wider information obligations in Art. 9 and reporting obligations imposed in Chapter III.

Irrespective of the rule in Art. 7, Articles 8 and 9 propose additional conditions to the liability exemptions. First, intermediary service providers need to take action on orders regarding specific items of illegal content and inform the issuing authorities without delay of the actions taken and the time when these were taken. For the orders to be actionable they need to contain a statement of reasons, URL(s) and, where necessary, other specifying information enabling the identification of the content as well as information about redress opportunities' given to the provider and the recipient of the service (the uploader) concerned. They also need to specify the territorial scope, be drafted in the language declared by the service provider and be delivered to the designated point of contact of the providers (see Art. 10 in the next section). This is without prejudice to procedural criminal requirements under national and EU law. Further details are laid down in Recitals 29 to 31.

Secondly, Art. 9 obliges providers to react to orders to provide specific information about one or more specific individual recipients of the service (users). Again, these orders need to fulfil certain requirements: they must contain a statement of reasons of the request and the redress available; the provider cannot be asked to provide information that is not already collected by them as part of their service; and the order must be drafted in the declared language of the provider. Recital 32 specifically excludes any information requests for aggregate information for statistical purposes or policy-making. It further clarifies that providers need to react to orders against illegal content and information requests from any competent national or judicial authority in the EU, i.e. even when this authority is outside their country of establishment. This is one reason why the DSA Proposal makes prescriptions on the content and procedural aspects of these orders (Recital 29 and 30) and clarifies their territorial reach (Recital 31). Providers should be able to deal with these orders effectively and efficiently and not be exposed to varying formats and procedural rules.

3. Assessment

The Commission kept the current generous conditions for exemptions from liability virtually unchanged in its Proposal, narrowing them only marginally with obligations to react to authority orders against specific illegal content and information orders about specific users. The due diligence obligations formulated in Chapter III, which will be discussed in the next section, apply in addition to, and independently of the liability exemptions regime and thereby constitute an additional layer of responsibility of providers that is separate from the question of their liability.

As can be derived from the Impact Assessment of the proposed act, the Commission had evaluated and discarded several other regulatory options.[200] Amongst these were options to impose additional due care or diligence obligations as *part of* the conditional regime for liability exemption or to replace the existing conditional liability regime entirely with positive obligations, which in case of non-compliance with these obligations would result in liability. Several commentators had already explored these kinds of responsibility systems.[201] The Commission noted in its Impact Assessment that incorporating additional due diligence or duty of care obligations into the current conditional liability exemptions could have led to providers making a calculated choice of 'opting' for non-compliance and submitting themselves to national liability charges if these are less expensive and onerous.[202] Meanwhile the option of creating exclusively positive obligations was discarded due the Commission's view of a potential con-

---

200 European Commission, DSA Proposal Impact Assessment Part 2, p. 162–166.

201 *Smith*, Enforcement and Cooperation between Member States, p. 30–34; *de Streel et al*, Online Platforms' Moderation of Illegal Content Online; *Nölke*, in: Blandin, Proceedings of the Workshop on "E-commerce rules, fit for the digital age", p. 11; *Quintel/Ullrich*, "Self-Regulation of Fundamental Rights? The EU Code of Conduct on Hate Speech, related initiatives and beyond", in: Petkova/Ojanen (eds.), 182, 193–195.

202 European Commission, DSA Proposal Impact Assessment Part 2, p. 165–166.

flict with the principles of proportionality and subsidiarity.[203] The now proposed combination of the liability privilege with separate, free-standing obligations and duties of providers has without doubt its advantages. First, it reflects the crucial position of content intermediaries in facilitating the exercise of fundamental rights. Secondly, it highlights at the same time their centrality in the fight against illegal online content by allocating separate obligations. Thirdly, the option chosen provides more clarity for those intermediaries that engage in activities that straddle the border between neutrality and "editorial control", such as certain types of content curation, by imposing clear responsibilities irrespective of the liability exemption. Whether the currently proposed separate obligations are capable to interfere with national (secondary) liability for intermediaries if these do not fulfil the conditions for exemptions remains to be seen. Also, the DSA Proposal would not allow for making compliance with the obligations and duties of Chapter III conditional for intermediaries to continuously profit from the liability exemption. It would only foresee sanctions, regardless of whether an intermediary is found liable for information or content or not. The exact link between the two pillars 'liability exemption' and 'compliance with obligations' would need to be further discussed.

The clarifications offered for the retained liability exemptions regime, namely on the occurrence of actual knowledge, are welcome and needed, especially since this will be backed by harmonised notice and action procedures in Art. 14 (discussed below). This fits conceptually with the new "Good Samaritan" wording in Art. 6, which protects intermediaries that voluntarily engage in proactive measures to prevent illegal content against disqualification from the liability exemptions. The belated addition of this original U.S. law principle (although not in the broad approach as there) to the proposed DSA may provide legal certainty. Whether it actively encourages responsible behaviour is, however, doubtful. Today, the fact that especially large platforms engage in proactive enforcement is undisputed and in their own interest. By contrast it is the transparency over the criteria of their proactive enforcement and its general compliance with public interests and fundamental values that is the much thornier issue. It is, however, also clear that failure to act on actual knowledge gained through such good faith investigations would incur liability. Art. 6 has therefore merely a reassuring function. It may be useful for intermediaries, especially for hosting services that do not face enhanced obligations as VLOPs.

---

203 Ibid., p. 161–162.

The retention of the prohibition of general monitoring was expected, because this provision is widely regarded as an important safeguard for fundamental rights. However, the blank assertion that nothing in the proposed act should be construed as to impose a general obligation to monitor or take proactive measures would appear rather to be a matter for courts to decide based on concrete facts at hand and not in such a bold statement. In addition, it is doubtful whether the qualification offered in Recital 28 that general monitoring would not cover any monitoring obligations in specific cases will provide the clarification needed and widely demanded.[204] The formulation in Recital 28 is unlikely to defuse the debate over whether monitoring in a specific case (or for specific content) necessitates a monitoring of all content. As a compromise, an affirmation of stay-down obligations could have been made that ties into CJEU case law. This could then be supplemented by a declaration that broader specific measures (as attempted in C-18/18, *Glawischnig-Piesczek*) would need to be in accordance with fundamental rights and, where available, sectoral rules that regulate the proportionality of such obligations. Different kind of content and practices triggers different fundamental rights mixes which should influence the scope of proactive (monitoring/filtering) measures. This was made, for example, clear by the iterations of AG Szpunar in *Glawischnig-Piesczek*, who stated that preventive measures imposed on intermediaries in cases of intellectual property infringements may have a different scope than those in cases involving defamation.[205] Case law of the CJEU has not been conclusive or easily applicable in this matter. In lack of a definition or consensus understanding of what (general) monitoring is, monitoring in a specific case may not be the answer that will solve this problem. On the other hand, in consequence of the interpretation by the CJEU of the currently already existing provisions of the ECD it is evident that measures by providers must be conceivable that have the effect of "keeping down" content once identified as illegal.

The fact that new obligations to react to authority orders concerning illegal content and to information orders were added as basic conditions for the availability of the liability exemptions (in Articles 8 and 9) shows the need to enable courts and authorities to require timely and consistent reactions especially in urgent cases. It is certainly an important development that national authorities may now file orders directly to providers regard-

---

204 Cf. on this aspect *Cole/Etteldorf/Ullrich*, Cross-border Dissemination of Online Content, p. 194–200.

205 CJEU, C-18/18, *Glawischnig-Piesczek*, para. 68–71.

less of where they are established within the EU. This is in the interest of achieving more timely removals and information in a notoriously fast moving area in which risks through cross-platform propagation of illegal content may rise exponentially with time. Importantly, these obligations are without prejudice to sectoral provisions, as for example the one hour reaction time to removal orders as foreseen by the TERREG Proposal (Recital 30) or national law in this respect (Recital 29). It will certainly be interesting to see how authorities will assess whether content that is illegal in their jurisdiction would also constitute illegality in other Member States as stated in Recital 31. However, this is not a matter of the liability exemptions scheme but of regulatory co-operation (see below) and a welcome addition in order to allow for a more effective cross-border enforcement of the law.

Art. 9 on information orders helpfully addresses a key demand by authorities and other stakeholders to define the circumstances under which intermediaries become liable for illegal user content if they do not disclose the identity of that user to supervising bodies in order for them to be able to take action. This will help improve enforcement efficacy against users that act in violation of the law. Making these liability exception conditions applicable to all intermediaries is a positive recognition that even technical services, such as IAPs, which are not the primary addressee for enforcement measures against illegal content dissemination, can be the target of actions taken by competent bodies.

Nevertheless, the positioning of the obligations to react to authority and court orders on illegal content and on information requests throws up additional questions. Articles 8 and 9 are systematically part of the (new) conditional liability exemptions regime. This can mean that competent authorities could pursue unresponsive intermediary service providers under the (not harmonised) liability rules of their respective national regimes for exactly that lack of responsiveness to the orders. This approach is not contradicted by Recital 17, which states that the conditions set down in Chapter II are merely meant to harmonise the liability exemptions but not to determine whether a provider can be held liable. The question of liability as is underlined in the Recital derives from applicable EU or national laws. If non-responsiveness to an order to act against illegal content or to provide relevant information is regarded as a basis for establishing liability according to such rules, then the liability exemptions do not prevent this. In addition, enforcement powers, as foreseen in Art. 41 para. 2 of the Proposal, allow the imposition of fines for violations of any obligation under the proposed Regulation. However, if violations of obligations to enforce orders should be regarded as a potential trigger for liability, as is mentioned above for the context of Art. 9, then this needs to be further clarified. As it stands, besides the introduction of new positive obligations for intermediaries through the provisions of Chapter III, it is maintained that Chapter II is rather aimed at limiting liability of such providers; this, however, may seem in contradiction to adding potential reasons for justifying an assumption of liability. Given the variety of remedies and enforcement tools available against (liable) intermediaries under various national and sector specific rules (IP infringements, defamation, hate speech), it should be clarified whether a violation of the orders mentioned in Chapter II can be regarded as another type of basis for liability. This is especially relevant in light of the fact that Recital 17 stresses that the exemptions provided for by Chapter II apply to any type of liability irrespective of the type of content and the subject matter of the laws concerned. The newly inserted Articles 8 and 9 should be more clearly addressed in relation to both the liability exemption provisions and the new pillar of due diligence obligations imposed in Chapter III. One of those obligations includes actions under Articles 8 and 9 to be mandatorily included in the transparency reporting of all intermediaries (Art. 13 para. 1 lit. a)) as well as the activity reports of the DSCs (Art. 44 para. 2 lit. a)).

Although the Proposal does not itself address "harmful" content in the sense of a definition, it should be re-assessed whether the future DSA should not underline clearly that Member States approaches to how such harmful content has to be treated – namely concerning the way it is disseminated in order not to realise its harmful potential – are possible, especially in using instruments foreseen also in the DSA. It has been rightly pointed out that for harmful content the challenge of reacting to it in a fundamental rights respecting way is more difficult than for illegal content, which is why the Commission has suggested already in the past to address this question through separate regulatory tools and responsibilities.[206] The regulatory approaches and methodologies for unlawful content in the DSA Proposal can be useful for adapting them also to the treatment of harmful content.[207]

---

206 European Commission, Communication from the Commission to the European Parliament, the Council, the European Economic and Social Committee and the Committee of the Regions Tackling Online Disinformation: A European Approach COM(2018) 236 Final 1, https://eur-lex.europa.eu/legal-content/EN/TXT/?uri=CELEX:52018DC0236.
207 Cf. on this approach also *Ullrich*, Unlawful Content Online: Towards a New Regulatory Framework for Online Platforms, p. 35.

V. Obligations of Intermediary Service Providers

1. Starting Point

A new act concerning intermediaries and content dissemination should spell out positive obligations for the relevant service providers outside and independently of the harmonised liability exemptions (reminding again that the exemptions are harmonised by the ECD so far, but not the liability conditions). Such separate positive obligations currently do not exist at a horizontal and overarching EU level and have only been vaguely referred to as a possibility under Member States' national laws. Recital 48 ECD currently allows Member States to lay down duties of care under national law for hosting providers with regard to the detection and identification of illegal activities. The practical actual use and significance of this Recital is, however, unclear, and some even allocate merely declarative value to it in the context of the prohibition of general monitoring.[208] Nevertheless there is a broad consensus that the imposition of new positive obligations on intermediary services providers, and hosting services in particular, is needed and would be adequate in order to stem the ongoing occurrence of illegal content online and the risks originating from it.

In view of the transnational nature of the internet and its intermediaries, it promises to be especially effective if these obligations are laid down at EU level. Given the variety of the intermediary landscape, the different businesses, architectures and technologies involved, it might appear difficult to set broad horizontal rules. However, horizontal obligations could be formulated as general principles of responsibilities and set structural requirements[209] of processes and systems that intermediaries would need to have in place in order to provide a safe platform ecosystem to users. Intermediaries could then be held accountable for complying with these broad obligations, while leaving the door open for sectoral regimes to complement these responsibility obligations as is deemed appropriate. A more detailed and prescriptive responsibility system should also provide more legal

---

208 *Senftleben/Angelopoulos*, The Odyssey of the Prohibition on General Monitoring Obligations on the Way to the Digital Services Act. The German Network Enforcement Act, e.g., explicitly relies in its Explanatory Memorandum on Recital 48 ECD by assessing the compatibility of the act with EU law; cf. Printed Papers 18/12356, p. 14 (http://dipbt.bundestag.de/dip21/btd/18/123/1812356.pdf).

209 *Woods/Perrin*, Online harm reduction – a statutory duty of care and regulator, p. 48.

certainty and reduce the need for interpretation and reliance on 'court made law' by the CJEU for questions of provider actions or orders imposed on them concerning treatment of content.

Thus, it would appear necessary to adapt the obligations according to the risk that intermediaries' operations pose with regards to the risk related to illegal content and activity. This should reflect the severity or impact of the harms and the likelihood of it occurring on the platforms. Such a layered or graduated approach could be defined along criteria. It could take market power or influence/impact of the intermediary on public opinion, the economy or society at large into account. Other possible criteria for scaled obligations relate to the size of an intermediary provider's service measured by the number of active users, the turnover/revenue or the market capitalisation. Responsibilities could also be formulated according to the business model, by introducing for example different levels of obligations on online content platforms such as social media networks or user-generated content sites, search engines, cloud service providers or internet access providers. These approaches could also be combined. It would be sufficient for the proposed act to look at the risk environments of the platform at a more general level with regards to, e.g., the risk to fundamental rights or broader public interests. The responsibilities could be refined and complemented by obligations at sectoral level that take account of more specific risks or harms. Current examples of such EU-wide, specific sectoral regimes are the highly relevant AVMSD, which imposes measures on VSP to mitigate risks originating from hate speech, terrorist content or content harmful for minors (see above B.). The AVMSD offers a toolset of risk mitigation measures in Art. 28b, relying on a co-regulatory approach, which could serve as an example for formulating general responsibilities in the new act while retaining the existing instruments specifically concerning VSP as lex specialis (see above E.I.1.c).

The new responsibility could usefully borrow from existing notions and examples of diligent operators, duty of care or due diligence that are already widely used in various other areas of EU law. Such approaches can be found in data protection law[210], financial regulation[211] or health and

---

210 For Example, Art. 35 GDPR.
211 Directive (EU) 2015/849 of the European Parliament and of the Council of 20 May 2015 on the prevention of the use of the financial system for the purposes of money laundering or terrorist financing, amending Regulation (EU) No 648/2012 of the European Parliament and of the Council, and repealing Directive 2005/60/EC of the European Parliament and of the Council and Commission Directive 2006/70/EC, OJ L 141, 5.6.2015, p. 73–117.

safety regulation[212], to name but a few. In all these areas responsibility and obligations are fixed by applying risk management approaches and imposing different level of obligations according to the riskiness of the business activity. For example, in the financial sector,[213] anti-money laundering legislation imposes due diligence measures on financial entities when establishing and/or maintaining a business relationship. These measures vary according to the risk profile of clients. That risk profile has to be established by the regulated entities themselves and may result in simplified, standard or enhanced due customer diligence. Under the GDPR, companies have to assess whether they engage in high-risk personal data processing activities and, if this is the case, whether they need to undertake a data protection impact assessment.[214]

Obligatory risk assessments can follow widely established and available criteria and methodologies and may already be obligatory or voluntarily used in other area by platforms, such as, for example, IT security or financial aspects for those platforms that enable or provide payment services as part of their business.[215] The advantage of these more general structural and procedural obligations is that regulators could supplement them with more detailed guidance and best practices that arise out of consultations between industry, regulators and civil society stakeholders.

While, thus, the obligations are expected to be broad, they should address the following key areas that are considered as most important for achieving a safe(r) online platform environment.

a. Reactive Obligations: Notice and Takedown and Dispute Settlement

One of the most frequently and early criticised issues of the current regulatory framework for online intermediaries was the lack of coherent and harmonised Notice and Takedown (NTD) procedures. This has notably impacted the actual knowledge standard but also led to fragmentation of practices according to national and sectorial provisions (where they exist)

---

212 Council Directive 89/391/EEC of 12 June 1989 on the introduction of measures to encourage improvements in the safety and health of workers at work, OJ L 183, 29.6.1989, p. 1–8, Art. 5, 6, 9.
213 Directive 2015/849, Art. 10–18.
214 Art. 5, 25, 32 para. 1, 35 GDPR.
215 *Ullrich*, in: IJLIT, 26 (3), 2018, 226, 226 et seq.

and to the imposition of platform NTD standards via their terms of service.

The submission of notices has also undergone significant changes over the last decade: it saw the emergence of automated and large volume notice submission systems, the automated NTD decision on the part of platforms, outsourced notice submissions and platforms creating expedited systems for preferential notifiers (especially in the area of copyright and trademark violations).[216] This automatisation has obscured the entire process. Laying out common structural and procedural obligations for such systems would appear to be necessary in order to safeguard basic standards of accountability and transparency for users. At the most basic level these obligations should include the minimum standards for the content of the notice, the response and information requirements to users, but also redress mechanisms. These information requirements should also extend to automated proactive removals so that users are aware of what can happen to content uploaded. This section may also include specific modalities for dispute settlement, through which basic principles of alternative dispute resolution (ADR) mechanisms would be specified.

b. Reactive Obligations: Trusted Flaggers and Law Enforcement Cooperation

Other reactive measures would include the obligation to involve trusted flaggers in the content moderation process, which happens retrospectively in the sense that pre-defined flaggers receive a special attention when highlighting the availability of problematic content. Trusted flaggers should be defined by the new act. They could include civil society organisations, business organisations or public bodies, such as internet referral units for terrorist content, that are acknowledged by EU or national registrations. Additional reactive obligations should see hosting services report and liaise with law enforcement authorities in cases of illegal content or activity that constitutes a serious crime.

---

216 *De Streel/Husovec*, The e-commerce Directive as the cornerstone of the Internal Market, p. 35 with further references to the studies conducted in this field.

c. Proactive Obligations: User Empowerment

The act should impose a well-defined set of proactive measures that could be limited to hosting providers above a certain size or impact. Such proactive measures can be regarded as prospective in nature as they have to be put in place in advance of an issue occurring.

A number of preventive proactive technical measures aimed of promoting a safe and secure interaction of users should be prescribed for hosting providers. On the architectural and design side these measures could include – duly streamlined with the sectoral provisions of the AVMSD – the following: effective age verification systems for harmful and other content restricted for minors, but also for verifying the age limitations that are imposed by the platform in general; parental control systems that help parents manage access of their children to content on platforms; user complaint mechanisms (outside of the regular NTD process) that would allow highlighting abusive practices or behaviour; content rating and notification tools. These systems could be evaluated by competent national regulatory authorities.

d. Proactive Obligations: Stay down, Know Your Customer and Sanctions

Platforms may be obliged to put measures in place that prevent the reappearance of previously notified content. This has been an endemic problem on platforms but was partly obscured as a requirement due to the unclear interaction with the general monitoring prohibition and not harmonised NTD requirements. This general approach could then be taken up and specified through sectoral legislation, whereby the manifest illegality of content should influence the scope of the preventive activities along established case law of the CJEU.[217]

Certain platforms, determined by size and/or business model, should be obliged to put Know-Your-Customer (KYC) procedures in place. These procedures would put providers in a position to identify service recipients that present a high risk with regards to the dissemination of illegal content. These measures have been demanded by stakeholders, namely in the area of the online sale via e-commerce platforms when dealing with traders

---

217 E.g., CJEU, C-18/18, *Glawischnig-Piesczek*; C-324/09, *L'Oréal and Others*; C-484/14, *Mc Fadden*.

or advertisers.[218] They have also been discussed in the context of managing the risks and harms attached to user anonymity in the context of online dissemination of hate speech, terrorist content, or disinformation. Apart from their deterrent effect on abusive and illegal behaviour, such adapted obligations would help in enforcing information obligations of providers and the potential liabilities in case of non-disclosure of such information (in Art. 9 of the proposed DSA). Extended user identification, and verification, on social media networks could help building more trustful and safe online communication spaces.[219]

Hosting services should have processes in place to effectively deal with users that repeatedly violate the platforms terms and conditions. These procedures could include the obligatory imposition and communication of suspension and account closure procedures. This has already been included in the recent P2B Regulation, which stipulates that online intermediation services have to have clear terms and conditions and sanction processes in place for businesses that repeatedly infringe the services' policies.

e. Proactive Obligations: Content Management

Obligations to engage in the proactive identification and removal of illegal or harmful content must be carefully and closely prescribed so as to not conflict with the prohibition of general monitoring or to not result in sidestepping of the NTD process. Although content identification and predictive tools using machine learning have improved significantly over the last two years, it will be important to put in place safeguards, such as effective redress tools and transparency requirements. While the accuracy of these automated tools is improving constantly, it is still not clear how exact these tools are when used by online platforms and whether they result in significant over- or under-blocking of content. Any endorsement of proactive measures should be dependent on the way human intervention is be-

---

218 European Commission, Summary of Responses to the Public Consultation on the Evaluation and Modernisation of the Legal Framework for IPR Enforcement (2016) 17, http://ec.europa.eu/DocsRoom/documents/18661; *Ullrich*, in: IJLIT, 26 (3), 2018, 226, 239–244.

219 *Babbs*, New Year, New Internet? Why It's Time to Rethink Anonymity on Social Media; *Zeno-Zencovich*, in: Koltay (ed.), Media Freedom and Regulation in the New Media World, p. 107–113; *Vamialis*, in: IJLIT 21/2013, 56, 56 et seq.; *Ullrich*, Unlawful Content Online: Towards a New Regulatory Framework for Online Platforms, p. 410–412.

ing used in order to safeguard fundamental rights compliance. It would therefore be important that any proactive content management obligations are tied to a strong structural and procedural framework.

This could be done through imposing risk management obligations under which intermediary services need to identify whether their business models, architectures and content management practices pose high risks to public interests and fundamental rights and values where it concerns the availability and spread of illegal (and harmful) content. In case providers identify such high risks, they would be required to take proportional (appropriate and necessary) measures to mitigate these risks. Under this procedural and structural framework any proactive measures can be applied in a specific manner to high-risk situations, which would not conflict with the prohibition of general monitoring. The proactive measures can therefore be directly justified by, and tied to, the legitimate aim of protecting public interest (public security, public health, democratic values, consumer protection) and fundamental rights (personality rights, privacy, freedom of expression and information). Such procedural frameworks could be implemented on a more technical level through harmonised technical standards.[220]

This co-regulatory solution allows for an adaptation to sectoral level and/or to the type of service providers. It could be justified to exclude small providers (such as start-ups) from these duties or parts of them. However, as a business management approach it should be applicable to all other hosting providers in the area. Medium-sized platforms or other intermediaries, but even small niche services, may be subject to high-risk content dissemination, so it will also depend on the potential impacts. The spread with which information propagates via any online platform, regardless of their size, would justify a broad approach when implementing new obligations.[221]

---

220 *Ullrich*, in: JIPITEC 8/2017, 111, 122, 126; *Cole/Etteldorf/Ullrich*, Cross-border Dissemination of Online Content, p. 202–205; *Ullrich*, Unlawful Content Online: Towards a New Regulatory Framework for Online Platforms, p. 385–389.
221 European Commission, Commission Staff Working Document, Impact Assessment. Proposal for a Regulation of the European Parliament and of the Council on Preventing the Dissemination of Terrorist Content Online, SWD(2018) 408 Final, p. 7–10.

f. Transparency, Reporting and Information Obligations

The opacity of content management and business practices and the lack of democratic oversight over how hosting providers, and especially online platforms, enforce policies and provisions on illegal content and harmful content has moved to centre stage in the debate over platform regulation. Transparency and reporting obligations are commonly seen as an important means to overcome risky content management practices by platforms. Transparency and reporting can only be a first step, aimed at bringing light into the harms encountered on platforms and how they are being addressed and in that way influence the design of responsible technology and platform architectures.[222] However, transparency can go a long way in driving accountability if the reporting and information obligations force providers to shed light on their internal risk management processes in a pertinent, understandable and comparable manner. This would allow regulators and the public to acquire the knowledge and expertise needed to participate in the formulation of responsible platform design and hold providers accountable effectively.

On a procedural level, transparency reporting should be regular and the format and content of reporting should be standardised, ideally based on a predetermined format. Providers should be obliged to provide defined data-sets about their content removal activities, which include quantitative information on automated removals and those following NTDs and orders by authorities and courts. It should also include data on response times following NTD, authority orders and notice submission by institutional notifiers, such as trusted flaggers or rights holders (and their representatives). The reports should further give insights into the number of counterclaims and their success (reinstatements of content), cases settled through ADR, sanctions against repeat infringers (temporary and permanent suspensions/ account closures) and the number of referrals to law enforcement.

Platforms should also put measures in place to inform users when content display rankings or recommendations are influenced by sponsored content that has been paid for by advertisers. This requirement would help in the identification of political advertising and disinformation but also inform users when consulting search engines or purchasing goods on online marketplaces.

Platforms with significant automated content management activities and predictive removal mechanisms should also be required to give inde-

---

222 *Mulligan/Bamberger*, in: CLR, 106, 2018, 697, 770–772.

pendent researchers access to their data-sets in order to allow for repro-
ducibility and verification of automated content decisions and the general
build-up of knowledge and expertise in this area. This can extend to verification of the use of commercial communications (advertisement) in content ranking and recommender mechanisms on these platforms. Data access should be standardised, enabling authorised, independent researchers
to analyse content and decision-making processes in defined formats,
through defined application interfaces at a regular basis. However,
providers should not be required to necessarily disclose the algorithms or
source codes where this would conflict with trade secrets protection. Useful examples for opportunities and potential obstacles to data reporting
and transparency obligations are the Memorandum of Understanding on
the sale of counterfeit goods on the internet and the Commission agreement with collaborative economy platforms to publish key data on
tourism accommodation.[223]

Providers that are subject to risk management and reporting obligations
should also undergo periodical audits that evaluate the measures taken.

2. DSA Approach

Chapter III (Sections 1–4, Articles 10–37) of the DSA Proposal imposes a
set of new, positive due diligence obligations on service providers and can
be regarded one of the key elements and novelties of the proposed new
framework for intermediaries and, more specifically, online platforms.
These due diligence obligations are created in a free standing way and independent from the conditional liability regime of Chapter II. Providers
that fall foul of conditional liability exemptions need therefore still to
comply with these free standing obligations, but any provider is now not
only shielded against liability, which could derive from the DSA liability
privilege regime, but has more extensive obligations directly resulting
from the proposed new EU legislative act.

The obligations apply in a layered, cumulative way. Section 1 (Art. 10–
13) spells out due diligence obligations for all intermediary service

---

223 Commission's Agreement with Collaborative Economy Platforms, https://ec.eur
opa.eu/commission/presscorner/detail/en/IP_20_194; European Commission,
Report on the Functioning of the Memorandum of Understanding on the Sale
of Counterfeit Goods via the Internet, SWD(2020) 166 final/2, https://ec.europa.
eu/docsroom/documents/42701. See also above E.I.1.b.

providers (mere conduits, caching and hosting services). Section 2 (Art. 14–15) applies to hosting providers, Section 3 (Art. 16–24) concerns online platforms and Section 4 (Art. 25–33) covers very large online platforms (VLOPs). Section 5 (Art. 34–37), finally, deals with other aspects of due diligence obligations and relates to regulatory approaches and tools that will be used in implementing and enforcing the new rules. The Commission justifies this layered approach with its mandate to improve the functioning of the internal market and facilitate a safe online environment. The rules should therefore be clear, balanced, harmonised and adapted to the different types and nature of intermediary service providers (Recitals 34 and 35; see also above E.I.1.a).

a. All Intermediary Service Providers (Art. 10–13)

At the most basic level, all intermediary service providers with an establishment in the EU are required to establish single points of contact (SPoC) that can be reached electronically by national authorities, the Commission and the new European Board for Digital Services (Art. 10). Information on how the SPoC can be reached must be made publicly available. Intermediary service providers with no establishment in the EU need to nominate a legal representative in one of the Member States where they are offering their services (Art. 11). That legal representative takes the functions of the SPoC but can also be held liable for non-compliance with the new act. Providers need to provide the name, address, email address and telephone number of their legal representative to the DSC in the Member State where their legal representative resides.

All intermediary service providers will have to indicate in their terms and conditions the restrictions on information/content that they impose on users (Art. 12). These restrictions should include mentioning of the content moderation policies, procedures and tools (including the use of algorithmic decision-making and human review). This information has to be provided in a 'clear and unambiguous language' and in an easily accessible format. In addition, the providers are held to apply these policies and measures diligently, objectively and proportionately, taking notably care that they respect fundamental rights principles of the CFR.

Finally, all intermediary service providers will need to publish at least once per year transparency reports on their content moderation activities (Art. 13). These need to include data on orders to act on illegal content and information received by authorities (under Art. 8 and 9), the number of notices received by type of illegal content, the basis for any action taken (whether based on the terms and conditions or on the applicable law) and the time taken to implement the request. In addition, all providers need to report on the number and type of voluntary content decisions that affect the visibility, availability and accessibility of content. The reports must also contain detail on complaints received with regards to content decisions, including data on reinstatements of content (or reversal of original decisions). An exception is provided for micro and small enterprises.

b. Hosting Service Providers (Art. 14–15)

This section establishes common NTD obligations for all hosting providers.

All hosting providers need to put notice and action processes in place (referred to as NTD procedures in this study) that allow for the easy, electronic notification of illegal content (Art. 14). These notices need to comply with a common format and contain the following information in order to be qualified as providing actual knowledge: the reasons for why the notifier considers content illegal; the exact URL(s) of the notified content; name and email address of the submitter; a good faith statement of the accuracy of the information provided. The provider will need to send the submitter a receipt of the notice and a message once the decision has been taken. Where this decision relied on automated means, this fact must be included in the information message. The decision will need to be taken in a timely manner.

Any content removal decision, whether motivated by a notice or by proactive measures, will need to be communicated to the recipient of the service (the uploader) (Art. 15). This message needs to include as a minimum: the reasons for the decision; their territorial scope; whether the decision was taken using automated means; the legal basis where illegal content is concerned; a reference to the relevant contractual provisions where the content violated the terms and conditions; the redress means available to contest the decision. All content removal decisions and their reasons need to be deposited in a publicly available database that will be managed by the European Commission.

The Commission explicitly applies this requirement to all hosting platforms in order to capture file sharing (peer-to-peer) and web hosting providers, ad servers or paste bins (Recital 40). No exceptions are provided for small and micro enterprises.

c. Online Platforms (Art. 16–24)

Online platforms need to comply with due diligence obligations relating to complaints and redress mechanisms, trusted flaggers, the misuse of their services, out-of-court settlements, serious criminal offences, traceability of traders, transparency reporting and the transparency of advertising. Art. 16 offers an exclusion for micro and small enterprises from this complete section, except if they would constitute a very large online platform (Recital 43).

Art. 17 and 18 essentially regulate common standards for complaints and redress mechanisms for online platforms. As a reminder, online platforms are defined as those hosting providers that offer online content dissemination services to the public. Art. 17 imposes harmonised obligations for internal complaints handling on online platforms. The provisions should ensure that users have adequate means to contest decisions taken by online platforms that negatively affect them (Recital 44). This comprises content removals as well as account suspensions or closures. Internal complaint mechanisms should follow basic standards of fairness, objectivity and timeliness. They impose, amongst other, obligations to reverse decisions where the illegality of the content has not been established and where the terms and conditions have not been violated. Users will have to be informed of the decisions taken following a complaint and of the possibility of using out-of-court dispute settlements. The decisions must not be based solely on automated means.

Art. 18 lays down requirements relating to the certification of ADR bodies by the DSCs of Member States. It gives users the right to choose any certified ADR body to settle claims in regard to decisions about content taken by an online platform. This Article stipulates that platforms will need to bear the arbitration costs where the conflict is settled against them, while users will not have to bear any costs incurred by platforms under any circumstances.

Art. 19 requires that platforms establish expedited mechanisms for processing notices submitted by trusted flaggers. Trusted flaggers need to be recognised as such by the DSC of the relevant Member State. A register of recognised trusted flaggers will be published by the Commission. Furthermore, the Article regulates procedures for dealing with trusted flaggers that file unsubstantiated or incorrect notices.

Art. 20 establishes common approaches that platforms need to put in place to protect against misuse of their services. Online platforms need to have suspension policies for repeat infringers. These suspensions will need to follow an established and openly accessible policy that provides the facts and circumstances that play a role in establishing misuse and suspension, as well as the duration of suspensions. The Article also requires that online platforms have processes in place to assess whether service recipients engage in misuse. It also provides common minimum parameters for this assessment: the number of notices submitted on an annual basis in relation to the total number of items, the gravity of the violation and the degree of intent involved.

Where platforms have suspicions of illegal activity being conducted on their platforms that amounts to serious criminal offences, they will need to inform law enforcement or judicial authorities of the Member State (Art. 21).

Art. 22 establishes specific conditions for online marketplaces regarding the traceability of traders. These KYC style requirements include gathering information on address details and bank account, an ID check, trade register numbers (where applicable) and a self-certification that the products supplied comply with EU law. This information will need to be verified for its veracity using reasonable efforts. Where the information is incomplete or cannot be adequately verified, the platform is held not to continue the business relationship with the trader. In addition, the online platform is held to design its web pages (called online interface) in a way that enables traders to comply with any other obligations arising out of pre-contractual information and with product safety information under EU law. This Article is, as proposed, limited to the specific type of intermediary that resembles a marketplace.

Online platforms have enhanced transparency reporting obligations (Art. 23) on top of the general obligations established for all intermediary service providers under Art. 13. These additional requirements relate to information about ADR disputes and their outcomes; the number of account suspensions following illegal content notifications; abusive notice submissions and unfounded complaints; and statistics on the use of automated content moderation, in particular their purpose, decision accuracy and safeguards applied. In addition, online platforms need to publish biannual data on their average monthly active users in each EU Member State. The Commission is empowered to lay down common formats for such reporting.

Art. 24 requires online platforms to clearly indicate advertisements to users and indicate the person who has commissioned the advertisement and the criteria that are used to determine the display of the advertisements to the user.

d. Very Large Online Platforms (Art. 25–33)

Art. 25 provides a definition and the criteria for determining the status VLOPs. According to that, a platform with 45 million equal or more average users in the EU will be considered a VLOP. These details are not of relevance for the purposes discussed here. The Commission will maintain an updated list of VLOPs.

Art. 26 and 27 impose obligations with regards to the management of systemic risks on VLOPs. The risk assessment obligations in Art. 26 oblige platforms to identify, analyse and assess at least once a year their services with regards to systemic risks relating to the use of their services. Three systemic risks are defined, but not as a final enumeration: the risks of dissemination of illegal content; negative effects on fundamental rights, with a special emphasis on the respect for privacy and family life, freedom of expression and information, the prohibition of discrimination and children's rights; and cybersecurity threats. VLOPs are advised to conduct their risk assessment with respect to the use of their content moderation and recommender systems and online advertising mechanisms, paying notably attention to the 'rapid and wide' dissemination of illegal content.

Art. 27 lays down a number of risk mitigation measures VLOPs may adopt in order to address the mentioned systemic risks. This includes adaptation of the recommender and content moderation systems, limiting advertisement displays, reinforcing internal controls processes and adjusting their cooperation with trusted flaggers and other platforms through codes of conducts and crisis protocols. Guidance has to be provided by the European Board for Digital Services (EBDS) on the risk assessment procedures for systemic risks and best practices by VLOPs.

VLOPs have to undergo annual audits on the compliance with all the due diligence obligations applying to them and any other commitments through code of conducts (Art. 35 and 36) and crisis protocols (Art. 38). These audits need to be conducted by independent and sufficiently qualified organisations. Art. 28 regulates the further modalities of the audit procedure as well as mechanisms in case of negative reports and deficiencies.

Art. 29 imposes additional transparency requirements with regard to recommender systems. VLOPs need to give a clear indication in their terms and conditions on the parameters behind their recommender systems as well as options to influence these parameters, with the possibility for users to apply these modifications through easily accessible functionalities.

Art. 30 imposes additional requirements for advertising transparency by which VLOPs have to create a publicly accessible repository of advertisements displayed by them. This contains, amongst others, the content of the advertisement, the person on whose behalf it is displayed and during which time period, the parameters where advertisements are targeted and the number of recipients and groups targeted.

Art. 31 provides modalities for vetted researchers to access data of VLOPs with the purpose of scrutinising the platforms' compliance with the act.

VLOPs will need to nominate compliance officers (Art. 32) that will be responsible for monitoring compliance of the platform with the proposed act. These compliance officers need to be adequately qualified and experienced to perform their activities. Their tasks consist mainly in cooperating with the responsible DSC, overseeing the platform's activities when the independent audit is conducted, advising management and employees of compliance obligations as well as monitoring the VLOP's compliance.

Going beyond the obligations of Art. 13 and 23 of the Proposal, VLOPs will need to provide annual transparency reporting every six months (Art. 33). In addition, they need to provide an audit implementation report following up on items identified from the annual audit. Where VLOPs are concerned over disclosure of confidential information and information that would pose other security risks, they may provide this information in a complete report only to the relevant DSC and eliminate that part of the information for the public report.

e. Additional Obligations (Art. 34–37)

These Articles specify the methods and tools that the DSC and the Commission may apply in implementing the due diligence obligations.

The Commission envisages the promotion of the development of industry standards for the development of processes for NTD systems and trusted flagger systems, online advertising transparency (Art. 30), data access requests (Art. 31), auditing and the interoperability of advertisement repositories regarding VLOPs.

Codes of conduct will be used as a means to address and mitigate systemic risks relating to VLOPs where these concern several platforms. Furthermore, the Commission aims to facilitate codes of conduct between platforms, advertisers and other stakeholders concerning additional requirements relating to advertising transparency (Art. 36). Finally, the Commission will facilitate the creation of crisis protocols with VLOPs and other platforms to address situations in which the EU experiences serious

crises that affect public security and/or public health. These crisis protocols, limited to 'extraordinary circumstances', would set out clear procedures and tasks of participants, safeguards and reporting to address these
situations.

3. Assessment

The DSA Proposal incorporates key positions and suggestions that have
been made by Member States' political bodies, civil society and industry in
the context of additional obligations of intermediaries. Overall, the comprehensive list of due diligence obligations proposed by the Commission is
to be welcomed. As stated in the previous sections, the separation of liability exemption conditions from free-standing obligations has its advantages
as it moves away from a retroactive evaluation of an individual situation to
introducing additional "permanent" obligations. It also brings possible
challenges with it. The detailed and comprehensive due diligence obligations formulated in the Proposal will need to stand the test of subsidiarity
and proportionality and therefore be individually assessed as to whether
they are necessary for the proper functioning of the single market. Member States could argue that some of these measures may be more adequate
if taken at national level, especially in light of their potential overlap with
media-oriented content regulation that takes place on Member State level.
They may even already be part of obligations at national level, such as, for
example, the requirement of social media networks under the German
Network Enforcement Act to have complaint handling systems in place.[224]
The interrelation of such rules, unless they are based on the implementation of provisions in Directives, such as the requirements for VSPs to deal
with user complaints as laid down in the AVMSD, is not addressed in the
DSA Proposal.[225] In contrast to the proposed DSA, the AVMSD or other

---

224 Gesetz zur Verbesserung der Rechtsdurchsetzung in sozialen Netzwerken 2017
(BGBl I p. 3352 (No. 61)), para. 3; *Cornils*, Designing Platform Governance: A
Normative Perspective on Needs, Strategies, and Tools to Regulate Intermedi-
aries, p. 70–82; cf. also Digital Services Act Proposal, Recitals 9–11.

225 The reason why this is relevant can be illustrated with an example from Germany: The provisions of the new German Telemedia Act, which regulate the
procedure for reporting user complaints as an implementation of the AVMSD,
are closely interlinked with the provisions of the NetzDG, whereby the NetzDG
– if applicable – also takes precedence over these provisions for VSPs. Cf. § 10a
Telemedia Act of 26 February 2007 (Federal Law Gazette I p. 179; 2007 I p.

relevant instruments such as the DSMD were set up as Directives, thus leaving Member States more leeway, for example, with regards to the obligations on VSPs under the AVMSD.

The gradual, cumulative allocation of obligations according to type, nature of activity and size of the intermediary is adequate as a policy approach and aimed at avoiding unnecessary burdens on some actors for whom the obligations could have a deterring effect. However, questions remain as to the distribution of due diligence obligations amongst the different intermediary categories, which appears to be highly complex.

Asking all providers to nominate SPoC or legal representatives (Art. 10 and 11) and requiring clear terms and conditions (Art. 12) with regards to content restrictions and the use of algorithmic tools makes sense, even for micro and small enterprises. This will force all companies, including start-ups, to clarify to customers, and potentially even to themselves, at an early stage their own values, tenets and processes with regards to responsible behaviour. At the same time, exempting micro and small enterprises from transparency reports is adequate. Having all intermediaries, including internet access providers (and caching services), to publish transparency reports over their content removal activities also appears adequate. Internet access providers have been concerned by the rise in automated take-down and filtering systems and dynamic injunctions, too,[226] and information about that would contribute to a better overall picture. Given their infrastructural significance, it is to be welcomed that they are included in transparency reporting obligations. The obligation would also shed light on the use of internet registrars/registries in the fight against unlawful content where they qualify for one of the intermediary service provider categories.

The definition of basic structural and procedural requirements for NTD (Art. 14) had been widely expected. Stronger harmonisation in this area has been pondered by the Commission for the last 10 years and took a very concrete shape in the Recommendation about Illegal Content Online.[227] Its significance for the determination of actual knowledge has been out-

---

251), as last amended by Article 12 of the Act of 30 March 2021 (Federal Law Gazette I p. 448).

226 *Quintais*, Global Online Piracy – Study Legal Background Report, p. 85–88; European Commission, Guidance on Certain Aspects of Directive 2004/48/EC of the European Parliament and of the Council on the Enforcement of Intellectual Property Rights, COM(2017) 708 Final, p. 21.

227 European Commission, Online Services, Including e-Commerce, in the Single Market. A Coherent Framework to Boost Confidence in the Digital Single Market of e-Commerce and Other Online Services, Accompanying the Document,

lined before. The actual requirements for the content of notices correspond to basic requirements already in place with larger platforms today. Likewise, the obligation to state reasons for content removals (through NTD or proactive tools) and give information about redress regarding removal decisions will contribute to better procedural safeguards for all users. Requiring hosting providers to publish this data in a publicly available database will help create useful empirical data and contribute to transparency and put pressure on the accountability of providers' content removal systems. If this database does indeed include details on whether decisions were made automatically or following a notice, the legal basis and/or the applicable terms and conditions, this will create valuable insights for civil society and regulators alike.

By contrast, excluding mere conduits (i.e. internet access providers) from these requirements is a missed opportunity. Internet access providers have been included in national laws and codes of conduct that regulate NTD. They are routinely sought out by rights holders and other damaged parties when it comes to blocking and removing illegal content. As noted above, dynamic injunctions or graduated response systems are primarily directed at internet access providers. Since the new NTD requirements are free-standing and not part of the conditions for liability exemption, it would have been possible to extend these Articles towards mere conduits and caching services. The explanation in Recital 40 that Articles 14 and 15 should apply to infrastructural hosting providers, such as webhosts or file sharing services, are further arguments for an inclusion of mere conduits into the scope of these Articles. An exemption could be provided for operators that provide free Wi-Fi hotspots as part of their business (such as restaurants or educational establishments).

Obliging online platforms to put in place complaint handling systems and out-of-court dispute settlements provides important procedural safeguards. The requirements spelled out in Articles 17 and 18 are broadly worded, underlining the general nature of the rights that are to be protected. It will be important to back up enforcement of these requirements with effective and concrete implementation and enforcement measures. Otherwise, broad terms such as 'undue delay', 'timely', 'easy to access' may lead to diverging implementations and lengthy court proceedings. Since the Proposal does not envisage the creation of industry standards in this

---

SEC(2011) 1641 Final, p. 46–47; European Commission, Commission Recommendation of 1.3.2018 on Measures to Effectively Tackle Illegal Content Online, C(2018) 1177 Final, Recitals 10, 11.

area, it will need to rely on codes of conduct. Whether these self-regulatory measures are, however, adequate and effective for an area with such importance for user rights and transparency is questionable.[228] It is also unclear how these requirements will interact with legislation at national sectoral level, for example with the German NetzDG, which already requires social media networks to put complaints management systems in place. The enhanced procedural framework for trusted notifiers (Art. 19) is in line with the Commission's previous iterations on this matter[229] and a very important clarification to make responses to (trusted) requests more efficient.

The obligations in Art. 20 (measures against abusive notices and counter-notices) are the first indication of more proactive risk management obligations. Until this part of the DSA Proposal, all due diligence obligations were largely ex-post, aimed at reacting to notifications and transparency. Being in a position to identify in a consistent manner the violation history of service recipients will require platforms to develop processes to monitor the compliance with terms, conditions and laws relating to illegal content in a more general manner. This Article was carefully worded and applies only to violations notified under the reactive notice and complaints-handling mechanisms and, as a consequence, not to voluntary measures taken. Here again it would have been appropriate to support a consistent and harmonised implementation into daily business practices of platforms through the development of standards.

Art. 22 puts more flesh on the bones of Art. 20, but only for platforms that function as online marketplaces. The more detailed requirements on the traceability of traders essentially establish KYC due diligence obligations on these platforms. In addition to the ability to identify repeat infringers, these platforms would need to verify traders (sellers) before starting a business relationship. These enhanced obligations are motivated by the pronounced impact of e-commerce on the internal market (notably the free movement of goods), on the one hand, and by the already existing due diligence requirements in the neighbouring areas of EU consumer law or anti-money laundering, on the other.[230] Arguably, this existing enforcement landscape makes it easier and legally justifiable to close the gap with

---

228 *Ullrich*, Unlawful Content Online: Towards a New Regulatory Framework for Online Platforms, p. 385–389, 372–374.

229 European Commission, C(2018) 1177 Final, Points 25–27; AVMSD, Art. 28 para. 2 lit. b, 3 lit. e.

230 Directive 2005/29/EC of 11 May 2005 concerning unfair business-to-consumer commercial practices in the internal market 2005, OJ L 149, 11.6.2005, p. 22–39; Directive 2015/849.

these neighbouring obligations. The violations targeted through this Article are intellectual property rights and consumer and product safety laws (Recital 49). Importantly, e-commerce marketplaces are required to design their websites in a way that allows traders to comply with pre-contractual information and with product safety requirements. This important passage provides a welcome and much needed tool for enforcement authorities in the area of product and food law to bring platforms to act as responsible actors when providing sellers with the opportunity to list products that pose specific safety risks and for which mandatory online information requirements exist.[231] Nonetheless, in light of dangers to user rights and fundamental values by the dissemination of illegal content and the difficulties that come with enforcement actions against users if their identity cannot be verified, it should be considered to extend elements of a KYC approach in a comparable way to content dissemination platforms. The platforms potentially would then have to be regarded as responsible for the content disseminated (or under the proposed regime: subject to sanctions) if they do not put user identification measures in place (or do not want to make available on a court's request information about their "clients").

Obliging online platforms to publish additional transparency data on their specific obligations is important, as is the obligation to publish details on the use of automated content moderation mechanisms. However, whether codes of conduct will be the right way to implement this requirement remains doubtful. It has become obvious that the obligation of providers to provide reliable and more complete data – especially as more decisions are done or based on algorithmic systems – to regulatory authorities, but also to the public, seems to be the most promising way to enable some form of control (or individual empowerment). If that is the case, then robust reporting obligations need to be in place.

By imposing more detailed risk management due diligence obligations on VLOPs, the Commission has squarely entered into the area of proactive obligations. The systemic risks formulated in Art. 26 para. 1 lit. a, b and c relate to what other commentators have defined as statutory harms.[232] Articles 26 and 27 rely on standard risk management methodologies which most of the VLOPs will already apply throughout various areas of their operations. The additional transparency requirements on online advertising, recommender systems and reporting relate to the specific systemic risks

---

231 *Ullrich*, Unlawful Content Online: Towards a New Regulatory Framework for Online Platforms, p. 299–325.
232 *Woods/Perrin*, Online harm reduction – a statutory duty of care and regulator.

that VLOPs need to report on. However, the risk assessment process is only addressed in basic terms in Art. 26. The brevity of Art. 26 stands in contrast to the potential impact that these risk assessments are likely to have. VLOPs are held to assess, notably, systemic risks emanating from their services relating to the exercise of certain fundamental rights laid down in the CFR (Art. 26 para. 1 lit. b). This implicit imposition of fundamental rights obligations on current actors is not new, but it is controversially discussed in the area of online platform governance. If the frequent criticism that current regulatory efforts outsource the decision-making procedure on fundamental rights to private corporate actors[233] is not to be repeated, then the DSA needs to put a more solid supervisory structure in place in order to ensure that these risk assessments comply with the policy objectives set out.

The risk mitigation measures that may be taken by platforms, mentioned in Art. 27 para. 1, offer some more indicative guidance. Yet they, too, are rather general. It appears unlikely that the annual reports on the assessment and mitigation measures of most common systemic risks, the publication of general guidelines or the sharing of best practices will be enough to ensure sufficient regulatory oversight.

Meanwhile, the possibility for the Commission in Art. 35 para. 2 to assemble stakeholders to draw up codes of conduct for systemic risk mitigation measures that have emerged across several VLOPs is a welcome step for including a self-regulatory approach, but it is again formulated rather vague and without defining the involvement of the regulatory authorities – or rather in this case the Commission and EBDS –, especially given the doubts over the usefulness of such codes. Given the repeated failure of existing examples for such tools to measurably enhance the responsibility of the practices of platforms, a commitment towards more structured co-regulatory approach would be preferable. The GDPR's privacy by design-principle, which is backed up by technical standards, is just one example of how fundamental rights objectives could be implemented into a more measurable and structured regulatory framework which allows for more regulatory oversight.

---

233 *Quintel/Ullrich*, "Self-Regulation of Fundamental Rights? The EU Code of Conduct on Hate Speech, related initiatives and beyond", in: Petkova/Ojanen (eds.), 182, 182 et seq.

In general, it is worth asking whether it is useful to apply these comprehensive obligations in Section 4 only to VLOPs.[234] As regards risk management, it can be argued that online platforms with less than 45 million users are also capable of causing systemic risks. Apart from that, the use of basic tools such as risk management will undoubtedly be familiar to most online platforms from other areas, be it with regards to fraud prevention, IT security or data protection.[235] Recommender systems and automated content moderation are used by all content dissemination platforms that rely on advertising revenue. Likewise, requiring access to data for scrutiny of compliance only from VLOPs may deprive researchers of valuable insights into upcoming risks emanating from new business models and content moderation practices. It would be useful to instil these enhanced responsibilities at an early level into all (new) online platform providers in order to build a safe and responsible online environment from bottom up. Only where burdens amount to a deterring effect when deciding on market entry or pose significant economic disadvantages, they should be avoided for some type of providers.

The audit obligations in Art. 28 may be a way, at least at a first stage, to create an oversight structure that monitors compliance with the obligations set out in the DSA for VLOPs. However, outsourcing these audits to other private actors that will be building their (new) verification and reporting processes bears inherent risks. The current design of Articles 26 to 28 bears the hallmarks of a future governance, risk and compliance – including fundamental rights aspects – system for online platforms. This should not be combined with a full reliance on private actor audits for the oversight function, because it would undermine the need for regulatory authorities to have the capacity to conduct the oversight. In other words, they should have to build their own capacities to effectively audit the auditor. There are recent examples that show the risks of relying too much on such types of audits instead of a regulatory authority's oversight.[236] It is therefore recommended that this solution should only be a supplementary first step of an otherwise closer involvement of authorities in auditing and

---

234 *de Posson*, Digital Services Act: Ensuring a Trustworthy and Safe Online Environment While Allowing Freedom of Expression.

235 *Ullrich*, Unlawful Content Online: Towards a New Regulatory Framework for Online Platforms, p. 417.

236 *Mulligan/Bamberger*, in: CLR, 106, 2018, 698, 718–719; *Cohen*, in: Theoretical Inquiries in Law, 17 (1), 2016, 369, 403–407.

assessing online platforms business and content management practices, which entails acquiring the necessary skills and capacities to do so.

Overall, the proposed layered allocation of due diligence obligations could have been simplified into obligations for all intermediary services providers, on the one hand, and online platforms, on the other, with the exception of requiring only VLOPs to provide independent audits. In the legislative process it is worth reconsidering whether all layers of differentiation as presented in the current Proposal are necessary or whether some obligations could not be extended to apply to all or more of the different layers of providers.

Regarding other provisions (Articles 34 to 37), the Commission favours codes of conduct as an overarching implementation tool. The use of standards is restricted to more technical areas of notice and action (including trusted flaggers), audits and information access and exchange requirements (i.e. in the area of advertising transparency). Given the history of past codes of conduct in this area, this is questionable.[237] More transparent, co-regulatory tools such as harmonised standards could provide for more transparency, consistency and accountability. Models of existing process and risk management standards could usefully be consulted.[238] At least, in the creation of codes of conduct and their oversight the role of regulatory bodies would have to be underlined if the solution of more binding standards is not chosen.

VI. Design and Structure of Supervision

1. Starting Point

a. Overall Structure of Supervision

The COO principle as the underlying institutional principle for the regulation of ISS, and thereby decisive also for the question of supervision and enforcement, has provided legal certainty and facilitated the use of the sin-

---

237 *Quintel/Ullrich*, "Self-Regulation of Fundamental Rights? The EU Code of Conduct on Hate Speech, related initiatives and beyond", in: Petkova/Ojanen (eds.), 182, 182 et seq.

238 For example ISO – ISO 31000 – Risk Management (ISO), https://www.iso.org/iso-31000-risk-management.html; ISO – ISO/IEC 27001 – Information Security Management (ISO), https://www.iso.org/isoiec-27001-information-security.html.

gle market freedoms. However, in the context of the increase in harms caused by online platforms that can trigger the public interest derogation possibilities, the procedures for such deviation from the COO principle should be clarified and streamlined. This is not only necessary in view of the complex and in practice hardly applicable nature of the derogation system provided by the ECD[239] but also by the successive encroachment of sectoral acts on the design of derogations provided by the ECD. These additions to exceptional measures in sectoral acts show the growing public policy relevance of platforms active in content dissemination. ·

These sectoral incisions have increased the variety of regulators and sectoral regulatory designs that may potentially need to be involved and participate – or taken into account – in a possible new supervisory structure of a reformed regulatory framework for intermediary service providers. The most important example of such an addition is the AVMSD, whose scope of application not only now extends to VSPs and the regulation of harms relating to hate speech, the protection of minors and beyond but also has introduced a more formalised cooperation system between national competent bodies in ERGA. This necessitates that, at least for the specific area of media content type of dissemination, the structure of ERGA and with it the Member States' reserved competence regarding media regulation, expressed also in the reliance on the COO principle, must be incorporated into the design of a new supervisory structure, or this structure has to allow for a comparable approach taking into consideration the specificities of content regulation.

Other sectoral influences will be introduced through TERREG, which imposes its own cooperation structure between Member States' competent authorities concerning cross-border content removal orders and allocates a coordinating role to Europol. This is despite the fact that the AVMSD would prevail in cases where there is a conflict with the TERREG.[240] Yet other supervisory set-ups are applicable in the consumer law context, where Member States retain significant national competencies in enforcement and through the formulation of codes of conduct, but where European cooperation is coordinated by the Commission through a consumer

---

239 *Cole/Etteldorf/Ullrich*, Cross-border Dissemination of Online Content, p. 174–176.
240 Art. 1 lit. c of the TERREG Proposal.

protection cooperation network.[241] Furthermore, in the area of product regulation new obligations have recently been formulated for ISS. The supervisory and enforcement structure in this area is characterised by distinct enforcement competences for national market surveillance authorities. This latter system is subject to readjustment with the Commission asserting more coordinating powers and the foundation of a Union Product Compliance Network for cross-border enforcement.[242] These sectoral set-ups will all influence the design of an overarching supervisory system and at the same time question whether such an overarching system can appropriately incorporate the existing approaches or whether it will not have to continue to rely on sector-specific supplementary enforcement rules.

This complexity would call for a more detailed allocation of supervisory tasks and also respect the specific options and mechanisms for derogation that exist in the sectoral provisions which would interrelate with the new framework. Especially emergency situations and possible enhanced and expedited powers of supervisory bodies need to be considered in a (re)design of supervisory structures for online intermediaries.

An allocation not necessarily by type of provider but according to obligations formulated by the new legislative act would be one possible solution. This would allow certain regulators to build up effective structures that correspond to their particular competence and expertise. For example, the supervision and enforcement of rules relating to transparency procedures and due care obligations of content moderation systems on online platforms could be allocated to the supervisory regulatory bodies already nominated by the AVMSD. In this context a future framework should rely on media authorities in the exercise of their mandates to protect public interests related to the formation of public opinion. By contrast allocating such regulatory tasks to other enforcement bodies would cause a conflict of competencies with the mandate of national media regulators (and ERGA) in cases where VSPs as one specific case of online platforms with special relevance for content dissemination are being supervised. Responsibilities relating to the traceability of traders and KYC obligations could be

---

241　Regulation (EU) 2017/2394 of the European Parliament and of the Council of 12 December 2017 on cooperation between national authorities responsible for the enforcement of consumer protection laws and repealing Regulation (EC) No 2006/2004, OJ L 345, 27.12.2017, p. 1–26.

242　Regulation (EU) 2019/1020 of the European Parliament and of the Council of 20 June 2019 on market surveillance and compliance of products and amending Directive 2004/42/EC and Regulations (EC) No 765/2008 and (EU) No 305/2011, OJ L 169, 25.6.2019, p. 1–44, Art. 7 para. 2.

an area in which the authorities and the network set up under the consumer acquis or product safety regulation as well as the Union product compliance network could be integrated.

With regards to overarching systemic risks caused by VLOPs, a stronger involvement of a dedicated, newly created regulatory body at EU level could be considered. This can be justified on grounds of effectiveness and the strong cross-border reach of VLOPs. However, this cross-border dimension alone does not justify the replacement of the general prevalence of administrative and procedural autonomy of the Member States nor can it disrespect the specific requirements of oversight for certain areas, such as content dissemination. Thus a more centralised approach would at least have to be strongly coordinated with national enforcement authorities. The format of such a structure could be modelled on existing institutions such as the Consumer Protection Cooperation (CPC) Network, the Body of European Regulators for Electronic Communications (BEREC), the EDPB or ERGA or combining elements of these. The joint characteristic of these co-operation bodies is their reliance on the national competent bodies. The central body convening these national authorities or bodies could intervene on issues that call for strong international cooperation or are too large to be dealt with by one authority. Apart from that, a central body could provide assistance and facilitate cooperation of national enforcement bodies.[243]

It is not new that a strictly and consistently applied COO principle brings with it certain risks of forum shopping with possible unwanted outcomes regarding regulatory standards.[244] Therefore, in order to ensure a consistent approach to tackling the most important regulatory issues, e.g. on removing illegal content, the standards that apply to intermediary service providers, their obligations and responsibilities should be harmonised across the EU so that regulatory enforcement is based on the same starting point. From that perspective, a Regulation would be the most adequate legislative tool in order to achieve this objective.[245] However, the existing examples which use the COO approach while enabling cooperation between regulators that are competent because of jurisdiction criteria and those that

---

243 In this direction also *Smith*, Enforcement and cooperation between Member States, p. 30 et seq, opting for NRAs regulating but in a network with overall coordination by a central EU Regulator.

244 *Cole/Etteldorf/Ullrich*, Cross-border Dissemination of Online Content, p. 254–255.

245 On the question of full harmonisation of the provisions for ISS, *Lomba/Evas* (EPRS study), Digital services act, p. 23.

are involved due to the effect of a given service on the territory they monitor show that a framework laid down in a Directive is not contrary to this goal.

Maintaining the COO principle in a new legislative framework should be accompanied by a strengthening of capabilities and competences of national regulators, notably those that have less clearly assigned tasks under national law so far. In addition, the cooperation between national authorities should ensure that the application of the COO principle does not hinder a joint approach to issues which are relevant for Member States beyond the place of establishment of the provider. Such a cooperation could also assist those regulatory authorities in the exercise of their tasks that are confronted with a concentration of many (large) providers established within their jurisdiction. In general, new supervisory tasks and powers, such as those relating to transparency obligations or auditing, should be clearly and expressly assigned both concerning the exercise of supervisory powers at the COO and in cooperating with other Member States' authorities.

In order to achieve more clarity on responsibility of supervisory authorities, the introduction of a public register of all intermediary service providers established in the EU with indication of the competent authorities should be foreseen. Such a database would enhance transparency of the applicable jurisdiction in advance of conflict situations.

b. Regulatory Powers and Sanctions

The monitoring of intermediary services is not only difficult in the current set-up because of a lack of clear allocation of competences to authorities or bodies. In addition, the insight into the functioning of the online platforms is in some context rather limited, which results in a difficulty of issuing targeted and appropriate supervision measures. For example, given the opacity of content moderation tools and business practices of online platforms, it appears adequate to give regulatory authorities special powers to have access to data that reveals the parameters and reasons of algorithmic content moderation processes that have been identified as causing harms. These powers could envisage access to decision-making procedures of the businesses, software documentation or internal reports that detail the motivations for implementing certain algorithms or content moderation features that facilitate or amplify harms caused by illegal content and activity.[246] In this context national regulators should also have powers to review and understand whether and how hosting providers are managing risks on their platforms that are related to illegal content. Regulators should be given powers and capabilities to audit these procedures with a view to establish whether the provider has complied with obligations that are set by the framework.

Beyond this example, as a general approach to the availability of data in order to measure compliance and in case of non-availability or the failure to produce the data to the competent authorities, there should be enforcement tools that can pressurize the intermediaries to comply with information requests. This also means that the designated bodies for the monitoring have to be equipped to do so and have to meet the conditions for the oversight, for example in the sensitive area of content-related monitoring.

The structure and detail of a unified sanctioning system in case of violation of obligations by online intermediaries depends on the actual set-up of the supervisory structures and the obligations. Arguably, if obligations on intermediary service providers were directly integrated into the current liability exemptions regime, this would work against a consistent and harmonised sanctions regime. Failure to comply with these obligations would make the provider liable under applicable Member State provisions. Freestanding obligations that are independent from the liability exemption protections, on the other hand, would facilitate the formulation of horizontally applicable sanctions. These sanctions could be linked to the size of the provider and impose fees as a percentage of worldwide turnover, such as done in the GDPR.[247]

Given the large size and international reach of some online platforms, it would appear problematic to generally assess and determine the true impact and harm caused by failure to comply with obligations from the perspective of individual Member States. In order to create a clear sanctioning regime and avoid multiple or uncoordinated sanctions that could conflict with the *ne bis in idem* principle, it seems preferable to have a framework

---

246 See generally on this European Parliament resolution of 20 October 2020 with recommendations to the Commission on the Digital Services Act: Improving the functioning of the Single Market (2020/2018(INL)), Whereas AA. et seq.

247 In this regard also *Smith*, Enforcement and cooperation between Member States.

for sanctions including fines and penalties at EU level.[248] The requirement for effectiveness of sanctions would hold national regulators accountable to formulate timely and adequate responses that act as a deterrent for further breaches; proportionality would hold regulators accountable to pass sanctions that respect the fundamental rights context of online intermediation; flexibility would ensure that regulators adapt their regulatory responses to the circumstances of the violation, the type of content and the platform concerned; a risk-based approach would allow regulators to prioritise their enforcement actions on those violations that pose the highest risk and cause the most harm; evidence-based decisions oblige regulators to acquire solid, fact-based evidence before passing sanctions; an obligation to co-operate would require from regulators to stay in regular contact with market participants so that any emerging risks can be addressed at an early stage. These requirements or a selection of them could be established in the EU regulatory framework in order to have a more unified approach to enforcement and a comparability of sanctions from the perspective of the providers.

c. Supranational Coordination and Cooperation

Given the cross-border nature of online intermediation and the wide reach of many platform activities, it is crucial, as described several times above, that cooperation between national regulatory authorities of the Member States is enabled and takes place in practice. Considering the potentially large number of competent authorities from different subject matter areas, structuring such cooperation remains just as important.

Several levels of cooperation can be envisaged. At the lowest level such cooperation could comprise a mere loose exchange of opinions resulting in voluntary and non-binding commitments. Action could be coordinated through joint decision-making procedures and cooperation overseen by an institution created at EU level. However, given the significance and breadth of the regulatory challenge ahead, this form of cooperation is unlikely to achieve the decisive and coordinated response needed. Under the review of the AVMSD, ERGA has developed from such a loosely structured cooperation forum into a more defined organisation with concrete tasks and mandates. A similar process of solidification, although as yet at a

---

248 *Schulte-Nölke et al.*, The legal framework for e-commerce in the Internal Market, p. 38.

less advanced level, can be seen through the emergence of the Union Product Compliance Network in the area of product regulation. The EDPB is an example of a supervisory structure established with more active powers, under which national data protection authorities come together to issue joint opinions and pass binding majority-based decisions. Even more institutionalised and solid central regulatory structures at EU level include the Single Supervisory Mechanism for banking supervision or the European Banking Authority, which, as an EU agency, even has the power to overrule Member States' regulatory authorities.

There are a variety of other regulatory models and institutions at EU level that could serve as examples: these include, but are not limited to, cooperation in the enforcement of consumer law; food safety enforcement cooperation, where the European Food Safety Authority (EFSA) acts as a scientific body that supports national decision making with scientific risk assessments and research; or BEREC in the telecommunications sector. Again, the actual model for cooperation chosen will depend on the set-up of involved authorities or bodies and the obligations that intermediary service providers will face as well as the sanctioning system put in place. The type of hierarchical structure chosen would also determine the reporting procedures for breaches with a cross-border element and the cooperation modalities in emergency situations, including an obligation to actually cooperate.[249] And it would also need to take into consideration possible specificities as they may exist in areas that have a more local, regional or national dimension in addition to the cross-border economic market dimension, such as is the case for media-type content.[250] This will necessitate a clear assignment or retaining of competence with existing regulatory bodies besides creating new structures in a hierarchy.

The current cooperation between providers and regulators has followed mostly the model of non-binding, self-regulatory measures, along codes of conduct or memoranda of understanding. The efficacy of these kind of agreements has been criticised as ineffective where they have been con-

---

249 *Lomba/Evas (EPRS study)*, Digital services act, p. 22, argue that an improved and more binding cooperation mechanisms would lead to reduction of administrative costs and inefficiencies and to a more effective and efficient enforcement of the ECD.

250 Advocating for centralised structures otherwise, for media and content context *de Streel/Husovec*, The e-commerce Directive as the cornerstone of the Internal Market, p. 35, 42, also underline the need to rely on existing national regulatory authorities for content oversight.

cluded only on the level of the providers.[251] One of the reasons for this could be the relatively generous regulatory framework of the ECD when it comes to the question of potential consequences for ISS because of violations of certain rules. When more wide-reaching obligations will be imposed on providers in the future, the form of public-private cooperation should eventually move towards a more hierarchical format which allows for results to be achieved that reflect the regulatory goal. While voluntary and informal cooperation will still be important in exchanging best practices, expanded obligations can better be effectively enforced through co-regulatory tools. These co-regulatory cooperation measures are likely to consist of mandatory reporting and transparency requirements, the exact format of which could be laid down through binding (technical) standards or codes developed by wider stakeholder groups consisting of industry, regulatory bodies and civil society. Harmonised technical standards could be a particularly useful, because well tested and proven, instrument to implement more technical requirements relating to transparency, on the one hand, and wider risk management and reporting standards, on the other.[252]

Enhancing the "public authority" element in the co-regulatory approach does not mean that cooperation between providers where standards or joint approaches are developed should not be upheld. But assuring the regulatory oversight of approaches that can be qualified as purely self-regulatory on areas where important public interests are at risk has surfaced as an important motivation for including intermediaries in the enforcement of rules in a way that reflects their position even if they are not the source, e.g., of the illegal content.[253]

---

251 Cf., e.g., with further references *Quintel/Ullrich*, "Self-Regulation of Fundamental Rights? The EU Code of Conduct on Hate Speech, related initiatives and beyond", in: Petkova/Ojanen (eds.), 182, 182 et seq.

252 *Ullrich*, Unlawful Content Online: Towards a New Regulatory Framework for Online Platforms, p. 385–389.

253 Against any further extension of liability privileges therefore *Smith*, Enforcement and cooperation between Member States, p. 13.

2. DSA Approach

a. Overall Structure of Supervision

The relevant provisions on the design and structure of supervision are mainly included in Chapter IV of the DSA Proposal, although provisions in the previous chapters also contain important elements as part of the overall functioning of enforcement, in particular concerning information and data gathering.[254]

Art. 38 para. 1 of the DSA Proposal leaves ("in principle"[255]) supervision essentially to the Member States. Member States shall designate one or more competent authorities as responsible for the application and enforcement of the rules proposed. Art. 40 of the DSA Proposal contains rules on jurisdiction in line with the set-up of supervisory authorities on national level: A provider should be under the jurisdiction of the Member State where its main establishment is located or, in absence of an establishment in the Union, where its legal representative resides or is established – the designation of a legal representative being an obligation for all intermediary services that are established outside of the EU according to Art. 11 of the Proposal.[256] However, Art. 40 does not itself – as is the case, e.g., in the AVMSD[257] – define relevant criteria when deciding about the place of establishment besides mentioning that it is the "main" establishment.

---

254 This includes in particular the provisions laid down in Art. 10 (establishing points of contact allowing for direct communication also with supervisory authorities), Art. 11 (designation of legal representatives for EU foreign providers, which is especially relevant in the context of supervision online regarding the dominance of EU foreign providers), Art. 13 (laying down transparency reporting obligations, which can be an important source for data gathering and assessment of supervisory authorities if they are implemented in a meaningful and concrete way) and Art. 38 (ensuring the designation of compliance officers by very large platforms which cooperate with the supervisory authorities).

255 Cf. Recital 72.

256 Where a provider of intermediary services fails to appoint a legal representative in accordance with Art. 11, all Member States shall have jurisdiction, but the acting Member State shall inform all other Member States and ensure that the principle of *ne bis in idem* is respected (Art. 40 para. 3). This, therefore, introduces a certain backstop mechanism to ensure the supervisory authority's ability to act even in cases of non-compliant providers.

257 Art. 2 para. 3 defines, relying on a graded layer of criteria such as the question where programme-related decisions are made, where for the purposes of the AVMSD a media service provider shall be deemed to be established in a Member State.

Rather, these clarifications are made by Recital 76 by referring to the head office or registered office and adding the condition that in this office "the principal financial functions and operational control are exercised". In case of non-establishment, as mentioned, the triggering element for jurisdiction is the location of the legal representative, and the incentive to appoint such a representative – besides being a legal obligation – lies in the fact that otherwise, according to Art. 40 para. 3 of the Proposal which in this respect is only of declaratory nature, all Member States have jurisdiction. For the latter case there is only a limitation introduced that there is an obligation for Member States to inform the other Member States if measures have been taken according to this assignment of jurisdiction and that it has to be ensured that there is no parallel imposition of measures that would be contrary to the *ne bis in idem* principle.[258]

Furthermore, according to Art. 38 para. 2, Member States shall designate one of the competent authorities as a DSC that acts as a central contact point and coordinates the cooperation of different supervisory authorities at national level if there are a number of supervisory authorities implied. The provision as part of EU law does not concretise how this coordination at national level would work. Alternatively, the DSC can also be foreseen as the sole authority responsible for the DSA application in a Member State. In both models, the DSC is in charge of organising the cooperation with other DSCs, the Board established in the DSA Proposal (European Board for Digital Services, see below), and the Commission at supranational level.

The DSC can be a new or existing national authority; thus, a merging of functions within an existing authority is not precluded.[259] Art. 39 lays down rules on the independence of DSCs and the effectiveness of the fulfilment of their tasks by obligating the Member States to ensure that they perform tasks impartial, transparent and in a timely manner, act with complete independence and free from any external direct or indirect influence and are endowed with adequate technical, financial and human resources. These resources shall enable them, in particular, to search for and obtain information which is located in their territory, including in the context of

---

258 Irrespective of the question whether choosing a Regulation as instrument for the DSA Proposal is appropriate (see on that above E.I.), it is unclear whether this suggests that Member States are altogether limited in addressing intermediaries that fall under the scope of the DSA Proposal by provisions in national law and, if so, whether such a limitation of Member State competency concerning third country providers would at all be possible.

259 Recital 75.

joint investigations.[260] Recital 74 clarifies that independence does not exclude, within constitutional limits, national control or monitoring mechanisms regarding their financial expenditure or being subjected to judicial review as long as this does not endanger reaching the objectives of the DSA. The possibility to consult other national authorities where appropriate, leaves the independence of the authority untouched.

Section 2 of Chapter IV of the Proposal lays down provisions regarding the European Board for Digital Services (EBDS), which is proposed to be established as an "independent advisory group of DSCs" serving primarily as a forum to coordinate cooperation, to support and issue guidance and to assist the DSCs amongst each other and the Commission in the supervision of VLOPs (Art. 47). According to Art. 48, the EBDS shall be composed of each Member States' DSC, "represented by high-level officials". In addition, other competent authorities entrusted with specific responsibilities for the application and enforcement of the DSA rules shall participate in the Board. Furthermore, other national authorities may be invited to the meetings provided that the issues discussed are of relevance for them. The DSA Proposal assigns the Commission with the chairing role for the EBDS, including giving administrative and analytical support while not granting it any voting rights regarding the decisions taken by the EBDS. Internal rules of procedure of the EBDS require consent by the Commission.

Finally, the DSA Proposal adds a fourth layer on the structure of supervision over intermediaries by introducing specific additional rules for VLOPs. These provide for an enhanced supervision system when VLOPs have been found by a DSC to infringe the provisions of Section 4 of Chapter III[261] or when the Commission or other DSCs suspect such an infringement. The Commission has the power to intervene in case the infringements persist and are not addressed sufficiently by the responsible DSC (Art. 51). Generally this means that a DSC of establishment[262] that comes

---

260 Recital 77.

261 Obligations to take on risk assessments and proportionate mitigations measures accordingly, to provide transparency and user-friendly options in recommender systems, to ensure advertising transparency, to provide data access and scrutiny, to designate compliance officers and to publish transparency reports in a specific manner.

262 Cf. the definition in Art. 2 lit. l: the DSC of establishment is the DSC of the Member State where the provider of an intermediary service or its legal representative is established. This is differentiated from the DSC of destination in lit. m: the DSC of any Member State where the intermediary service is provided.

to a decision finding a VLOP to have infringed the above-mentioned provisions shall integrate the views on the matter of the Commission and the EBDS and follow the elements of the enhanced supervision system as laid down in Art. 50 in the further steps vis-à-vis the concerned platform. The enhanced supervision system mainly foresees a limitation of the role of the DSC of establishment and an inclusion of the European Commission and also of the EBDS, which are given specific powers regarding supervision of VLOPs. Both can act on their own initiative and trigger the mechanism of Art. 50, but the DSC of establishment's competence to act on its own behalf ends after completing the participation procedure with its final opinion communicated to the Commission, the EBDS and the VLOP concerned about the compliance of the VLOP (Art. 50 para. 4). Pursuant to that communication, the DSC of establishment shall no longer be entitled to take any investigatory or enforcement measures in respect of the relevant conduct by the VLOP except on request of the Commission. It is the Commission that is instead subsequently holding the relevant investigative powers, the power to initiate formal proceedings as well as the enforcement powers, with partial involvement of the EBDS, while the involvement of the DSC is mainly limited to information rights and obligations.

Mechanisms of self-regulation can be found in particular in Art. 34 to 37 in the context of the introduction of due diligence obligations, which are then partly addressed in the supervision section, e.g. regarding the tasks of the EBDS in Art. 49 para. 1 lit. e. According to this, the Commission shall support and promote the development, implementation and also updating of voluntary industry standards set by relevant European and international standardisation bodies, in particular regarding certain mechanisms of the proposed Regulation (Art. 34)[263], and shall encourage and facilitate the drawing up of codes of conduct at Union level in order to contribute to the proper application of the proposed Regulation, taking into account in particular the specific challenges of tackling different types of illegal content and systemic risks (Art. 35), especially in the field of online advertising (Art. 36). In addition, as a very specific reaction to unusual circumstances, the Commission (on recommendation by the EBDS) shall encourage and facilitate VLOPs and, where appropriate, other online platforms, with the involvement of the Commission, to participate in the drawing up, testing and application of so-called "crisis protocols", for addressing crisis situa-

---

263 E.g., the electronic submission of notices (Art. 14), the auditing of VLOPs (Art. 28) or the interoperability of ad repositories (Art. 30 para. 2).

tions strictly limited to such extraordinary circumstances[264] affecting public security or public health (Art. 37). Articles 34 to 37 do not contain specific indications on the question of the binding force or enforceability of these mechanisms; thus, they follow general rules on a lack of binding force. However, a regular monitoring and evaluation of such measures is foreseen, and Recital 67 mentions that codes of conduct need to be implemented in a "measurable" way and be "subject to public oversight".

In addition to the different layers of supervisory structures and instruments, the Commission has the power to adopt delegated acts referred to in Articles 23, 25, and 31, as is further detailed in Art. 69. In accordance with the rules foreseen for such implementing powers, a "Digital Services Committee" is set up which convenes Member States' representatives and the Commission.

The DMA Proposal, on the other hand, takes a much more centralised approach and allocates the powers regarding the supervision over gatekeepers exclusively to the European Commission. It is the Commission that decides on the designation of gatekeepers and has the relevant regulatory powers to assess, monitor and enforce the proposed provision. In doing so, the Commission shall be assisted by the Digital Markets Advisory Committee. This Committee is established as required by Regulation (EU) No 182/2011[265] and composed of representatives of the Member States. It is not a specific body such as the EBDS under the DSA Proposal, but the main role of these types of bodies is to ensure that the adoption of implementing acts by the Commission is subject to the control of Member States. In addition the Digital Markets Advisory Committee shall give opinions on certain individual decisions of the Commission, but it is not equipped with regulatory powers.

---

264 Recital 71 clarifies that this could entail any unforeseeable event, such as earthquakes, hurricanes, pandemics and other serious cross-border threats to public health, war and acts of terrorism, where, for example, online platforms may be misused for the rapid spread of illegal content or disinformation or where the need arises for rapid dissemination of reliable information.

265 Regulation (EU) No 182/2011 of the European Parliament and of the Council of 16 February 2011 laying down the rules and general principles concerning mechanisms for control by Member States of the Commission's exercise of implementing powers, OJ L 55, 28.2.2011, p. 13–18.

b. Regulatory Powers and Sanctions

With regard to the regulatory authorities to be established at Member State level according to Art. 38, the DSA Proposal at first sight does not, in contrast to the specific provision for the DSC (Art. 41), contain any concrete specifications with regard to regulatory powers. However, in Recitals 79 and 80 there are references to the basic principles of effective law enforcement to be established by the Member States. They highlight the importance of respecting the principle of proportionality, the fundamental rights to an effective remedy and to a fair trial, including the rights of defence, and the right to respect for private life by mentioning that the regulatory measures proposed in the DSA, for which the Commission is in charge, could serve as "an appropriate point of reference" for an area which otherwise remains in the procedural autonomy of Member States.

Art. 41 contains more concrete provisions on the minimum powers ("at least") of DSCs. These include powers of investigation (right to information and to carry out on-site inspections vis-à-vis providers and their business partners under certain circumstances; powers to ask any member of staff or representative of providers to give explanations and to record the answers) and enforcement powers (powers to accept the commitments offered by providers in relation to their compliance and to make those commitments binding; powers to order the cessation of infringements and, where appropriate, to impose remedies; powers to impose fines and/or periodic penalty payment and to enforce them; powers to adopt interim measures to avoid the risk of serious harm).

In addition, Art. 41 para. 3 provides for *ultima ratio* powers in cases where all other powers to bring about the cessation of an infringement both under the Regulation and other EU or national law have been exhausted without bringing an end to the infringement which causes serious harm. Firstly, they can involve the management body of the provider by requesting within a deadline to "examine the situation, adopt and submit an action plan setting out the necessary measures to terminate the infringement, ensure that the provider takes those measures, and report on the measures taken". Secondly, for cases that entail a "serious criminal offence involving a threat to the life or safety of persons" they can request the competent judicial authority to order the temporary restriction of access to the service for end users or even, if that is not possible, to the website or app (or comparable software, see definition of "online interface" in Art. 2 lit. k) of the provider overall.

According to Art. 41 para. 6, Member States shall ensure that any exercise of these powers is subject to adequate safeguards laid down in the applicable national law in conformity with the CFR and with the general principles of Union law. In addition, recipients have the right to lodge a complaint with their "home" DSC, which is forwarded to the DSC of establishment to be assessed, and, where appropriate, to further transmit it to another competent body (Art. 43). Importantly, the proposed Regulation also foresees powers of DSCs other than that of establishment to request action by the competent DSC; if there is a lack of action or a result of investigation that differs from the position of the requesting DSC, the matter can be forwarded to the Commission, which in turn can request the DSC of establishment to revisit the matter and ultimately can replace the DSC's powers with its own (see below).

Although these powers of DSCs in principle also apply in relation to VLOPs, they are limited by the Commission's powers established for this category of platforms. Essentially they are rather restricted to find in the case of breaches of specific obligations for VLOPs (Chapter 3, Section IV) an infringement based on the DSC of establishment's investigative powers, whereby already then the Commission's and EBDS' views are to be included. In the further procedure the DSC coordinates the communication with the VLOP concerned using its information rights while being obliged to inform Commission and EBDS according to the procedure under Articles 50 and 51. However, DSCs of establishment are in such cases not entitled to enforcement powers concerning the specific conduct (Art. 50 para. 4), which are instead shifted to the Commission, as is also the case if there is non-activity of the normally competent DSC (Art. 51 para. 1). But even outside the cases of a possible breach of obligations that only affect VLOPs, the normally competent DSC of establishment can practically hand over the procedure with regard to a VLOP (but concerning general obligations of it) to the Commission by a request under Art. 46 para. 2.

When it comes to sanctions for the violation of obligations by intermediaries as part of the enforcement mechanism, Member States have to lay down rules on penalties for such breaches (Art. 42) to accompany the powers foreseen for DSCs (Art. 41). These penalties have to be effective, proportionate and dissuasive while the cap is included in the Proposal: they may not exceed – but can go up to – 6% of the annual income or turnover of the providers or, in case of violations of procedural measures (e.g., supply of or failure to correct incorrect, incomplete or misleading information), 1% and for periodic penalty payments 5% of the average daily turnover in the preceding financial year per day.

Regarding regulatory powers and the sanctioning of VLOPs as far as the specific obligations imposed on them are concerned, it is the Commission which is equipped with various means to investigate and address the compliance of VLOPs. It can carry out investigations, including through requests for information (Art. 52), conducting interviews (Art. 53) and onsite inspections (Art. 54). Interim measures can be adopted in urgent cases due to the risk of serious damage for recipients (Art. 55), and the Commission can make binding[266] commitments offered by VLOPs to ensure their compliance (Art. 56) as well as monitor compliance – irrespective of individual cases – with the Regulation in general, which includes the right to receive access to, and explanations relating to, databases and algorithms used by the platforms (Art. 57). In case of non-compliance, the Commission is equipped with a set of different powers to react against VLOPs: It can adopt non-compliance decisions and impose fines in case of violation of the relevant provisions of the proposed Regulation or interim measures and commitments (Art. 58 and 59) as well as for violations of procedural requirements. Furthermore, the Commission is granted the possibility to impose on VLOPs (and, under certain conditions, their business partners) periodic penalty payments. The caps for these types of penalties are the same as for sanctions imposed by the DSCs, namely 6%, 1% and 5% of the relevant factors as described above for Art. 42. The Proposal sets limitation periods of five years for the imposition of penalties (Art. 61) and for their enforcement (Art. 62). To ensure the respect of fundamental rights, Art. 63 and 64 contain procedural guarantees, in particular the right to be heard and of access to the file as well as the publication of decisions (the latter with regard to the rights and legitimate interests of the VLOP).

As mentioned above, the Commission has regulatory powers under the DSA Proposal outside the rules that apply only to VLOPs. This applies in cases of cross-border cooperation under Art. 45 para. 7 if the Commission concludes that the activity of a DSC of establishment in a cross-border case is incompatible with the DSA. The Commission can oblige the respective DSC to continue the investigation and re-assess the matter before potentially being able to take over the case handling.

---

266 Although there is the possibility to reopen the proceedings in cases of changed circumstances, in cases where the VLOP is not acting compliant with its commitment or when the former decision was based on false information, Art. 56 para. 2; this follows the commitments-provision in Art. 9 Regulation (EC) 1/2003.

In contrast, the EBDS is not granted with regulatory powers. Rather its activities are limited to measures of support, coordination and advice with its general tasks (Art. 47 para. 2) to contribute to consistent and effective cooperation, to coordinate and contribute to guidance and analysis of the Commission, DSCs and other competent authorities on emerging issues across the internal market and to assist the DSCs and the Commission in the supervision of VLOPs. This general description of tasks is added with more details in Art. 49, which lists "in particular" the tasks of issuing opinions, recommendations or advice to DSCs and supporting and promoting the development and implementation of European standards, guidelines, reports, templates and codes of conduct. The DSA Proposal does not in the substantive part specifically address to what extent these measures should have a binding character or within the framework of which evaluation they should be taken into account. In Recital 90 it is underlined that the regular rules apply, according to which opinions, requests and recommendations are not legally binding, whereas any disregard of them needs specific explanation and shall potentially be used as indicator by the Commission when assessing whether a Member State is fulfilling its obligations resulting from the proposed Regulation. Further, according to Art. 49 para. 1 lit. d), the EBDS can trigger the intervention and opening of proceedings by the Commission laid down in Art. 51 by advising the Commission to do so.

Regarding the DMA Proposal, on the other hand, the Commission has a set of powers according to Chapter IV to conduct market investigations with the purpose of examining if there are new services or new practices relevant for the scope of the proposed Regulation. Besides that, the regulatory powers granted to the Commission are very similar to those in the DSA (requests for information, powers to carry out interviews and take statements as well as to conduct on-site inspections, interim measures, commitments vis-à-vis stakeholders, non-compliance decisions). The penalty cap is higher (10% of total turnover in the preceding financial year) compared to the DSA and the respective provisions (Art. 26–29 DMA Proposal) are more concrete in regarding the different treatment of violations of different provisions. Besides this, however, the DMA Proposal also provides for possibilities and limits for fines and periodic penalties. In this context, Art. 35 clarifies that the CJEU has unlimited jurisdiction to review such Commission decisions and that it can cancel, reduce or increase the fine or periodic penalty payment imposed.

c. Supranational Coordination and Cooperation

The DSA Proposal provides for several layers of cooperation mechanisms interconnecting the different levels of supervision (national regulatory authorities, DSCs and the Commission).

The main forum for a regular cooperation in general matters concerning the regulation of digital services in the sense of the DSA Proposal is supposed to be the EBDS, which – as explained above – is composed of the DSCs of the Member States under the chairmanship of the Commission. Besides the exchange of information, the development of guidelines and standards and the coordination of cross-border regulatory matters shall be achieved in the Board. Art. 44 should also be read in this context. It obliges DSCs to publish annual activity reports giving an overview of numbers and subject matters of orders taking action against illegal content and information orders under Art. 8 and 9 DSA Proposal, in which the DSC has to include the activity of all competent supervisory authorities of the given Member State. The DSCs shall make the annual reports available to the public and communicate them to the Commission and the EBDS, giving the necessary information to the latter in order to exchange on regulatory practices.

Different cooperation mechanisms concerning concrete investigations, procedures and decisions can be found throughout numerous provisions of the DSA Proposal.[267]

Art. 45 and 46 of the DSA Proposal concerning cross-border matters are key in that respect. Art. 45 provides for procedures of cross-border cooperation between DSCs. As explained above, this provision shall respond to the situation that a DSC is of the opinion that the competent DSC (of establishment) should be acting because of an assumed infringement of relevant provisions of the DSA by a provider under its jurisdiction. It can then request the DSC of establishment to assess the matter and take the necessary investigatory and enforcement measures to ensure compliance (Art. 45 para. 2). Where such an assumed violation is regarded to concern at least three Member States, the EBDS has the right to approach the DSC of establishment with the same goal. The resulting obligation of that DSC is the need to investigate and communicate within a given timeframe its as-

---

267 "Cooperation", esp. in cross-border situations, is a recurring theme in the accompanying Explanatory Memorandum to the DSA, too. It is one of the main elements of the DSA Proposal according to Art. 1 para. 1 lit. c) which concerns "cooperation of and coordination between the competent authorities".

sessment of the situation and possible planned measures whereby it has to take "into utmost account the request or recommendation" of the other DSC or EBDS. If the time limit is not met or the requesting DSC or the EBDS do not agree with the assessment, the matter can be referred to the Commission, which shall then assess the matter within three months after having consulted the DSC of establishment and, unless it had referred the matter itself, the EBDS. If the Commission concludes that the measures envisaged by the DSC of establishment are incompatible with the proposed provisions of the DSA, it shall request the DSC of establishment to further assess the matter and take the necessary investigatory or enforcement measures. Again, there is a strict time-delay of two months from that request to provide the Commission with information about the measures taken.

However, Art. 45 does not contain any indications as to what extent this last decision of the Commission is binding or what happens if the measures ultimately taken by the DSC of establishment do not correspond to the Commission's assessment. This is different compared to the situation for VLOPs where the Commission cannot only initiate proceedings (Art. 51 para. 1) but also adopt decisions pursuant to Articles 58 and 59 in cases where the DSC of establishment did not take appropriate measures. This difference is acknowledged by Recital 85, which also refers to the Commission's powers for a general monitoring of Union law compliance by the Member States and the possibility of infringement procedures, thereby clarifying that no direct (other) consequence derives from the different opinion of the Commission (again: except if a VLOP is concerned).

Meanwhile, Art. 46 para. 1 highlights the possibility of joint investigations of DSCs by stating that such investigations could be coordinated by the EBDS and that the results shall be made available to other DSCs. Art. 46 para. 2 establishes the right of the DSC of establishment at any time to request the Commission to take the necessary investigatory and enforcement measures to ensure compliance of a VLOP, thereby delegating the procedure voluntarily to the EU level.

Outside of these separately regulated procedures in specific cases, however, other provisions of the DSA Proposals also contain repeated references to the interplay between the various participating regulatory bodies. This is, for example, the case regarding the procedure set out in Art. 50 et seq. concerning possible violations: once the Commission initiated proceedings against a VLOP, the DSC of establishment concerned should be precluded from exercising investigatory and enforcement powers so as to avoid duplication, inconsistencies and risks from the viewpoint of the principle of *ne bis in idem*[268], but also because that DSC originally had the possibility to act by itself. However, on request of the Commission, the normally competent DSC shall assist the proceedings, inter alia by providing the Commission with all necessary information and assistance to allow it to perform its tasks effectively, whilst conversely the Commission should keep it informed about the exercise of its powers. In that regard, the Commission should, where appropriate, take account of any relevant assessments carried out by the EBDS or DSCs concerned (without prejudice to its own investigatory powers). Articles 51 para. 3 and 52 para. 5, as well as other proposed rules[269], contain provisions on the exchange and use of information. Because of the importance of this exchange, the DSA Proposal provides in Art. 67 for the establishment of an information sharing system by the European Commission to enable reliable and secure communication between DSCs, Commission and the EBDS.

Cooperation mechanisms are foreseen also with regard to the risk mitigation obligations of VLOPs. According to Art. 27 para. 3, the Commission, in cooperation with the DSCs, may issue general guidelines in relation to specific risks, in particular to present best practices and recommend possible measures. But the cooperation between EBDS and Commission extends also to the publishing of reports concerning systemic risks (Art. 27 para. 2).

Finally, the DSA Proposal also provides for special rules on the cooperation of the Commission with national courts (Art. 65) and for the adoption of implementing acts on practical arrangement of the proceedings (Art. 66).

As the powers under the DMA Proposal are concentrated in the Commission, other supervisory authorities do not have a place alongside it, and Member State participation is only foreseen within the framework of the proposed Digital Markets Advisory Committee, which is only granted review powers and no regulatory powers of its own. There are also no cooperation mechanisms included in the DMA Proposal as would concern possibly affected national authorities. Art. 33 is noteworthy in this context, as it gives the Member States – when there are three or more intending to do

---

268 Recital 98.
269 According to these other provisions, DSCs have to notify the Commission of the out-of-court dispute settlement bodies that they have certified (Art. 18 para. 5), have to inform the Commission and the EBDS on entities awarded as trusted flaggers (Art. 19 para. 3) and have to verify, at least every six months, if a platform under their jurisdiction has to be qualified as a VLOP and communicate that decision to the Commission (Art. 25 para. 4).

so – the right to request a market investigation by the Commission if they consider that there are reasonable grounds to suspect that a provider of core platform services should be designated as a gatekeeper. This right is assigned to the Member States, not to specific authorities of the Member States. Besides that, Art. 1 para. 7 of the DMA Proposal underlines that national authorities shall not take decisions which would run counter to a decision adopted by the Commission under the proposed Regulation. It is suggested that instead Commission and Member States shall work in close cooperation and coordination in their enforcement actions. Regarding the implementation of the latter, the Commission may adopt implementing acts according to Art. 36 para. 2 DMA Proposal.

3. Assessment

The DSA Proposal picks up the demand for an updated and cooperation-enabling supervisory framework in order to ensure a better monitoring of rules applicable to online intermediaries especially in cases of cross-border dissemination. The inclusion of a sanctioning regime raises the promise of a more robust enforcement. However, it stops short of two important aspects in terms of supervisions: taking into consideration the specificities of certain areas of online activity irrespective of the goal to reach a horizontally applicable framework and relying more on administrative structures on the level of Member States.

The fact that the DSA refers to existing legislative acts of the EU with an effect on the online intermediaries as lex specialis – such as the VSP provisions of the AVMSD – seems insufficient when it comes to ensuring in a clear way that the specifics of content dissemination online are reflected in the regulation and the regulatory oversight. If the suggested approach is retained to create a Regulation and not to foresee rules for supervisory structures that apply specifically to online content dissemination or carve-outs to ensure that the horizontal rules do not overlap sector-specific solutions, then it is even more essential to uphold the role of administrative structures at Member States' level that are experienced in responding to these specifics. This leaves untouched the possibility and need for enhanced forms of cooperation between these Member States' authorities and bodies.

The current draft takes a centralising approach also concerning the supervision. Interestingly enough, however, it does not do so by relying on the creation of new bodies with decision-making power but instead assigns an entirely new role in the "platform market observation" to the European Commission. Firstly, it needs to be pointed out that procedural autonomy which includes the design of the administrative structures in a given field remains in the competence of the Member States. These are indeed bound, as clearly set out in the CJEU's jurisprudence on the principles of effective implementation of EU law and sincere cooperation, by the task of taking all efforts to ensure that the applicable provisions of EU law are realised in an efficient way. But besides this general obligation it is still, from the outset, a responsibility to create the necessary structures – or use existing structures by empowering them accordingly – that is in the hands of the Member States. Secondly, the approach chosen is also not reflective of other comparable sectoral approaches under EU law. As examples of different intensities of cooperation, for ERGA, BEREC or the EDPB, which are all the joint "bodies" on EU level contributing to the enforcement of sectoral EU rules, there is the same characteristic: it is national authorities coming together in a joint body which are then assigned certain cooperation tasks, but it is not a delegation of the powers of national institutions to the Commission.

There is one area for which the executive power distribution is significantly different, which is in the enforcement of EU competition law. Therefore, even though the DMA is not based on competition law as legal basis but the single market harmonisation clause, too, it is not surprising that in an instrument that is reflective of competition law instruments and that addresses the few, biggest and therefore most relevant gatekeepers, the enforcement powers are (in the Proposal) accordingly vested in the Commission. It is a different matter for the scope of application of the DSA, which is why here it should be carefully reconsidered not only whether the instrument of Regulation is the appropriate choice but also whether the prominent role of the Commission is adequate. Although the Commission does not have voting rights in the foreseen EBDS, it chairs that new board, thus giving it a strong steering role, especially as it also provides the analytical support and needs to consent to the internal rules of procedure. For VLOPs there is an even stronger similarity to the DMA approach, as the Commission for those platforms can receive or take investigatory and decision-making powers.

Irrespective of the cross-border dimension of online business activity and specifically content dissemination, it is not only possible but recommendable to rely on the Member States level for enforcement. This is more in line with the competence framework of allocation of powers to Member States or the EU respectively and, in addition, there is a comparability to the regulation of media-type content for which national, regional and even local specificities may play a role. Such need of potentially differing Member State approaches is, for example, clearly integrated in the AVMSD, which relies on the national regulatory authorities (NRAs) for enforcement but creates cooperation structures between them.

These enhanced forms of cooperation are indeed needed, and needed urgently, in a clear and effective manner. The cross-border nature of dissemination plays a role in that respect, as the reliance on only a regulatory "home base" for businesses that offer services across the Union finds its limit in the need for effective protection of public interest goals. In order to avoid a permanent deviation from the COO principle if an efficient joint approach to cross-border matters is not found, it is the right way forward to institutionalise cooperation forms. The DSA Proposal goes in that direction, but it is not very clear in the assignment of powers to the cooperation structures or in the procedures; so it is questionable whether with the proposed provisions and the introduction of an EBDS, which is only a very loose form of cooperation, a more effective enforcement across borders would be achieved. It is to be welcomed that there is a sort of "accountability" of each DSC to the DSCs of other Member States and that in case of a contradictory assessment of a given situation under certain circumstances other concerned bodies can "step in". However, such a request for action on the side of a DSC of establishment would, according to the current Proposal, lead to the Commission receiving the powers to continue the procedure instead of, e.g., the EBDS. There are no specific avenues for expedited procedures or even joint decisions created, even though procedural steps are now linked more to time limits.

The DSA Proposal should leave untouched the possibilities for organising cooperation by national bodies outside of cooperation structures that assign the decision-making power to the Commission or from the outset foresee that the decisions in matters of joint interest are taken by the concerned authorities, e.g. in a majority voting in a consistency procedure, as was introduced in the GDPR's new joint body EDPB. For certain types of providers it could also be envisaged that a joint body has exclusive competence for decision, e.g. because of the relevance of the intermediary concerned across all or a significant part of EU Member States. It is not clear why in such cases it should automatically be the Commission entrusted with this task, because for such an approach a regulatory structure would have to be built up. In other areas where a structure for joint supervision and decision-making was deemed necessary, this was created in addition to, and outside of, the Commission.

For content dissemination platforms and the comparable regulatory setting for audiovisual media services, a closer look at the role of NRAs, but more importantly of the joint cooperation body institutionalised only in 2018 with the reformed AVMSD, would give examples of how a cooperation mechanism can be designed. ERGA discussed how a more efficient enforcement of rules concerning providers that fall under the scope of application of the AVMSD could be achieved. For that purpose, the national NRAs assembled in ERGA agreed on a Memorandum of Understanding[270] detailing on which bases and how (in practice) cooperation will take place in order to achieve speedily and efficient reactions in enforcement.[271] The commitments listed in this Memorandum under 1.3. give evidence to the agreement on a joint basis of why and how the providers should be regulated and show that an efficient cooperation does not mandatorily need a centralisation. The introduction of an accelerated mutual assistance procedure (in 2.1.4.) is intended to increase the speed of investigations and reactions especially to the dissemination of illegal content. Section 4.4. acknowledges that a Memorandum cannot have any binding legal force and that such a binding legal text would not fall within the current remit of ERGA, but this form of cooperation that is aligned to the needs and possibilities of cross-border work could be a blueprint for legally binding cooperation mechanisms in a new legislative framework. The legislative act could limit itself to designate the authority to create such types of more concrete cooperation mechanisms by the regulatory authorities concerned without having to list the details. Such an approach would combine the need for an effective cross-border law enforcement while retaining the role of national authorities. Currently, the role of the proposed EBDS is designed in a rather loose form, especially compared to the enhanced position the Commission is proposing for itself. If all regulatory authorities concerned are mandated by a legislative framework to cooperate and decide jointly, this can have a positive effect compared to a "merely" loose form of cooperation, as can be seen in the difference of the former A29-WP of the Data Protection Directive in comparison with the EDPB under the GDPR.

---

270 MoU of 3.12.2020, https://erga-online.eu/wp-content/uploads/2020/12/ERGA_Memorandum_of_Understanding_adopted_03-12-2020_l.pdf.

271 Already the Rules of Procedure of ERGA (Version 10.12.2019) introduce strict time limits for certain joint decision-making procedures (fast track adoption procedure, Art. 13).

A further aspect of the supervisory structures as proposed by the DSA needs to be considered carefully: as mentioned, a lex specialis rule alone will not ensure that there is no overspill of new regulatory structures under the DSA into sector-specific areas such as the AVMSD. Besides referring to that Directive generally, a more specific clarification of the role of NRAs and their cooperation forum under AVMSD, which would remain untouched by the DSA, would be welcomed. This could include the clarification that the DSC, and with that the national representative for the EBDS, can be the same as the institution representative that takes seat in ERGA. The DSA does not go into detail of the set-up of national regulatory authorities involved in the oversight of intermediaries besides an independence requirement and some further indications. Here it could be considered whether it is not advisable – if no sector-specific supervisory solutions are included – to include similar expectations to the set-up of the national authorities as is the case for AVMS-NRAs.

The Proposal would force Member States to focus their oversight structures on one (coordinating) DSC. Even though other authorities can exist and cooperate with the DSC and even sit in the EBDS besides the DSC, such a concentration in one regulatory body may not be an adequate solution for structures in federal systems or where there are no convergent regulatory authorities. It is fully understandable that a precise allocation of representation facilitates the communication between all involved parties, but as it is acknowledged that there is a complex web of interacting authorities already on national level, it is not an obvious solution to expect the assignment of one "super-authority" for intermediary supervision, be it an existing, merged or newly created authority.

The procedures for cooperation as well as the further detailing of the procedure by delegated acts of the Commission suggest the possibility of a further enhancement of the role of the Commission. This needs to be critically reviewed in order not to create contradictions to existing supervisory approaches and cooperation forms that impact the online sector (at least as well). The procedures are of a multilayer nature and set up in a complex way concerning the involvement of the DSC of establishment, the other DSCs, the EBDS and the Commission. In the further legislative procedure a careful assessment should be made for any type of violation of the substantive provisions of the proposed Regulation in order to see whether the new structures (if they were to be retained) facilitate or rather complicate the procedures, especially in cross-border cases, and whether or not they sufficiently ensure the consideration of specific contexts, such as media-type content dissemination. The procedures should result in an improvement of the enforcement in urgent situations compared to the situation foreseen under the ECD. As, for now, those rules would stay in place and the new rules – at least for content-specific matters – would not on first sight lower the hurdles for cross-border action of competent authorities, it should be re-discussed on how to accelerate the procedure and make it less complex when, e.g., one regulatory authority has to rely on the involvement of another when investigating or issuing an order against illegal content disseminated by a provider under foreign EU jurisdiction. This analysis of the proposed procedures should include a scrutiny of the involvement of independent public authorities in the assessment of the risk management processes of providers without relying solely on audits by private parties.

For content dissemination intermediaries, the starting point of reforming the ECD framework – which is addressed in the DSA – was to ensure that the rules (and their enforcement) concerning this dissemination are applicable in a more or less equal way in the online environment as they are for the offline situation. This should be the prime guiding principle when deciding about the final supervisory structure in a DSA, which in the initial Proposal is not yet achieved.

F. Looking Ahead

In an overall assessment of the situation concerning the regulatory framework for online content dissemination on the level of the European Union, there are several findings to be highlighted. With the two Proposals for a DSA and a DMA the Commission has responded, after a long period of reluctance to address the issue more broadly beyond sectoral approaches, to the widely acknowledged need for reforming the rules concerning online platforms. As was analysed extensively in a previous study of the authors, the reliance on the ECD as a horizontal framework regulating the ISS resulted in negative outcomes: the way the rules were applied and interpreted did not allow for an efficient response to the dissemination of illegal and harmful content online nor a cross-border enforcement of the standards laid down in the ECD and the EU legislative framework altogether.[272] The purpose of this follow-up study was to identify the legislative options for responding to the pressing need of reforming the current framework and propose ways forward. This was done by evaluating the way that the DSA Proposal addresses the issues and suggesting – where appropriate – in which way the Proposal should be further adapted in the course of the legislative procedure ahead.

Without any doubt, the Proposals are to be welcomed: they promise in the final outcome to be the basis for a sustainable regulatory framework for the digital sector and can put the EU in the position of setting standards in a way that was already successfully done with the GDPR.[273] The Proposals are ambitious not only because they are aimed at addressing intermediaries in total but because they identify specific categories of providers that are essential for the connection between businesses and users and are then under special scrutiny as gatekeepers (in the DMA) or that have such an impact that they have to comply with specific additional obligations (as VLOPs in the DSA). As a condition for that, and in line with more recent legislative approaches such as the GDPR or the VSP provisions in the AVMSD, neither the applicability of the proposed Regula-

---

272 *Cole/Etteldorf/Ullrich*, Cross-border Dissemination of Online Content.
273 In this sense also *Ukrow*, Die Vorschläge der EU-Kommission für einen Digital Services Act und einen Digital Markets Act, p. 57.

tions nor the jurisdiction depends on an establishment of the concerned providers in an EU Member State.

However, a number of concerns exist which should be taken into account in the further shaping of the Proposals. Partly, these are connected to the approach chosen in the two Proposals, and for other issues there is a more specific need to clarify some of the suggested new rules. One of the more fundamental concerns relates to the way this new framework, which mainly means the DSA, would affect the regulation of content intermediaries. Because of the relevance of such platforms for the dissemination and availability of media and communication content more generally, it is justified to pay specific attention to these, and they are in the focus of this study. As much as a horizontally applicable framework for ISS promises a unified and overarching approach to any type of such intermediary service as covered by the DSA Proposal, it can also be problematic in addressing specificities of certain categories of platforms or services. The basic rules can and should apply to any type of ISS, but the requirements for rules that impact media and communication content are different to that of a marketplace where goods and services are traded. Considering the Member States' retained power to regulate the media, from the outset it should be questioned whether a Regulation is the appropriate instrument to introduce the new rules. Beyond that principal question, the current version of the Proposal does not yet sufficiently take into account the existing framework for supervision and enforcement of rules concerning content dissemination. In view of the goal that the same rules should apply (and be enforced) for content online as for content offline, there should be a further clarification of how the new general rules relate to existing or future rules specifically enacted for regulating content dissemination. This also concerns existing supervisory structures that have an established experience of dealing with the sensitive balancing of fundamental rights when tackling content matters. With the still new AVMSD in transposition stage, the cooperation structures – namely in a body such as ERGA – stemming from a media services approach should rather be reinforced by the new approach than questioned when creating new overarching authority structures with a focus on one major DSC per Member State.

The proposed DSA takes into account the position of intermediaries which, due to network effects, in many cases have acquired dominant market power and generally provide a crucial function between providers of services and end users. It imposes on certain types of platforms due diligence obligations that add a second, free standing pillar next to the question of liability for information hosted (to mention only the most important category besides providers offering mere conduit or caching services) by recipients of the service. The liability exemption chapter is transferred from the ECD to the proposed DSA with very few changes and by adding some clarifications about what type of orders can be imposed on providers under the liability exemptions. As the set of these rules included in Chapter II on the liability of the providers of intermediary services are in addition of any outcome regarding the liability exemptions, it is important to have a clear integration of those obligations of providers also in the enforcement procedures. In addition, there appear to be links between the conditions for liability exemptions and the allegedly free-standing due diligence obligations of Chapter III. This relation needs to be clarified because any intermediary that is found liable will also face the remedies and sanctions under national and applicable sectorial Union law, and it is important to clarify the enforcement steps in case of violation of the obligations to follow orders mentioned in Chapter II in connection with that matter.

The idea of being able to deal under certain circumstances with issues emanating from providers with an establishment outside of a given EU Member State, as far as the regulatory authority observes a negative impact of a – possibly targeted – service, is the right approach. However, this necessitates adequate structures and procedures, and again it is advisable to reconsider whether the institutional set-up of the current Proposal can sufficiently respond to this need, as has been shown in this study.

The Proposal relies in parts on enforcement tools that emanate from the self-regulatory approaches to include online platforms by ways of codes of conducts and memoranda of understanding. These kind of arrangements have, previously, only had limited success. The use of standards and more incisive oversight measures, such as audits, is applied in a rather limited way in the current Proposal. Standards could be used more broadly across areas such as risk management, and it should be reconsidered to expand such reliance on standards also for other platforms than only the category that have to observe the strictest measures. Meanwhile, outsourcing of audits to the private sector alone can be problematic if it is not accompanied by a solid public oversight framework in the proposed DSA. Apart from that, the layered approach to due diligence obligations could be simplified by extending obligations solely defined for VLOPs to online platforms in general.

Especially concerning the oversight structures, the current approach of the Proposals has to be criticised. At least for the approach in the DSA it is not sufficiently explained why the cross-border treatment of cases, when a competent regulatory authority does not act in a way that ensures efficient enforcement of the rules, should move from a joint forum of national regulatory authorities to the Commission. Generally speaking, existing regulatory structures should be taken more into account and an inclusion of the Member States' competent authorities and bodies should be sought, not only in cases that fall under their jurisdiction but also when it comes to resolving conflicts in cross-border cases. The Proposals already foresee a certain set of expectations about the set-up of authorities involved in the supervision of intermediary services providers. It should, however, be considered whether the strict criteria that, for example, apply to the regulatory bodies in the audiovisual media sector or to the data protection authorities, especially concerning independence from state powers, supervised entities and private parties and with regard to assignment of powers and capacities enabling efficiency, should not be more clearly integrated also in the current Proposal. As already mentioned, the cross-border dimension of the problem does not necessarily call for a centralised body on a supranational level but for efficient cooperation between authorities confined to their borders as well as with the bodies and institutions on EU level. In extending the approach of the Proposal it should be considered to upgrade joint bodies with decision making powers in a kind of consistency mechanism when there are disputes about the enforcement in specific cases and vis-à-vis specific providers.

Assuming that the new ruleset will stand in principle for a long period of time and will shape the digital intermediaries market at least for a decade, the suggested rules should be seen as a good basis which can be improved in the legislative procedure in order to reach a solution that responds in a promising way to the challenges previously identified.

Bibliography

Albath, L.; Giesel M.: Das Herkunftslandprinzip in der Dienstleistungsrichtlinie – Eine Kodifizierung der Rechtsprechung? In: EuZW 9 (2), 2006, p. 38–42.
Cited: *Albath/Giesel*, in: EuZW 9(2), 2006, 38, p.

Babbs, D.: New Year, New Internet? Why It's Time to Rethink Anonymity on Social Media, in: Inforrm's Blog, 2020, https://inforrm.org/2020/01/31/new-year-new-internet-why-its-time-to-rethink-anonymity-on-social-media-david-babbs/.
Cited: *Babbs*, in: Inforrm's Blog, New Year, New Internet? Why It's Time to Rethink Anonymity on Social Media.

Blandin, L.: Proceedings of the Workshop on "E-commerce rules, fit for the digital age", Study for the Committee on Internal Market and Consumer Protection, Policy Department for Economic, Scientific and Quality of Life Policies, European Parliament, Brussels, 2020.
Cited: *speaker*, in: Blandin, Proceedings of the Workshop on "E-commerce rules, fit for the digital age".

Blanke, H.-J.; Mangiameli, S. (eds.): The Treaty on European Union (TEU), Berlin 2013.
Cited: *author*, in: Blanke/Mangiameli.

Büllesbach, A.; Gijrath, S. J. H.; Poullet, Y.; Prins, J. E. J. (eds.): Concise European IT Law, 2nd edition, Alphen aan den Rijn 2010.
Cited: *Büllesbach et al. (eds.)*, Concise European IT Law.

Cappello, M. (ed.): Media pluralism and competition issues, IRIS Special, European Audiovisual Observatory, Strasbourg 2020, https://rm.coe.int/iris-special-1-2020en-media-pluralism-and-competition-issues/1680a08455.
Cited: *author*, in: Cappello (ed.), Media pluralism and competition issues.

Chapuis-Doppler, A.; Delhomme, V.: Regulating Composite Platform Economy Services: The State-of-play After Airbnb Ireland, in: European Papers, 5 (1), 2020, p. 411–428.
Cited: *Chapuis-Doppler/Delhomme*, in: European Papers, 5 (1), 2020, 411, p.

Cobbe, J.; Singh, J.: Regulating Recommending: Motivations, Considerations, and Principles, in: European Journal of Law and Technology (EJLT), 10 (3), 2019, https://ejlt.org/index.php/ejlt/article/view/686.
Cited: *Cobbe/Singh*, in: EJLT, 10 (3), 2019.

Cohen, J.E.: The Regulatory State in the Information Age, in: Theoretical Inquiries in Law, 17 (1), 2016 p. 369-411.
Cited: *Cohen*, in: Theoretical Inquiries in Law 17 (1), 2016, 369, p.

Cole, M.: Gestaltungsspielraum der EU-Mitgliedstaaten bei Einschränkungen der Dienstleistungsfreiheit, in: Zeitschrift für Medien- und Kommunikationsrecht (AfP), 52 (1), 2021, p. 1–7.
Cited: *Cole*, in: AfP 52 (1), 2021, 1, p.

Cole, M.: Zum Gestaltungsspielraum der EU-Mitgliedstaaten bei Einschränkungen der Dienstleistungsfreiheit. Eine Untersuchung am Beispiel einer Regelung bezüglich der Medienvielfalt in Deutschland, Saarbruecken 2020, https://emr-sb.de /wp-content/uploads/2020/06/Zum-Gestaltungsspielraum-der-EU-Mitgliedstaate n-bei-Einschr%c3%a4nkungen-der-Dienstleistungsfreiheit.pdf.
Cited: *Cole*, Zum Gestaltungsspielraum der EU-Mitgliedstaaten bei Einschränkungen der Dienstleistungsfreiheit.

Cole, M.: Die Neuregelung des Artikel 7b Richtlinie 2010/13/EU (AVMD-RL), Saarbruecken, 2019, https://emr-sb.de/wp-content/uploads/2019/12/emr-gutacht en_neuregelung-des-artikel-7b-avmd_11.2019.pdf.
Cited: *Cole*, Die Neuregelung des Artikel 7b Richtlinie 2010/13/EU (AVMD-RL).

Cole, M.: The AVMSD Jurisdiction Criteria concerning Audiovisual Media Service Providers after the 2018 Reform, Saarbruecken, 2018, https://emr-sb.de/study-av msd-jurisdiction-criteria/.
Cited: *Cole*, AVMSD Jurisdiction Criteria after the 2018 Reform.

Cole, M.: The Country of Origin Principle – From State Sovereignty under Public International Law to Inclusion in the Audiovisual Media Services Directive of the European Union, in: Meng, W.; Ress, G.; Stein, T. (eds.), Europäische Integration und Globalisierung – Festschrift zum 60-jährigen Bestehen des Europa-Instituts, Baden-Baden 2011.
Cited: *Cole*, The Country of Origin Principle.

Cole, M.: Europarechtliche Rahmenbedingungen für die Pluralismussicherung im Rundfunk, in: Freiheitssicherung durch Regulierung: fördert oder gefährdet die Wettbewerbsaufsicht publizistische Vielfalt im Rundfunk?, Baden-Baden 2009, p. 93 - 130.
Cited: *Cole*, Europarechtliche Rahmenbedingungen für die Pluralismussicherung im Rundfunk, 93, p.

Cole, M.; Etteldorf, C.; Ullrich, C.: Cross-border Dissemination of Online Content: Current and Possible Future Regulation of the Online Environment with a Focus on the EU E-Commerce Directive (Schriftenreihe Medienforschung der Landesanstalt für Medien NRW 81), Baden-Baden 2020, https://www.nomos-elibrar y.de/10.5771/9783748906438/cross-border-dissemination-of-online-content.
Cited: *Cole/Etteldorf/Ullrich*, Cross-border Dissemination of Online Content.

Cole, M.; Iacino, D.; Matzneller, P.; Metzdorf, J; Schweda S.: AVMS-RADAR: AudioVisual Media Services – Regulatory Authorities' Independence and Efficiency Review: Update on recent changes and developments in Member States and Candidate Countries that are relevant for the analysis of independence and efficient functioning of audiovisual media services regulatory bodies (SMART 2013/0083), Study prepared for the Commission DG CNECT by the EMR and the University of Luxembourg, Brussels 2015, https://op.europa.eu/en/publicatio n-detail/-/publication/9860f65c-8776-11e5-b8b7-01aa75ed71a1/language-en.
Cited: *Cole et al.*, AVMS-RADAR.

Cole, M.; Ukrow, J.; Etteldorf, C.: On the Allocation of Competences between the European Union and its Member States in the Media Sector. An Analysis with particular Consideration of Measures concerning Media Pluralism, Saarbruecken 2020, https://www.rlp.de/de/regierung/staatskanzlei/medienpolitik/rundfunk kommission/aktuelle-studien-gutachten/.
Cited: *Cole/Ukrow/Etteldorf*, On the Allocation of Competences between the European Union and its Member States in the Media Sector.

Constantin, S.: Rethinking Subsidiarity and the Balance of Powers in the EU in Light of the Lisbon Treaty and Beyond, in: Croatian Yearbook of European Law and Policy (CYELP), 4, 2008, p. 151–177.
Cited: *Constantin* in: CYELP 4, 2008, 151, p.

Cornils, M.: Designing Platform Governance: A Normative Perspective on Needs, Strategies, and Tools to Regulate Intermediaries, Algorithm Watch, Berlin 2020, https://algorithmwatch.org/wp-content/uploads/2020/05/Governing-Platforms-le gal-study-Cornils-May-2020-AlgorithmWatch.pdf.
Cited: *Cornils*, Designing Platform Governance: A Normative Perspective on Needs, Strategies, and Tools to Regulate Intermediaries.

de Posson, V.: Digital Services Act: Ensuring a Trustworthy and Safe Online Environment While Allowing Freedom of Expression, in: Disruptive Competition Project, 20th January 2021, https://www.project-disco.org/european-union/01202 1-dsa-ensuring-a-trustworthy-and-safe-online-enviornment-while-allowing-freedo m-of-expression/.
Cited: *de Posson*, Digital Services Act: Ensuring a Trustworthy and Safe Online Environment While Allowing Freedom of Expression.

de Streel, A.; Broughton Micova, S.: Digital Services Act: Deepening the internal market and clarifying responsibilities for digital services, Brussels 2020, https://c erre.eu/wp-content/uploads/2020/12/CERRE_DSA_Deepening-the-internal-mar ket-and-clarifying-responsibilities-for-digital-services_Full-report_December2020 .pdf.
Cited: *de Streel/Broughton Micova*, Digital Services Act: Deepening the internal market and clarifying responsibilities for digital services.

de Streel, A.; Husovec, M.: The e-commerce Directive as the cornerstone of the Internal Market. Assessment and options for reform, Luxembourg, 2020, https://w ww.europarl.europa.eu/RegData/etudes/STUD/2020/648797/IPOL_STU(2020)6 48797_EN.pdf.
Cited: *de Streel/Husovec*, The e-commerce Directive as the cornerstone of the Internal Market.

de Streel, A.; Defreyne, E.; Jacquemin, H.; Ledger, M.; Innesti, A.; Goubet, M.; Ustowski, D.: Online Platforms' Moderation of Illegal Content Online, Study for the committee on Internal Market and Consumer Protection, Policy Department for Economic, Scientific and Quality of Life Policies, European Parliament, Luxembourg 2020, https://www.europarl.europa.eu/RegData/etudes/STU D/2020/652718/IPOL_STU(2020)652718_EN.pdf.
Cited: *de Streel et al.*, Online Platforms' Moderation of Illegal Content Online.

Diaz Crego, M.; Manko, R.; van Ballegooij, W.: Protecting EU common values within the Member States. An overview of monitoring, prevention and enforcement mechanisms at EU level, EPRS | European Parliamentary Research Service, Brussels, 2020, https://www.europarl.europa.eu/RegData/etudes/STUD/2020/652088/EPRS_STU(2020)652088_EN.pdf.
Cited: *Diaz Crego/Manko/van Ballegooij (EPRS study)*, Protecting EU common values within the Member States.

Dreyer, S.; Heyer, R.; Seipp, T. J.; Schulz W.: The European Communication (Dis)Order. Mapping the media-relevant European legislative acts and identification of dependencies, interface areas and conflicts. Hamburg 2020 (Working Papers of the HBI No. 52), https://hans-bredow-institut.de/uploads/media/default/cms/media/8engbt7_AP52BKM_Mapping-Gutachten_en.pdf.
Cited: *Dreyer et al.*, The European Communication (Dis)Order.

European Parliament: The Future of Money, Study for the Committee on Economic and Monetary Affairs, Policy Department for Economic, Scientific and Quality of Life Policies, European Parliament, Luxembourg, 2019, https://www.europarl.europa.eu/RegData/etudes/STUD/2019/642364/IPOL_STU(2019)642364_EN.pdf.
Cited: *author*, in: European Parliament, The Future of Money.

European Regulators Group for Audiovisual Media (ERGA): Report on the independence of NRAs, 15 December 2015, available at http://erga-online.eu/wp-content/uploads/2016/10/report_indep_nra_2015.pdf..
Cited: *ERGA*, Report on the independence of NRAs.

Evas, T.: Civil liability regime for artificial intelligence. European added value assessment, Study of the European Parliamentary Research Service, Brussels, 2020, https://www.europarl.europa.eu/RegData/etudes/STUD/2020/654178/EPRS_STU(2020)654178_EN.pdf.
Cited: *Evas (EPRS study)*, Civil liability regime for artificial intelligence.

Geiger, C.; Jütte, B.J.: Platform liability under Article 17 of the Copyright in the Digital Single Market Directive – Automated Filtering and Fundamental Rights: An Impossible Match, forthcoming in: GRUR International 2021, https://papers.ssrn.com/sol3/papers.cfm?abstract_id=3776267.
Cited: *Geiger/Jütte*, Platform liability under Article 17 of the Copyright in the Digital Single Market Directive.

Grabitz, E.; Hilf, M.; Nettesheim, M. (eds.): Das Recht der Europäischen Union: EUV/AEUV, Vol. 71, Munich, 2020.
Cited: *author*, in: Grabitz/Hilf/Nettesheim.

Haarkötter, H.: Journalismus.online: Das Handbuch zum Online-Journalismus, Cologne 2019.
Cited: *Haarkötter*, Journalismus.online: Das Handbuch zum Online-Journalismus.

Hadzhieva, E., Impact of Digitalisation on International Tax Matters, Study for the Committee on Financial Crimes, Tax Evasion and Tax Avoidance, Policy Department for Economic, Scientific and Quality of Life Policies, European Parliament, Luxembourg 2019, https://www.europarl.europa.eu/RegData/etudes/STUD/2019/626078/IPOL_STU(2019)626078_EN.pdf.
Cited: *Hadzhieva*, Impact of Digitalisation on International Tax Matters.

Harrison J.; Woods, L.: Jurisdiction, forum shopping and the 'race to the bottom', Cambridge 2007.
Cited: *Harrison/Woods*, Jurisdiction, forum shopping and the 'race to the bottom'.

Helberger, N.; Pierson, J.; Poell, T.: Governing Online Platforms: From Contested to Cooperative Responsibility, in: The Information Society, 34, 2018, p. 1–2.
Cited: *Helberger/Pierson/Poell* in: The Information Society, 34, 2018, 1, p.

Hörnle, J.: Country of Origin Regulation in Cross-Border Media: One Step Beyond the Freedom to Provide Services?, in: International & Comparative Law Quarterly, 54 (1), 2005, p. 89–126.
Cited: *Hörnle*, in: International and Comparative Law Quarterly, 54 (1), 2005, 89, p.

Iacob, N.; Simonelli, F.: How to Fully Reap the Benefits of the Internal Market for E-Commerce?, Study for the committee on the Internal Market and Consumer Protection, Policy Department for Economic, Scientific and Quality of Life Policies, European Parliament, Luxembourg 2020, https://www.europarl.europa.eu/RegData/etudes/STUD/2020/648801/IPOL_STU(2020)648801_EN.pdf.
Cited: *Iacob/Simonelli*, How to Fully Reap the Benefits of the Internal Market for E-Commerce?

Joint Research Centre (European Commission): Multimedia information society, Brussels 1997, https://op.europa.eu/en/publication-detail/-/publication/4da834e3-011d-11ea-8c1f-01aa75ed71a1/language-en/format-PDF/source-140486803.
Cited: *Joint Research Centre*, Multimedia information society.

Jungheim, S.: Medienordnung und Wettbewerbsrecht im Zeitalter der Digitalisierung und Globalisierung, Tuebingen 2012.
Cited: *Jungheim*, Medienordnung und Wettbewerbsrecht im Zeitalter der Digitalisierung und Globalisierung.

Koltay, A. (ed.): Media Freedom and Regulation in the New Media World, Alphen aan den Rijn, 2014.
Cited: *author*, in: Koltay, Media Freedom and Regulation in the New Media World.

Kuczerawy, A.: Intermediary Liability and Freedom of Expression in the EU: from Concepts to Safeguards, Cambridge 2018.
Cited: *Kuczerawy*, Intermediary Liability and Freedom of Expression in the EU: from Concepts to Safeguards.

Lavi, M.: Evil Nudges, in: Vanderbilt Journal of Entertainment and Technology Law (JETLaw), 21 (1), 2018.
Cited: *Lavi*, in: JETLaw, 21 (1), 2018.

Lievens, E.: Protecting Children in the Digital Era: The Use of Alternative Regulatory Instruments, Leiden/Boston 2010.
Cited: *Lievens*, Protecting Children in the Digital Era: The Use of Alternative Regulatory Instruments.

Lomba, N.; Evas, T.: Digital services act. European added value assessment, Study of the European Parliamentary Research Services, Brussels 2020, https://www.eu roparl.europa.eu/RegData/etudes/STUD/2020/654180/EPRS_STU(2020)654180_ EN.pdf.
Cited: *Lomba/Evas (EPRS study)*, Digital services act.

Lopatka, R.: Subsidiarity: Bridging the gap between the ideal and reality, in: European View, 18 (spring), 2019, p. 26–36.
Cited: *Lopatka*, in: European View, 18 (spring), 2019, 26, p.

Madiega, T.: Reform of the EU liability regime for online intermediaries: Background on the forthcoming digital services act, In-depth analysis of the European Parliamentary Research Service, Brussel 2020, https://www.europarl.europ a.eu/RegData/etudes/IDAN/2020/649404/EPRS_IDA(2020)649404_EN.pdf.
Cited: *Madiega (EPRS study)*, Reform of the EU liability regime for online intermediaries.

Matulionyte, R.: Enforcing Copyright Infringements Online: In Search of Balanced Private International Law Rules, in: Journal of Intellectual Property, Information Technology and Electronic Commerce Law (JIPITEC), 6 (2), 2015, p. 132–145.
Cited: *Matulionyte*, in: JIPITEC, 6 (2), 2015, 132, p.

Montagnani, M. L.; Trapova, A.: New Obligations for Internet Intermediaries in the Digital Single Market – Safe Harbors in Turmoil?, in: Journal of Internet Law (JIL), 22 (7), 2019, p. 3–11.
Cited: *Montagnani/Trapova*, in: JIL, 22 (7), 2019, 3, p.

Mulligan, D.; Bamberger, K.: Saving Governance-By-Design, in: California Law Review (CLR), 106, 2018, p. 698–772.
Cited: *Mulligan/Bamberger*, in: CLR, 106, 2018, 698, p.

Nettesheim, M.: Normenhierarchie im EU-Recht, in: Europarecht (EuR), 41 (6), 2006, p. 737–772.
Cited: *Nettesheim*, in: EuR, 41 (6), 2006, 737, p.

Nordemann, J. B.: Internal Market for digital services: Responsibilities and duties of care of providers of digital services, Study for the European Parliament Committee on the Internal Market and Consumer Protection, Policy Department for Economic, Scientific and Quality of Life Policies, European Parliament, Luxembourg 2020, https://www.europarl.europa.eu/RegData/etudes/STUD/2020/64880 2/IPOL_STU(2020)648802_EN.pdf.
Cited: *Nordemann*, Internal Market for digital services: Responsibilities and duties of care of providers of digital services.

Oster, J.: Communication, defamation and liability of intermediaries, in: Legal Studies, 35, 2015, p. 348–368.
Cited: *Oster* in: Legal Studies, 35, 2015, 348, p.

Penney, J. W.: Internet surveillance, regulation, and chilling effects online: a comparative case study, in: Internet Policy Review (IPR), 6 (2), 2017, https://doi.org/10.14763/2017.2.692.
Cited: *Penney*, in: IPR, 6 (2), 2017.

Petkova, B.; Ojanen, T. (eds.): Fundamental Rights Protection Online: The Future Regulation of Intermediaries, Cheltenham 2020.
Cited: *author*, "title", in: Petkova/Ojanen (eds.), p.

Quintais, J.: Global Online Piracy – Study Legal Background Report, Amsterdam 2018, https://www.ivir.nl/publicaties/download/Global-Online-Piracy-Study-Legal-Background-Report.pdf.
Cited: *Quintais*, Global Online Piracy – Study Legal Background Report.

Quaglio, G.; Miller, S.: Potentially negative effects of internet use, In-depth analysis of the European Parliamentary Research Service, Brussels 2020.
Cited: *Quaglio/Miller (EPRS analysis)*, Potentially negative effects of the internet use.

Rowland, D.; Kohl, U.; Charlesworth, A.: Information Technology Law, 5th edition, London 2016.
Cited: *Rowland/Kohl/Charlesworth*, Information Technology Law.

Sartor, G.: New aspects and challenges in consumer protection, Study for the committee on the Internal Market and Consumer Protection, Policy Department for Economic, Scientific and Quality of Life Policies, European Parliament, Luxembourg 2020, https://www.europarl.europa.eu/RegData/etudes/STUD/2020/648790/IPOL_STU(2020)648790_EN.pdf.
Cited: *Sartor*, New aspects and challenges in consumer protection.

Savin, A.: EU Internet Law, Cheltenham 2014.
Cited: *Savin*, EU Internet Law.

Schulte-Nölke, H.; Rüffer, I.; Nobrega, C.; Wiewórowska-Domagalska, A.: The legal framework for e-commerce in the Internal Market, Study for the committee on the Internal Market and Consumer Protection, Policy Department for Economic, Scientific and Quality of Life Policies, European Parliament, Luxembourg 2020, https://www.europarl.europa.eu/RegData/etudes/STUD/2020/652707/IPOL_STU(2020)652707_EN.pdf.
Cited: *Schulte-Nölke et al.*, The legal framework for e-commerce in the Internal Market.

Schwartz, I.: Subsidiarität und EG-Kompetenzen – der neue Titel „Kultur"-Medienvielfalt und Binnenmarkt, in: AfP, 24 (1) 1993, p. 409–421.
Cited: *Schwartz*, in: AfP 24 (1), 1993, 409, p.

Senftleben, M.; Angelopoulos, C.: The Odyssey of the Prohibition on General Monitoring Obligations on the Way to the Digital Services Act, Amsterdam 2020, https://www.ivir.nl/new-study-the-odyssey-of-the-prohibition-on-general-monitoring-obligations-on-the-way-to-the-digital-services-act/.
Cited: *Senftleben/Angelopoulus*, The Odyssey of the Prohibition on General Monitoring Obligations on the Way to the Digital Services Act.

Smit, S. J.: SME focus – Long-term strategy for the European industrial future, Study for the committee on Industry, Research and Energy (ITRE), Policy Department for Economic, Scientific and Quality of Life Policies, European Parliament, Luxembourg 2020, https://www.europarl.europa.eu/RegData/etudes/STUD/2020/648776/IPOL_STU(2020)648776_EN.pdf.
Cited: *Smit*, SME focus – Long term strategy for the European industrial future.

Smith, M.: Enforcement and cooperation between Member States in a Digital Services Act, Study for the Committee on Internal Market, Policy Department for Economic, Scientific and Quality of Life Policies, European Parliament, Luxembourg 2020, https://www.europarl.europa.eu/RegData/etudes/STUD/2020/648780/IPOL_STU(2020)648780_EN.pdf.
Cited: *Smith*, Enforcement and cooperation between Member States.

Sohnemann, N.; Uffrecht, L. M.; Hartkopf, M. C.; Kruse, J. P.; Noellen, L. M.: New Developments in Digital Services, Study for the committee on the Internal Market and Consumer Protection, Policy Department for Economic, Scientific and Quality of Life Policies, European Parliament, Luxembourg 2020, https://www.europarl.europa.eu/RegData/etudes/STUD/2020/648784/IPOL_STU(2020)648784_EN.pdf.
Cited: *Sohnemann et al.*, New Developments in Digital Services.

Spindler, G.: Internet Intermediary Liability Reloaded – The New German Act on Responsibility of Social Networks and its (In-) Compatibility with European Law, in: JIPITEC, 8 (2), 2017, 166-179.
Cited: *Spindler*, in: JIPITEC, 8 (2), 2017, 166, p.

Svantesson, D.: European Union Claims of Jurisdiction over the Internet: An Analysis of Three Recent Key Developments, in: JIPITEC, 9 (2), 2018, p. 113–125.
Cited: *Svantesson*, in: JIPITEC, 9 (2), 2018, 113, p.

Ukrow, J.: Die Vorschläge der EU-Kommission für einen Digital Services Act und einen Digital Markets Act. Darstellung von und erste Überlegungen zu zentralen Bausteinen für eine digitale Grundordnung der EU, in: Impulse aus dem EMR, Saarbruecken 2021, https://emr-sb.de/wp-content/uploads/2021/01/Impulse-aus-dem-EMR_DMA-und-DSA.pdf.
Cited: *Ukrow*, Die Vorschläge der EU-Kommission für einen Digital Services Act und einen Digital Markets Act.

Ukrow, J.: Indexierung des Rundfunkbeitrags und Stabilität der deutschen Rundfunkfinanzierung. Ansätze einer europarechtlichen Risikoanalyse, in: UFITA, 83 (1), 2019, 279–330, p.
Cited: *Ukrow*, in: UFITA, 83 (1), 2019, 279, p.

Ullrich, C.: Unlawful Content Online: Towards a New Regulatory Framework for Online Platforms, Luxembourg 2020.
Cited: *Ullrich*, Unlawful Content Online: Towards a New Regulatory Framework for Online Platforms.

Ullrich, C.: New Approach meets new economy: Enforcing EU product safety in e-commerce, in: Maastricht Journal of European and Comparative Law (MJ), 26 (4), 2019, p. 558–584.
Cited: *Ullrich*, in: MJ, 26 (4), 2019, 558, p.

Ullrich, C.: A Risk-Based Approach towards Infringement Prevention on the Internet: Adopting the Anti-Money Laundering Framework to Online Platforms, in: IJLIT, 26 (3), 2018, p. 226–251.
Cited: *Ullrich*, in: IJLIT, 26 (3), 2018, 226, p.

Ullrich, C.: Standards for Duty of Care? Debating Intermediary Liability from a Sectoral Perspective, in: Journal of Intellectual Property, in: JIPITEC, 8 (2), 2017, p. 111–126.
Cited: *Ullrich*, in: JIPITEC, 8 (2), 2017, 111, p.

Vamialis, A.: Online Defamation: Confronting Anonymity, in: IJLIT, 21 (1), 2013, p. 56–62.
Cited: *Vamialis*, in: IJLIT, 21 (1), 2013, 56, p.

van Eecke, P.: Online Service Providers and Liability: A Plea for a Balanced Approach, in: Common Market Law Review, 48 (5), 2011, p. 1455–1502.
Cited: *van Eecke*, in: Common Market L. Rev., 48 (5), 2011, 1455, p.

van Hoboken, J.; Quintas, J. P.; Poort, J.; van Eijk, N.: Hosting intermediary services and illegal content online. An analysis of the scope of Article 14 ECD in light of developments in the online service landscape, SMART 2018/0033, Amsterdam 2018, https://www.ivir.nl/publicaties/download/hosting_intermediary_services.pdf.
Cited: *van Hoboken et al.*, Hosting intermediary services and illegal content online.

Vlassis, A.: The review of the Audiovisual Media Services Directive. Many political voices for one digital Europe?, in: Politique européenne, 56 (2), 2017, p. 102–123.
Cited: *Vlassis*, in: Politique européenne, 56 (2), 2017, 102, p.

Waldheim, S.: Dienstleistungsfreiheit und Herkunftslandprinzip: Prinzipielle Möglichkeiten und primärrechtliche Grenzen der Liberalisierung eines integrierten europäischen Binnenmarktes für Dienstleistungen, Göttingen 2008.
Cited: *Waldheim*, Dienstleistungsfreiheit und Herkunftslandprinzip.

Woods, L.: The proposed Digital Markets Act: overview and analysis, in: EU Law Analysis, 14 January 2021, http://eulawanalysis.blogspot.com/2021/01/the-proposed-digital-markets-act.html.
Cited: *Woods*, The proposed Digital Markets Act: overview and analysis.

Woods, L.: Overview of Digital Services Act, in: EU Law Analysis, 16 December 2020, http://eulawanalysis.blogspot.com/2020/12/overview-of-digital-services-act.html.
Cited: *Woods*, Overview of Digital Services Act.

Woods, L.; Perrin, W.: Online harm reduction – a statutory duty of care and regulator, Dunfermline 2019, https://d1ssu070pg2v9i.cloudfront.net/pex/carnegie_uk_trust/2019/04/08091652/Online-harm-reduction-a-statutory-duty-of-care-and-regulator.pdf.
Cited: *Woods/Perrin*, Online harm reduction – a statutory duty of care and regulator.